PAST IMPERSONAL

PAST Impersonal

Group Process in Human History

Rudolph Binion

NORTHERN

ILLINOIS

UNIVERSITY

PRESS / DEKALB

Published by the Northern Illinois University Press, DeKalb, Illinois   60115

Manufactured in the United States using acid-free paper

All Rights Reserved

Design by Julia Fauci

Library of Congress Cataloging-in-Publication Data

Binion, Rudolph, 1927–

Past impersonal : group process in human history / Rudolph Binion.

   p.   cm.

Includes bibliographical references and index.

ISBN-13: 978-0-87580-345-6 (clothbound : alk. paper)

ISBN-10: 0-87580-345-8 (clothbound : alk. paper)

1. Social groups—History. I. Title.

HM711.B56 2005

302.3'094—dc22

2005007277

Contents

"The light of common day

to which we are accustomed

may blind us to what is going on in the dark,

and the roots of everything are underground."

—**George Santayana**

Preface

All human history is people doing things. I say "doing things" in the progressive mode in order to suggest ongoing actions. What people have once done is of course past. But it is past in the way that, say, old loves are past and yet present in new ones. Whatever we do, we tend to act out of our past, whether thoughtlessly or (in Kant's deft phrase) under the idea of freedom. Most of what we do is accordingly what we have already done and even redone, twisted as far beyond recognition as that idea of personal freedom may require.

But the pasts out of which we act all differ. How, then, do numberless disparate individual actions by numberless disparate individuals ever add up to world history? No historic calculator could handle the arithmetic if the prime movers of human affairs were a globeful of individuals each acting out of a different past. Historians dodge the difficulty in various slippery ways. One way is to tag dominant or influential personalities as history makers and discount the multitudes as compliant or suggestible. Another is to focus on trends—to smaller peasant plots, or to secularism, or to births out of wedlock—and reduce the interests and motives involved to a manageable few. Yet another is to abstract modernization, say, or nationalism, or decadence, from patterns of historic change and to treat the abstractions as impersonal forces producing those patterns. But however historians explain the past, their explanations invariably turn on most or usually all individual actions running to type or balancing off. Not even for a mass-minded, historical-minded Marxist do the masses act out of a shared consciousness; Marxist class consciousness, if achieved, is so much individual awareness of class interests identical across the board; in Marxist theory, such class interests motivate large-scale action only by their parallel effects on individuals. All in all, action by groups past or present has heretofore been no more than a figure of speech. "Germany followed

Hitler" is short for Germans, or most Germans, following Hitler for any of a variety of individual reasons laid out in clusters by historians of the sorry event. Taken literally, the concept of a shared, sustained German or other collective identity pursuing an inner determination of its own looks on the face of it like a so-called fallacy of composition best fit for massive deconstruction. Yet such collective acting out, alias group process, is sober fact.

My purpose in this book is to demonstrate this sober fact by showing several historic group phenomena to have been just that: doings by groups, due in each case to the felt needs of the groups as such. Because as a rule a group's highest priority is its members' welfare, group purposes often overlap with individual pursuits. Even then the two remain radically distinct, with the group's members all the less mindful of its power over them or indeed of its very existence in its own right. That existence and that power are easiest to see in retrospect and from the outside. But whoever has once seen the group effect in the past will see it in the present by the same token—will recognize the main groups and group mechanisms operant in yesterday's and today's world alike. Deep-felt group identities come alive only slowly and never quite die, cohering most tightly around common wounds that fester instead of healing. The deadliest dangers from groups today are yesterday's dangers potentiated. Such continuity, intensifying along its way, is the name of the historic game. Once the missing group dimension of history is supplied, today's bad news will be no big news. Then I will have made my point.

This book has been in preparation since the 1970s as, in working from one broad-based historical monograph to another, I kept seeing the fact of group process confirmed and gradually came to distinguish its main forms. Ideally I would have gone on doing monographs on group process for some decades more before venturing to synthesize my findings. But at the turn of the millennium I resolved to face up to my own mortality and pull my findings together however tentatively while the pulling was good. To this end, I have reworked some earlier research, often drastically, and conducted some new research, above all on the Black Death as a showcase for my three main modes of group process in action together.[1] I deliberately chose as broad a range of illustrative historic material as I could in order to make my basic point as strongly as possible: that groups lead lives of their own. I was encouraged and assisted in my efforts by Deborah Hayden with her nimble wits and especially Alice Binion with her sharp eye for style and matchless expertise in art history: both pushed tirelessly for more clarity than I could achieve. Robert Aldrich and Stephen Kern helped shape the work at a formative stage, and William S. Koehler gave it an invaluable once-over when I wrongly thought it was done. It is much in the debt of all five.

PAST IMPERSONAL

Group Process

My subject is both conspicuous and easy to miss: group process in human history. Group process is the psychohistorian's term for actions in concert that run their course independently of individual volition, or again for people doing things together that have purposes and meanings for them collectively which are unknown to them as individuals.[1] As will be shown shortly, a European couple contracepting around 1900, a Frenchman thrilling to a cavalry charge around 1800, a European chuckling at monsters around 1300, were playing bit parts in group performances beyond their ken. Such collective, impersonal actions on a large scale pervade human history. Because historians feel just as self-propelled as anyone else, they tend like anyone else to mistake group process for a confluence or interplay of individual pursuits, for a combination or resultant of numberless personal doings. It is urgent to correct that mistake in order for history to be seen straight as the generative source of today's troubled world.

I specify group process in *human* history because group process suffuses the rest of animal history as well. But its terms of reference differ in nonhuman species. When a nonhuman animal acts to the advantage of its group or community rather than itself, biologists speak of "group selection" and call it "altruistic." On the other hand, biologists regard nonhuman animal communities as functionally equivalent to organisms—as "superorganisms," with the animals composing them as their organs. This equivalence is troublesome, for an organ does not serve an organism to its own detriment the way an animal will commonly serve its community to its own detriment. One natural historian, the radical group selectionist V. C. Wynne-Edwards, saw partway around this difficulty when in 1962 he argued a social stratification within animal communities such that underlings instinctively sacrifice for their superiors as the need arises.[2] After

Wynne-Edwards, evolutionary biologists mostly turned against such so-called group selection on the ground that within any group, social stratification or no, egoists would fast supplant whatever sacrificers might ever emerge among them. But group selection has staged a comeback in recent years on the higher ground that groups strengthened by altruists have a competitive edge against groups composed of egoists only.[3]

Even on that higher ground, the idea of a subset of animal altruists standing ready to deprive or endanger themselves however the group welfare might dictate—to breed or feed less, to abandon territory, to tackle predators—raises prickly problems of versatility and intentionality. Take a sudden communal need to breed less: for starters, are birds or bugs, let alone bacilli, even aware, as "group selection" would require, that their reproductive acts are reproductive? A simpler hypothesis avoids that whole line of trouble: that while the members of a group are all equally attuned to its needs, those members meet them first in any given case who are most tractable or most amenable in that particular case. "Group selection" would then hold in reverse, with the group as such selecting its sacrificers instead of being selected by them. This is in fact how group process does operate in human societies, with no communal altruism showing in adaptive birth control, belt-tightening, or migration, and precious little even in volunteer armies. In sum, biological theory in its present pass has nothing much to teach historians about how the human animal engages in group action unsuspectingly.[4]

For all their self-will, humans regularly serve group purposes unawares even while pursuing private purposes, about like particles acting differently from the bodies they compose. Selfhood is a rarity and a luxury in nature. Animals socialized to the hilt perform unthinkably intricate maneuvers together unthinkingly while by the same token they are pathetically helpless on their own. Army ants cut off from their group singly or even in small clusters go crazily self-destructive: they just run circles until they die.[5] As for humans, suicide and madness only appear to detach them from society. However personal and idiosyncratic case by case, suicide and madness register statistically as group functions, their rates strikingly constant, and with the slight inconstancies patterned to boot. This regularity was the ground for Émile Durkheim's argument from human suicide rates, in his masterly *Suicide* of 1895, that a "collective consciousness" dictates social conduct in all its interdependent varieties. Ever since Durkheim, more obvious social pathology such as crime has been the social statistician's delight by virtue of its easy correlation with other social series, poverty foremost. Social normalcy among humans is harder to grasp as group process because of the rich rationalizations that surround its works, obscuring their instinctual basis: witness the rhetoric of debate and dispute over labor laws or zoning laws approximating those in force among reptiles or rodents. Humans rationalize their groups' foreign agendas too, if more flimsily. Army ants forage for dear life; humans wage war for higher causes.

Radically individualized as is human consciousness, group pressure can penetrate and even overwhelm it in crowds—the subject of Gustave Le Bon's classic *The Crowd*, dated 1895 like Durkheim's *Suicide*—or again in wartime, when "everyone's individual lives are so swallowed up in the one great tragedy that one almost ceases to have personal experiences and emotions."[6] Conversely, individuality can be spontaneously surrendered to a group out of a "need to feel included or integrated, ultimately protected and nurtured, by the overall entity that is so much more powerful than oneself."[7] Even an ad hoc, experimental group can induce tenacious delusions in successive newcomers to it.[8] Such phenomena attest the ascendancy of groups over their members without, however, revealing much about how groups behave. How groups behave, or group process, is best inferred, not from how group ascendancy is refracted in individual consciousness, but from a comparative study of group doings or showings in history. Such group doings or showings will be seen in all cases to have aims and meanings unknown to the individuals involved.

Group process in human history appears to split three main ways with respect to its function. The chief one of the three comprises actions in concert tending to promote, sustain, or defend a group's vital interests, beginning with the dynamic cohesion that makes it a group in the first place. Such actions are best called "adaptive," as in evolutionary biology, with the difference that a human group's vital interests are as often moral as material. In a second, "maladaptive" mode of group process, fateful out of all proportion to its frequency, a human group will relive a traumatic adaptive failure. Such reliving might be seen as a variant of adaptation tending to undo or reverse the earlier failure, except that it never succeeds. It has no known counterpart in nature: even the lemmings' legendary periodic self-destruction en masse comes without a traumatic original.[9] The third leading mode of group process, neither functional nor dysfunctional, is the symbolic expression of a group's changing, multifaceted outlook on life. This mode may have an original in communal display by animals over and beyond any mating purpose. Its finest flowering in human societies is art, which, in Oscar Wilde's proud word, is quite useless. These three basic modes of group process do not comprise the whole range of group functions—far from it. The regularity of rates of madness and suicide, for instance, suggests a group attrition factor apart from natural death. Again, groups may singularize themselves by such senseless predictables as numbers of letters mailed without postage. But I would distinguish such fringe tokens of group identity from the group process proper that I have subdivided three main ways. In whichever of these three ways a group determination operates, it does so in concealment and through individuals each acting for reasons strictly personal.

Group process in the adaptive mode shows most distinctly, and hence most instructively, in reactive adjustments to changing existential needs.

Historical demography provides exemplary illustrations of such adaptive adjustments where physical challenges to a population's welfare are met in kind, directly and literally, in all animal simplicity. Fertility adjustments in particular are privileged peepholes into our animal basics in the bulk. A compelling object lesson in adaptive group process at work is the European fertility transition (to call it by its technical name) whereby deliberate, large-scale birth control, after taking a head start in revolutionary France (the theme of chapter 3 below), invaded the conjugal abode across the rest of Europe as well beginning in the mid-1870s.

As Malthus made his name arguing, population would burst all bounds if it grew unchecked. Until the fertility transition in Europe, the leading natural check on population there as elsewhere was early death from disease or malnutrition. The leading artificial check was the institution of marriage combined with a stigma on illegitimacy. Not only was breeding normally confined to wedlock; parenthood was the defining purpose of wedlock, with natural, or unrestricted, fertility accordingly the conjugal norm. Sex for its own sake was proverbially extramarital; so was the contraception that ordinarily went with it. European populations would control their numbers above all through women's marriage rates and ages: roughly half of fertile women were married at any given time, and their age at first marriage fluctuated around twenty-five. Marital fertility varied both regionally and socially with the incidence of breast-feeding, which tends to lengthen the intervals between successive pregnancies (as mothers can hardly have failed to realize deep down). Over and beyond breast-feeding, deliberate marital birth control was practiced by occasional isolated offenders and even systematically within certain distinctive subgroups, though nowhere did the results weigh significantly into the aggregate. In such odd cases, the most usual intentional curb on natural fertility in marriage was, by all indications, less frequent intercourse, dignified as "continence." The apparent runner-up was premature male withdrawal, ordinarily reserved for fornication or adultery. Abortion probably followed next, with condoms, known since antiquity, trailing in fourth place until after their popularization as prophylactics during World War I. The rhythm method, diaphragms, and the pill were all still in the future. By and large, the premodern European population held steady within the limits of available resources, with the marriage rate (and, a distant second, in- and out-migration) rising or falling to offset the ups and downs of famine, pestilence, and warfare.

By the turn of the eighteenth into the nineteenth century, mortality, child mortality foremost, had begun its steady decline in Europe. The result was not just a huge actual population increase, but an exponentially mounting potential increase such that, had the aggregate growth rate as of the 1870s held steady, total numbers in Europe would have more than sextupled within another three generations[10]—an unthinkable prospect. The stock adaptive device of adjusting marriage rates and ages on top of increased emigration was no match for such a massive incipient groundswell. In these circumstances, Europeans as a whole adopted the French expedient: they cut back on births within marriage as much as they could short of self-extinction and as fast as they could without social disruption.

This cutback—sudden, steep, smooth, and steady—provides a model instance of adaptive group process at work. Married couples having less taste or less use for parenthood cut back first, with no measurable variables (such as educational level, social status, religion or irreligion, urban or rural walk of life) consistently distinguishing the early or late starters across Europe. In no known cases did couples control births with the conscious aim of averting a continental disaster. Individual motives varied with circumstances and mind-sets. More to the point, they were causally irrelevant: thus the typical aim of easing family budgets had been around from time immemorial without a fertility plunge ensuing. The transition was not rigorously in sync from nation to nation across the continent, but neither was it from region to region within nations. Its near simultaneity overall, with even the French roughly in step despite their earlier start and their official anxiety about depopulation, is what marks it as a European event[11]—all-European and only European. As a group adaptation it was, then, a perfect success, though one that came at a high moral cost in guilt over the defilement of marriage, as will be seen in chapter 2.

How did Europeans pick up unawares in the 1870s on their urgent, coercive group need to multiply less? The answer, however it reads in biological theory, would seem to lie with a relic of their species' evolutionary past: with a group reflex against threats, external or internal, to the group's viability. If so, what triggered that European reflex was presumably the perception, unmistakable in all social spheres by the 1870s, of dangerously more children surviving to marriage age.[12] But whatever it was that cued young European couples into the need for reproductive retrenchment, they sensed and met that need with no more clarity about it than the dumbest social insects have about the whys and wherefores of the numberless intricate vital operations they perform collectively. For human as for other animal groups, adaptation is not second nature, but first.

The polar opposite of an adaptive reflex by human groups is much less obviously of evolutionary origin: their felt need to invite or contrive an intensified renewal of disasters that overwhelm them. Such traumatic reliving has been more closely explored in individuals than in groups even though in its group form, possibly the older of the two, it is equally conspicuous in the historic record, and far more portentous. It resembles a repeated adaptive effort to absorb a devastating existential blow. Where a group is caught painfully short, it may struggle to cope by obsessive recall or by phobic precautions after the fact. More distinctively, it will instead relive its traumatic reverse any number of times as if in an effort to master it. I say "as if" because the evidence from human groups is inconclusive as to whether they ever do even begin to master a trauma that cuts deep enough to entail reliving. A traumatized individual who relives certainly finds no closure as a result; such reliving resolves instead into a painful, pointless routine that must therefore cast doubt on its adaptive purpose. A traumatized group in the throes of maladaptive reliving will act no less in unison than one conducting successful adaptive maneuvers. Typically, it will relive in a mood of both resignation and gloomy foreboding. Emotionally it will be right back in the original misadventure to all intents and purposes except for this dim, diffuse presentiment of the dire outcome impending. Many participants will be reminded of the traumatic original that is being relived; none will be aware of the reliving itself.

A trauma will sharpen group identity, but for a group to be traumatized in the first place it must preexist in at least some form and measure. No merely adventitious assemblage thrown together however brutally, as in a hostage-taking, will relive the experience in group formation. Even so, humans are the species most prone to group trauma. For nonhuman groups exclude joint memberships, whereas humans as a rule identify strongly enough on several sides and several levels at once to incur a group trauma on any one of them. Nor need the group affiliations behind an adaptive group reflex be exclusive either: when deliberate birth control went domestic throughout Europe, Europeans were at one on that gut level even though nationalism was then tearing the continent apart on the bloody surface.

A case discussed by Joel Markowitz in 1969, a chronic reliving *en groupe* of a bloody military fiasco,[13] illustrates the traumatic process graphically because the successive relivings involved have been literal and, except for the last one, straight. Straight, literal reliving by human groups is exceptional because humans mentalized their evolutionary heritage early along, fitting it out with a loose and twisty subjective lining. The human ideational world cut in on the species's adaptive functions and dysfunctions alike even as human groups and individuals acquired the means to relive a trauma figuratively, substituting for key elements or reversing key relations. Already in the earliest histories on record, age-old rituals of evident traumatic origin were played out in symbols as subtly configured as those in dreams. Markowitz's is a less evolved, less convoluted scenario, perhaps because the trauma replayed was born of brutal battle. At all odds it has been replayed every time on its native ground, the battlefield, and has been replayed faithfully short of a single, final turnabout. I shall summarize Markowitz's detailed account of it selectively for my present, merely definitional purpose.

The armored noble horseman was the guardian of feudal Europe, drawing great prestige and huge privileges from his military function. The Franks established their vast feudal empire under Charlemagne in the year

AD 800 through their mastery of cavalry shock tactics. Invincible in frontal assaults, the Franco-Norman mailed cavalry attained legendary status by the time its armed horsemen conquered England in 1066. The legend gradually faded, however, after 1180, when the Welsh longbow proved able to pin an armored horseman to his mount. Warfare adjusted pragmatically thereafter in England and across Europe except only in France. The obstinate French warrior aristocrats for their part were traumatized at Courtrai in 1302 when common foot soldiers destroyed a whole army of them cavalierly attacking head-on across a swamp. "Subjected to enormous fear, humiliation, and feelings of hopelessness,"[14] their proud raison d'être cruelly undercut, the obsolescent knights took refuge in denial as they flagrantly repeated that traumatic, suicidal frontal attack over and over thereafter, snatching defeat from victory again and again despite ever more dizzying numerical odds in their favor. As they did so, English men-at-arms duly massacred them by the thousands at Crécy in 1346, at Poitiers in 1350, and at Agincourt in 1415, each time at only negligible cost to themselves. Even then, such noble French horsemen as remained still denied their vulnerability to the longbow and blamed their defeats instead on native English prowess. "Bypassing the hopeless nobility, France finally raised the first professional army of the Middle Ages: 9,000 men equipped with the world's finest artillery"[15]—who, still seeing the English through the nobles' eyes as inherently doughtier, attributed their own startling victories not rightly to their newly improved equipment and tactics, but wrongly to divine favor gained for them by their devout leader, Joan of Arc.

With the tardy demise of the noble cavalry in France, the proud mailed horseman's traumatic syndrome went into latency for four whole centuries. Only after the revolution of 1789 did it reemerge—and it reemerged to afflict the entire body politic, what with French solidarity then soaring within the nation in arms and soon within a new, Napoleonic empire reminiscent of Charlemagne's. For over a century beginning with the wars of the revolution and Napoleon, the French military command was prey to a recurrent fatal impulse "to hurl cavalry (especially) and infantry (later) in hopeless frontal assaults against well-defended infantry" while neglecting "more legitimate uses of cavalry" for scouting or communication.[16] Napoleon himself lapsed into this obsolete, ruinous tactic against his own better judgment whenever the battle odds were in his favor: it finally destroyed him at Waterloo. Napoleon III in turn likewise lost his empire through a disastrous head-on cavalry charge at Sedan. This bloody traumatic routine escalated still further in the course of World War I (despite occasional lapses into sanity), climaxing in 1917 with mutinies in the ranks. Against all reason, the nation at large wildly endorsed the *attaque brusquée* and the *offensive à outrance* all along as alone suitable to French *cran*, to French *élan*, to *furor Gallicae*.

Then after World War I the traumatic syndrome went into simple reverse. "Post-World War I thinking . . . was *exactly opposite* to the previous attitude" and "*was as bizarre in degree* in a defensive direction."[17] Just when motorized transport (trucks, tanks, airplanes) had made the offensive newly feasible for a highly mobile army with heightened firepower (as the Germans in particular realized), the French dug in defensively behind the Maginot Line—their string of fixed fortifications to the east with, as a clincher, a fatal gap along their Belgian border that practically ensured their defeat in 1940. This was the *attaque brusquée* and the *offensive à outrance* on their flip side. In the familiar French saying, the more it had changed, the more it was the same.

Markowitz aptly likened one peculiarity of this group dysfunction, that the mailed horsemen's trauma went all-national upon resurfacing after four centuries, to a local virus suffusing a whole organism after a prolonged remission. Another of its peculiarities, that extra-long remission itself, highlights the mystery of how a trauma is transmitted across the generations. Psychohistorians may soon discover how. Meanwhile, though, the riddle of transmission does not gainsay the fact of transmission any more than the law of inverse squares was inoperant until quantum field theory finally began to show how gravitation is transmitted. A further, albeit far lesser, peculiarity of the Courtrai trauma is that, except under the first Napoleon, it was relived spontaneously, with no leader manipulating it unconsciously to his own traumatic ends. Such traumatized leaders fill the annals of historic group reliving. Typical was Leopold III, king of the Belgians, who resolutely steered Belgium on a military disaster course in 1936–1940 at the helm of state just as he had earlier accidentally driven his queen to destruction at the wheel of his automobile: all the while Belgium on its side relived behind him the devastating German invasion of 1914.[18] Reliving of the sort, with leaders' and followers' traumatic agendas interlocking, is exclusive to the human breed as far as can be told.

The third symbolic mode of group process comprises broad intellectual and cultural developments that run their clear course regardless of the diverse personal reasons why individual thinkers or artists run along. How does this mode in turn relate to the fundamentals of group life? From a classic inquiry in this vein by Walter Abell, I shall extract his analysis of a single theme prominent in medieval art and legend: the theme of the monster-hero conflict.[19]

In the hallucinatory imagery of the Dark Ages, grim and gruesome monsters of primeval ferocity preyed on humankind with surpassing malignancy. Huge and fierce in sculpture, they were fully as redoubtable and loathsome in legend, with many an embattled hero succumbing to them as in *Beowulf* or the *Saga of the Valsungs*. Such beasts spilled over into early Romanesque art, there to claw or gnash helpless victims gaping in panic. This "nightmarish phantasmagoria"[20] flickered even longer in legend: wit-

ness Eilhart von Oberge's late-twelfth-century Tristan only barely van-
quishing a loathsome dragon—which, however, for all its nastiness, was a
somewhat circus-like vestige of a condemned species. For "from a Dark Age
phase in which hero and monster were equally matched, there was a gradual rise of the hero-savior line, [and] a gradual decline of the monster line,
until by Gothic times the savior had become all-powerful and the demons
and monsters subservient."[21] In the process, "omnipotent monsters dominating shadowy and helpless gods" yielded ever so slowly to "an omnipotent God and his attendant hosts dominating comparatively helpless
demons."[22] Thereafter, dislodged from their church portals and capitals, reduced to subserving divine justice by herding the damned to hell, "the de-
graded and powerless monsters made a last inglorious stand"[23] as gargoyles
and chimeras on the outlying stations of cathedrals. Heroes correspondingly triumphed over monsters "with a delightful athletic vigor,"[24] as
when a Saint George would casually, almost inattentively, stab a lizard-like
dragon to death, or when Perceval in Malory's *Le Morte d'Arthur* "slew his
dragon almost without combat, giving it but a single 'buffet.'"[25] Seen in reverse perspective, back down the centuries from the vantage point of the
Gothic with its "small monsters helplessly pinned beneath the feet of
saints, . . . the negative beings increase in importance and power" while
"the positive imagery of saints and heroes decreas[es] from the calm domi-
nance of the Gothic saint and savior to the grim resolution of the Dark
Age hero who must fight a foe at least as strong as himself and who is
killed by the monsters as often as he kills them."[26] Known Germanic
myths reach no farther back historically, but the few extant fragments of
archaic Germanic art conceal their subjects in abstractions suggestive of
monster fantasies too horrendous to be depicted outright.

By the logic of extrapolation, such unrecorded early monster fantasies
came of "a traumatic psycho-social situation."[27] For "no elaborate argument is necessary" to establish the historical basis of the later, recorded
monster fantasies, tracing as they do a steady progression from a cheerless
to a cheery outlook on the human condition.[28] Warfare and marauding
were chronic throughout the Dark Ages: their horrific human costs show
through chroniclers' glimpses of "the flight of a dispossessed people, the
devastation of rural areas, the siege and destruction of cities, and the brutality, famine, and plague by which such events were frequently accompanied or followed."[29] Nor was the incessant strife bodily only: "intellectual
and spiritual conflicts were likewise rampant and were often the cause of,
or the excuse for, physical violence." Thus "during the Dark Ages, even as
in Neolithic times, the inroads ascribed to the monsters of fantasy in no
whit exceeded the dangers and difficulties suffered by men as sober facts of
history."[30] Even so, these Dark Age minuses were offset by pluses—by ad-
vances in agriculture, technology, arts and crafts, learning, governmental
organization, and legal order. Besides, what were Dark Ages for the victims

in those brutal days were for the victors "transfused with all the radiance of new hope and new achievement."[31] Increasingly in the new millennium a "sense of growth, progress, present achievement, and future promise vividly permeated large sections of society and generated a 'boom' psychology on a heroic scale."[32] Eventually everything prospered together: population, agriculture, commerce, finance, nations, cities. Marauding and pillaging were checked; land was massively reclaimed; the arts and sciences flourished. With the extension and solidification of the material base of life and the expansion of the civic and personal realms went soaring spirits—"a psychology of triumph and exaltation, of relief from one-time dangers, of rejoicing in new-found power and security."[33] By the grand thirteenth century, remote cathedral grotesques were the last lingering relics of an obsolete symbolism of fear overwritten "with the disdain and amusement of newly acquired confidence."[34]

Finely articulated, deftly evidenced, richly illustrated, Abell's argument carries full conviction. Even that Gothic "psychology of triumph and exaltation, of relief from one-time dangers, of rejoicing in new-found power and security," gives no pause, however brief, such as Markowitz's headlong horsemen may give in likewise presupposing a thousand-year affective group memory. For one can more readily empathize with Abell's successive monster-slaying medievals as if with a single, long-lived individual than one can with Markowitz's cavalry group perpetually rerunning its disaster course. It helps on Abell's side that medievals did share individually in the existential tensions that they gradually surmounted, first shuddering and later scoffing at their resultant fantasms, whereas French champions of the cavalry charge after Courtrai never saw it straight as the grim fatality it was: their group imperative was at a deeper remove from consciousness. Nonetheless Markowitz's and Abell's group psychology are both individual psychology writ large. Individuals too relive traumas unknowingly, and so do individuals' fearful phantasms fall away with the anxieties that produce them. In no group process, though, is the group a mere aggregation of individuals; on the contrary, its reality is distinct and indeed primordial.

How do the three hypothesized modes of group process add up? As has just been noted, groups act like individuals—or perhaps, phylogenetically put, individuals take after groups. Groups act on and through their members. They act to sustain their composite welfare both physical and moral—in a word, adaptively. They also act dysfunctionally to relive existential blows and expressively to no practical end. They preserve—somehow, somewhere—the memory traces inherent in all three functions. And in all three functions their members think, feel, and act as individuals while conducting their group business unawares. These first findings about group process are especially cursory and blurry as first findings go. But for even this much schematizing, a single, skimpily sketched case for each of the three defined modes of group process hardly suffices. More and fuller case studies are needed.

Seven such fuller studies follow: two in each of the three main modes of group process by turns, then a seventh in all three modes together. The two in the adaptive mode deal respectively with the moral cost of the great European fertility decline and the moral cause of its prototype dating from nearly a century before. The first shows that when Europe as a whole followed the French lead and normalized marital contraception, a crisis of collective guilt ensued that found expression above all in the fiction of the time. And the second shows that the late-eighteenth-century French and American original of that demographic revolution was a spinoff of the kindred political revolutions waged in both nations at that same time—a repeal, on grounds of human freedom, of the age-old constraint on wives to reproduce to capacity. Next, two large-scale traumatic relivings are explored, one a mostly physical trauma relived in kind, and the other a mostly mental trauma relived more figuratively than physically. In the former case, the German defeat in World War I under dictator and warlord Erich Ludendorff was replicated under a fiercer dictator and warlord, Adolf Hitler, who relived a trauma of his own in the bargain. And in the latter case, the experience of the messianic hopes raised across Europe by the French Revolution and dashed by the Reign of Terror was relived across Europe through Romanticism in its myriad forms from reverie to revolt. The two studies in cultural group process that then follow concern, first, the thousand-year rise and fall of figural thinking in Christendom as it shows through the iconography of the Massacre of the Innocents evolving into the Pietà, and second, the five-hundred-year progression of the summum bonum in the Western scheme of values from rags to riches—from the medieval ideal of saintliness to ever worldlier criteria of personal worth. A final empirical study considers these three chief modes of group process operating together as Europe coped with the mega-trauma of the Black Death both adaptively and maladaptively, even while in art the slow transition already under way from otherworldly to this-worldly perspectives ran its course unaffected. In conclusion, with these seven additional examples of group process in action to draw on, a more informed effort will be made to pull the loose threads of our analysis tighter.

CHAPTER ONE

The Guilty Family

Group process rides roughshod over whatever individual sentiments or scruples would bar its way. In late-nineteenth-century Europe the adaptive imperative of fertility retrenchment left a trail of moral casualties behind it as it overrode Europe's inveterate resistance to birth control in marriage. The guilt felt deep down by even the most unresisting couples was creative: it found an outlet above all in the imaginative literature of the time, thereby easing the moral transition from "natural fertility" to "planned parenthood." That European literary guilt trip is the subject of this first of two chapters illustrating the workings of group process in the adaptive mode.

In the years 1879–1914 European fiction took a searching look at entrenched social institutions, scrutinizing the family in particular with a premium on boldness. Indeed, the bolder its approach, the broader and stronger did its appeal tend to be. At first the aim was to turn up problems that might be solved or evils that might be remedied. But a depressive, defeatist, even destructive mood fast carried the day. By the 1890s any ambitious fiction that probed domestic life, as most fiction then did, was apt to present it as a pernicious mistake, and the more pernicious the deeper the probing had gone.

This fictional assault on the family, along with marriage as the familial breeding ground, was only rarely explicit, as when a Tolstoy or a Shaw fell to pamphleteering within a novel or a play. Nor were authors' own statements of purpose in prefaces or elsewhere authoritative, for even a work of creative genius may convey a message other than its author intended. To tease arguments out of fiction can be tricky, but such a massive fictional trend as this antifamilial one is unmistakable. At the same time, the charges leveled at the family within that trend do not add up to a coherent indictment. Rather, they are like so many swipes taken at it from various standpoints and different angles. Those swipes scored no quick knockout, but they did eventually deflate the received familial ideal.

Europeans targeted the family in literary fantasy just when, in those decades before World War I, it was thriving among them in public esteem and popular sentiment as perhaps never before. Even so, that onslaught against it was not fiction only; it was the down side of Europeans' restructuring of the family through their widespread adoption of birth control within marriage. This collective demographic doing by Europeans and, even more, their shared innermost feelings about it are my present subject. Both show through Europe's fictional case against the family when that case is seen as a whole and seen as social fantasy. So my argument starts with that case spelled out in some detail from fictional intimations and implications mostly as hazy as they are strong.

A Darwinist-sounding fictional charge against human family life that cut deep at the time was that it constricted and confined a species naturally free and loose. This was the force of Ménalque's famed exclamation in André Gide's *The Foods of the Earth* (1897): "Families, I hate you!"[1] Gide's whole generation learned this reason for hating families from Henrik Ibsen. And Ibsen's supreme representation of human domesticity as a false departure from nature was *The Wild Duck* (1884). In this dramatic masterwork, a stunted household shares quarters with a captive, wounded wild duck lodged in a fake forest set in a garret. A visitor from the woodlands asks the grandfather, a broken outdoorsman, how he can ever "live in the midst of a stuffy town, between four walls."[2] By way of reply the grandfather points self-contentedly to those indoor, make-believe woodlands where the lamed duck has been growing fat in its confinement. His dreamy, washed-out son explains: "She's been in there so long now that she's forgotten the true wild life; it's as simple as that."[3] In Ibsen's deft symbolism, that hapless duck stood for the human animal in captive domesticity, maimed and degenerating. In his earliest notes for the play Ibsen specified: "Human beings are sea creatures—like the wild duck—not land creatures." And he added hopefully: "In time, all people will live on [the sea], when the land becomes swallowed up. Then family life will cease."[4]

Ibsen taught Europe first off to look at marriage, the basis of its family life as far back as it knew, as an unequal partnership that turned the woman into a mere wife and mother, thereby arresting her personal development. As Ibsen saw it, woman may have been man's rib to begin with, but her domestication had made her into man's appendix. "You are first and foremost a wife and mother," her husband admonishes rebellious

Nora in *A Doll House* (1879), and Nora replies: "I don't believe that any longer."[5] Never could Nora have told her husband, for all his uxorious doting, that he was first and foremost a husband and father: such was the disparity built into their domestic setup. But the trouble with their marriage could, and at first mostly did, seem to onlookers across Europe to lie elsewhere—in the husband's patronizing sexism, or in a wife's legal disadvantages—and to be remediable accordingly through moral or legislative reform. Indeed, even in slamming the door on her "playpen"[6] with a resounding bang, Nora leaves it figuratively open to "the greatest miracle" of a true marriage with that same husband at some future time.[7] That tiny residual crack of an opening was unreal to her, to be sure: as she puts it at their grand moment of truth, "I no longer believe in miracles."[8] And Ibsen's dramas thereafter left no room for wishful thinking by his audiences about a woman's fulfillment within marriage whatever her husband's character or her relative rights: "Marriage . . . has ruined the human race" was his simple verdict.[9] For the basic problem in Ibsen's sight was that very institution, designed as it was for a woman to make a home for a man and to bear and rear his children. In marriage so conceived, the woman was perforce subordinate psychologically, an instrument of her husband and family, with no more satisfactory way to rebel against that subordination than to renounce sex and maternity. While some Ibsenite women after Nora, beginning with Mrs. Alving in *Ghosts* (1882), merely submit and suffer for want of a viable recourse, angry Rita in *Little Eyolf* (1894) reacts with an erotic possessiveness such that she inadvertently cripples and later kills the child that has become her husband's emotional refuge from her.

Ibsen's deadly Rita at least loves her man, however badly. But marital love was literarily in short supply at this juncture. Leo Tolstoy's wife-killer in *The Kreutzer Sonata* (1887/1889) loathes his victim just because of his carnal bond with her: his situation as husband and father by its very nature incites the jealousy that prompts his deed. Tolstoy represented his bloody hero as exceptional only in that with manic consequence he acts out the murderousness that husbands otherwise repress. For Guy de Maupassant, marriage spelled the death of love, but not by dint of a Tolstoyan dialectic of lust and shame; rather, the role of wife and mother was for Maupassant inherently inimical to love with its need for freedom. His "Adieu" (1884) is a lament over a former mistress's comedown to wifery and motherhood, and in his "Once Upon A Time" (1880) a grandmother sighs back to a mythic golden age when marriage was for breeding children while love was free outside. For Anton Chekhov too, love ended where domesticity began. But Europe's harshest view of matrimony and parenthood in those years was August Strindberg's. As against Romantic visionaries early in the nineteenth century, who had seen what wasn't there, Strindberg led a fin-de-siècle psychic breed that, like his autobiographic Sunday Child in *The Ghost Sonata* (1907), saw what was there but no one else saw, in this instance not at any rate until he had flooded it with a lurid light. What Strindberg saw was primarily the battle of the sexes, a deadly struggle for power infusing the physiology and psychology of love. Marriage was the choice arena for that struggle; children were its born instruments; jealousy was its chief weapon. In *The Father* (1887) a wife drives her husband insane with doubt over his paternity of their child. In *Miss Julie* (1888) a father and mother have fought out their love and hate through their daughter, Julie, who consequently winds up a suicide. *Dance of Death* (1901) features an aging couple long since locked in a suffocating stranglehold on each other. *The Ghost Sonata* picks apart a respectable home pervaded by "crimes, deceit, and falsity of every kind."[10] Of a brother and sister born within a parental standoff in *The Pelican* (1907), the one sets fire to the family home in the end while the other cries as they perish together: "Everything has to burn up or we'll never get out of here."[11]

In *Miss Julie* and especially *The Ghost Sonata,* sexual struggles for power spill over into financial swindles and social impostures rather more than was usual with Strindberg, who saw money-grubbing and prestige-seeking as mere displacements from the basic genital tug-of-war. But to numberless literary contemporaries of Strindberg's the home was as much an economic as an affective unit, one as productive of conflicts and hatreds over property as over sex. For Émile Zola in *The Earth* (1887), family life was primarily an economic scramble, with lust itself subserving greed. Out of greed in various guises the peasant protagonist marries his cousin, rapes her sister, kills his mother, and burns his father alive. Comparably, Mikhail Soltykov-Shchedrin's *The Golovlevs* (1880) is a grim saga of a sanctimonious kulak draining his whole family bloodless, his miserly mother and his own three sons inclusive, until, alone at last, he dies begging forgiveness on his mother's grave. But fictitious peasant families could just as well spawn murderous rivalries over sex and land intermixed, as in Vładisław Stanisław Reymont's *The Peasants* (1902–1908) or Ludwig Thoma's *The Widower* (1911). As a rule, the familial power play was brutally aboveboard in such earthy novels, whereas in a bourgeois literary setting, even one magnified expressionistically by a Strindberg, it would remain devious and insidious.

Within that power play the strong might abuse the weak with impunity behind closed doors. As the son tells the mother in *The Pelican:* "You yourself know how you murdered my father by driving him to despair, which isn't punishable by law."[12] Like the son and daughter in *The Pelican,* Strindberg's Miss Julie and Ibsen's little Eyolf were casualties of their parents' matrimonial tangles. *The Child* by Jules Vallès (1879) was the original novelized cry of protest from a battered child whose father was, as he put it, "master of me as of a dog."[13] A touching unsentimentalized successor to Vallès's self-styled little rebel was the child heroine of Gerhart Hauptmann's *Hannele's Ascension* (1893), who flees her brutal stepfather into suicide accompanied by naïve visions of paradise. The weak might also abuse the strong *en famille* through an exploitative dependency. Thus in Franz Kafka's *The Metamorphosis* (1912) an overtaxed young family provider at the breaking point takes refuge in the mad idée fixe that he has become a bug—surely as stark an image as was ever drawn of the family as alienating and dehumanizing.

But the parental violence done to children in the fiction of the time was not usually either exploitative or battering. Rather, the child suffered under the governance of one or another set of elders who, however well-meaning, simply could not bridge the fundamental divide between children or even adolescents and themselves. Shortly before this surge of fictional family-bashing, Ivan Turgenev's *Fathers and Sons* (1861) had posited the generation gap as a perennial difference in outlook and values between oldsters and youngsters ("It used to be Hegelians," grumbles an outmoded uncle, "and now it's nihilists"[14]) that is in no way limited to the family system and that the generational cycle itself smoothes away in the end. By the fin de siècle that gap had turned into an abyss, one expressively dramatized by Frank Wedekind in his tragedy of sex among schoolchildren, *Spring Awakening* (1891), with its authority figures (parents, teachers, a preacher) shown as seen from below—as Grand Guignol grotesques, utterly uncomprehending and inaccessible. George Bernard Shaw had it in *Misalliance* (1910) that "there's a wall ten feet thick and ten miles high between parent and child,"[15] and prescriptively: "No man should know his own child. No child should know its own father. Let the family be rooted out of civilization! Let the human race be brought up in institutions!"[16] Shaw's staged bantering was in tune with Oscar Wilde's in *An Ideal Husband* (1895): "Fathers should be neither seen nor heard. That is the only proper basis for family life."[17] Otherwise, though, the ground tone was downbeat by and large wherever the theme of parental sins was sounded.

Dependent on parents at a vast existential remove from them, the fictional children of the time, especially single children, could feel desolately, desperately at loose ends. They might retreat inwardly: novelistic explorations of painful inner aloneness at home culminated in Marcel Proust's *Swann's Way* (1914) with its narrator's remembrance of having craved ever more affection as a pampered child. A classic tale of an unpampered juvenile exile within his family, coping outwardly as best he could, was Jules Renard's beloved *Little Redhead* (1894). But failure to cope was more the rule. It takes the hero of Samuel Butler's *The Way of All Flesh* (1884, published posthumously 1903) a whole sordid youth to shake loose from his household puritanism even after he has recognized his loving, controlling parents as "the most dangerous enemies he had in all the world."[18] The heroine of Gabriele Reuter's *Well-Born* (1895) grows up helplessly aware of "an unbridgeable gap between parents and children."[19] Before her mother in particular "she was a mere worm,"[20] foreshadowing Kafka's hero in *The Metamorphosis*. Her all too proper upbringing leaves her a sexual cripple. In

John Gabriel Borkman (1896) late Ibsen depicted a youngster up against a father, mother, and mother's twin sister, each needing and using him differently until he shouts: "I can't take it any longer!"[21] and flees to a femme fatale waiting in the wings to bear him off into the stormy night.

Still more damning for the family than such stunted lives were the child suicides that may even have outnumbered them in the fiction of the time. Marie von Ebner-Eschenbach's novelette *The Honor Pupil* (1897) was typical, even stereotypical. It told of an overstrained schoolboy who drowns himself rather than face his father and mother—the one a bully, the other a drudge—when he has flubbed a history test crucial for retaining his privileged standing. After his burial the brutalized wife reassures the broken husband that he had only meant well by the boy in driving him over the brink.[22] Child suicide came into three of the other works already cited *(The Wild Duck, Spring Awakening,* and *Hannele's Ascension)*—and adult suicide due to abusive parenting, another literary specialty of this period, into four more *(The Golovlevs, Miss Julie, The Pelican,* and *The Metamorphosis).* Suicides of the latter sort were central to Gerhart Hauptmann's dramas in particular. A daughter commits one in his *Before Dawn* (1889) for fear of degenerating like her father. In his *Lonely People* (1891) a conscientious son can find no other way out of the pious parental abode that is stifling him. And in his *Michael Kramer* (1900) a homely, offbeat young sculptor takes that escape from his father's philistine contempt for him as a butt of everyone's ridicule.

Even in Hauptmann the inevitable generational conflict did not inevitably end with the child's suicide. A potentially deadly reactive animus of children against their parents was still more the rule of the day, and Hauptmann followed this rule in *The Peace Dinner* (1890) about a son estranged from his father for six years after striking him in the face: they are reunited for a Christmas dinner at which the old fight flares up anew, the father this time collapsing fatally. Such an animus might be controlled, as by the son whose father tells him in *The Wild Duck:* "Gregers, I believe there is no one in the world you hate as much as you do me."[23] Parricide itself might be strictly verbal, as in this pithy exchange between mother and daughter from *Dance of Death:* "Your father is stricken." "Alot I care." "My own Judith!"[24] But words could presage deeds. "Not an hour went by in which my fingers didn't itch to strangle him," declares the heroine of Arthur Schnitzler's *The Call of Life* (1905) about her leech of a father,[25] whom she then proceeds to overdose with morphine. Schnitzler's heroine craved sexual emancipation, and indeed sex usually mixed into the generational war in one form or another, including sexual rivalry from Fyodor Dostoevski's *The Brothers Karamazov* (1879/1880) to the Reymont and Thoma novels. Nor did the parent-child animus always originate below the great parent-child divide: in *The Father* and again in Hermann Sudermann's drama *Home* (1893) a father takes a gun to his daughter.

J. M. Synge spoofed this fictional battle of the generations in his comedy *The Playboy of the Western World* (1907). There a stranger on the run enchants a whole village by relating how he split his father's skull in a scuffle after refusing to marry an ugly widow for the money his father wanted. His sex appeal soars. "There's a great temptation in a man did slay his da," explains a widow on the make.[26] She too had slain her da, she avows, but only by "a sneaky kind of murder did win small glory with the boys."[27] The lionized fugitive gloats: "Wasn't I a foolish fellow not to kill my father in the years gone by."[28] The girl who falls for him hardest has a suitor who laments: "Oh, it's a hard case to be an orphan and not to have your father that you're used to, and you'd easy kill and make yourself a hero in the sight of all."[29] The hero's charisma promptly vanishes when the father appears with a bandaged head in hot pursuit of his assailant. The son smites him again in a new scuffle, but now this apparent murder seen from close up strikes the villagers as a mere "dirty deed."[30] They are about to turn him in for it when the father reappears, bloody and somewhat bowed. The son leads him off triumphantly, lording it over him and therewith resolving the generational conflict—alas, for this one play alone.

Not only for the varieties of strife endemic to it was the family the villain of countless novels and plays of the time. Another grievance against the family current among fictionists then was that it had wrongly moralized, even sanctified, itself to cover up the carnality at its core. This charge resonated with old-style ascetical Christian sermonizing, and it is notable that Ibsen, who had no use for Christianity otherwise, first declared against the family through his stern preacher Brand (*Brand* 1866)—a dubious mouthpiece perhaps, for he winds up being swept away by an avalanche while a voice proclaims that God is charity. But the view of family life as so much window dressing for the act of lust and shame led Leo Tolstoy into the outright Christian asceticism whereby, in *The Kreutzer Sonata,* he represented conjugality as bestiality. His uxoricidal hero at least posed an alternative to the family in passing: that the human race should just die out as did the dinosaurs.

Romanticism had already mocked bourgeois domestic proprieties alongside its cult of the simple, homey virtues. Thereafter, from Gustave Flaubert's *Madame Bovary* (1857) through Tolstoy's *Anna Karenina* (1875/1877) to Theodor Fontane's *Effi Briest* (1894/1895) the novel showed increasing sympathy for mismated women victimized by the moral premium placed on marriage and motherhood. Ibsen's *Hedda Gabler* (1890) gave this mounting distaste for the familial ethos imposed on women a wrenching twist. Although its heroine is married and pregnant throughout, the play bears her maiden name to point up how miscast she was for that wifely and motherly role she was expected to play. Close behind the grand show she puts on, she despises her husband, writhes at his one relative who visits them, loathes their home styled ruinously to her taste, and haughtily refuses to acknowledge her pregnancy. Nor will she seek relief the common way, in love affairs: she recoils from sex itself as much as from the risk of scandal, always harder on a woman. Feeling trapped, she reacts with a nihilistic vengeance, in an orgy of destructiveness. She tempts a reformed alcoholic off the wagon, burns a great work by him in manuscript, gives him a revolver to kill himself with, and shoots herself in turn with its twin. Her would-be lover's curtain-ringer over her dead body is eloquent on the code of constraints that she too, like Nora before her, ultimately broke with a bang: "Such things just aren't done."[31]

The familial ethos enjoined love within the home, and this injunction was faulted on several scores in the fiction of the time. For one thing, it could work as a sexual stimulant under a sexual taboo—a setup for suffering. Actual incest freely enjoyed in Zola's *The Earth* or Thomas Mann's *The Blood of the Walsungs* (1905) got off easier morally than incest recoiled from in Ibsen's *Ghosts,* incest inflicted in Hauptmann's *Before Dawn,* or incest frustrated in Kafka's *The Metamorphosis.* Next, doting short of incest could be an intolerable drag: "Mother! How often I've almost wished and hoped you wouldn't care for me so deeply," exclaims the son in Ibsen's *Ghosts.*[32] But hardest hit was the duty to love even the hateful within the family on pain of remorse. In *Ghosts* again a preacher asks a mother: "Have you forgotten that a child should love and honor its father and mother?" and the mother replies: "Oh, don't let's talk so abstractly! Let's ask: should Osvald love and honor Captain Alving?"[33] The answer is no, as Mrs. Alving knows. Yet she has lied to her Osvald in letters out of a felt need to keep the paternal image clean, and she admonishes him shortly afterwards in the preacher's very idiom: "Shouldn't a child feel some love for its father no matter what?" Osvald duly replies in his mother's own vein: "Do you really cling to that old superstition—you, so enlightened otherwise?"[34] With further Ibsenite irony the family circle then closes around Osvald like a noose as he falls prey to the same degenerative disease as did the father he rejects. Gerhart Hauptmann in *The Peace Dinner* repeated this fatalistic scheme of Ibsen's. "Do you think I feel any special respect for my father, huh? Or maybe I love him, maybe I feel filial gratitude?" scoffs a son who is a prey to his father's own mental deterioration.[35] Both Ibsen and Hauptmann meant physical inheritance, but this was no less a metaphor for children's affective ties to their parents against their better judgment. Longest-winded against "compulsory affection" among the familial pieties was Shaw, that would-be perfect Ibsenite, in his preface to *Misalliance,*[36] and in this play itself a child of a happy marriage exclaims: "Oh home! home! parents! family! duty! how I loathe them! How I'd like to see them all blown to bits!"[37] Shaw's debt here was to Samuel Butler as much as to Ibsen. Butler's hero in *The Way of All Flesh* matures only by coming to terms with his wrenching dislike for both his parents. A sidelong glance at the animal kingdom convinces him, moreover, that the human family is against nature: "The ants and the bees, who far outnumber men, sting their fathers to death as a matter of course," he observes with envy.[38] Hard as it was to face unlovable parents as just that, their moral ascendancy could otherwise be devastating as in *Well-Born* or deadly as in *Miss Julie.*

The moralization of the family entailed as a further penalty the need to maintain appearances. *The Ghost Sonata* carried this need to a ludicrous extreme what with the members of a household always "saying the same things or saying nothing at all so as not to give themselves away,"[39] for they are bound together like all good families by "crimes and secrets and guilt."[40] From *The Wild Duck* to *The Ghost Sonata,* the effort to clear the air of such stifling falsity turned tragic ever and again.

The little heroine of *What Maisie Knew* by Henry James (1897) is a personified contradiction of the moralized, moralizing family. Maisie's closest novelistic lineage was that of Oliver Twist, a child who, while cut adrift from his family, runs a moral obstacle course unscathed: at the juvenile end of this line was Hector Malot's *Without A Family* (1878). Maisie, though, is no orphan, virtual or actual. Rather, she grows up as the only child in an ambiance averse to family life—an aversion underscored by her playboy stepfather's repeated empty protests that he really is a family man at heart. Maisie's divorced parents first shunt her back and forth to spy on each other, then slough her off on governesses, before finally abandoning her to a stepmother and stepfather who have used her to get together. Even while precociously exposed to the facts of life, not least through her mother's steady turnover of lovers, Maisie develops a dignity and strength of character such that, on adolescing, she is able to walk away from the affluent stepfather she adores, and into the custody of a straight-laced governess, when he declines to give up his self-willed mistress for her. This child of an antifamily within a greedy and promiscuous milieu scales that Jamesian height all on her own.

In the long view of it taken at the time, the family appeared as an overarching reality, one with a constraining inner dynamic independent of the wants and needs of its members. A preserve for old wounds rather than old joys, it could exact tribute for them years or even generations later, as when a daughter in *The Wild Duck* commits the suicide flubbed by her grandfather, then by her father, before she was born, and with the same revolver to boot. Its inertial coherence is such that it can, and repeatedly does, outlive its affective bonds and utilitarian functions until its "life spring" sickens and dries up as in *The Ghost Sonata,*[41] or else its values become unlivable and hence destructive as in Hauptmann's *Lonely People.* Encrusted family codes victimizing family members were the stock-in-trade of countless novelists of the time, among them John Galsworthy beginning with *The Country House* (1907). A naïve period piece in this vein is François de Curel's drama *The Fossils* (1892) about a young aristocrat dying of some wasting disease even as his family faces extinction: in extremis he marries his father's and his own mistress to legitimate her newborn son while his sister pledges her life to helping the improper mother raise the boy properly. But surely the family spirit (Ibsen's "ghosts") celebrated its grimmest fictional triumph in Zola's *The Earth* through a pregnant peasant wife raped by her cousin and murdered by her sister: in dying she covers up their crime, and even disinherits her husband from distant parts for their benefit, out of "a deep family sentiment stronger than hatred or the need for revenge."[42]

With his Rougon-Macquart novels, begun in 1871, about a widely ramified family, Zola pioneered the post-Darwinist notion, which swept the fictional field, that the family was the vehicle for degeneration in the species, or for short that decadence inhered in families. "I tell you, his father was a disgusting fellow who kept mistresses and the like; and so, you see, the son has been sickly since childhood," remarks Nora in Ibsen's *A Doll House*,[43] and that son himself later adds: "in every last family to some extent this inexorable retribution takes place."[44] This incidental, even extraneous, theme of *A Doll House* of 1879 was central to Ibsen's *Ghosts* three years later, with its legitimate son paying a steeper price at a younger age for his father's sins than did that father himself. At the same time, that blood taint in *Ghosts* passes an illegitimate daughter by as far as the play discloses. Conversely, in *The Wild Duck* ten years later a teenager is already going blind like her natural father—this, however, within what is thought to be a legitimate family, which thus legitimated the degeneration. Syphilis and alcohol came into the degenerative process quite commonly in the 1880s without ever being essential to it. Thus dissipation sped the hapless breed in Hermann Bang's *Hapless Breeds* (1880) along its Darwinian way down. The Galovlevs in *The Galovlevs* drink and whore when they degenerate, not vice versa. Hauptmann gave up on vice fermenting degeneration inside of the one year from *Before Dawn* (1889) to *The Peace Dinner* (1890). Strindberg for his part had no use for ferments, from his pseudo-Darwinist preface to *Miss Julie* on—though in *The Ghost Sonata* he did help out degeneration through a cook draining the vital juices from the family's food. By the time of Gabriele D'Annunzio's *The Virgins of the Rocks* (1895) or Thomas Mann's *Buddenbrooks* (1900), the family progressively devitalized down the generations was a literary cliché, including heightened awareness and sensitivity among the terminal brood. End-of-the-line neurotic aestheticism ran from Jens Peter Jacobsen's *Niels Lynhe* (1880) through Joris-Karl Huysmans's *Against the Grain* (1884) to Hauptmann's *Michael Kramer* (1900) and Rainer Maria Rilke's *The Notebooks of Malte Laurids Brigge* (1910). A masterly last word on decaying houses, their sapped energies drained by their own musty rules of life, is Eduard Graf von Keyserling's *Evening Houses* (1914).

Even this depressing theme of the ever more baleful family heritage could inspire a comedy. In Harley Granville-Barker's *The Voysey Inheritance* (1905) an heir apparent to his father's investment firm learns that the old man has been defrauding his clients for years. He covers up until the father's death, prepared to declare bankruptcy then after indemnifying the neediest victims. But the other Voyseys back away from his effort at restitution. Worse, his accountant tries to blackmail him while two wary old family friends press him to pay up their depleted accounts. In papering over the firm's deficit until he can make it good, he acquires a taste for juggling, faking, and swindling such as his father had acquired from his own father before him. And he grows manlier in the process until the girl cousin who had once despised him as a callow fool can return his love. As he had told the assembled family fast upon his father's burial: "You've the poison in your blood, every one of you," adding: "Who am I to talk? I daresay so have I."[45]

Such were some of the damning imputations against the family that pervaded European fiction in the few decades before World War I. To exemplify them I have barely skimmed the enormous literature involved.[46] This literature ran to type, theme for theme, from its finest showings on down to the penny thrillers of the day featuring "unhappy couples and hapless marriages."[47] And it ran to type Europe-wide if not quite on the supply side, at all odds on the consumption end: even the most sophisticated fiction in this vein found vast and eager markets throughout the continent. Its message hardly varied with authors' or readers' gender,[48] class, or nationality, so to approach it along such dividing lines would be to miss the whole for the parts, the forest for the trees, the river for its currents and crosscurrents. Fiction friendlier to the family in this same period was swamped, besides trailing *A Doll House* and its numberless sequels in both esteem and popularity.[49] Nor did that fictional quarrel with the family that began with *A Doll House* cease with the advent of World War I, but it no longer dominated the scene thereafter.

This European groundswell against the family in literary fantasy was wholly unprecedented, despite occasional earlier ripples. Marriage and the family had come into previous creative works almost always as a mere setting and not a subject proper. Resentments and rivalries galore, only no inveterate generational estrangement, had pitted children against parents in older drama and verse, folklore and farce. In Greek tragedy, familial calamity—the curse on the house of Atreus, Oedipus' parricide and incest, Phaedra's deadly lust for her stepson—was never made to look like an upshot of familial existence per se. The troubadours already sang the antithesis of love and marriage, but marriage was no less the precondition for their lyrical adultery. Possibly John Ford blamed the incest in *'Tis Pity She's A Whore*, as did Shelley for sure in *The Cenci*, but neither blamed it on the dynamics of family life; Shelley indeed saved his strictures against marriage for his anarchistic tracts.[50] Molière's *Tartuffe* lampooned the bossy father, and Jane Austen's *Pride and Prejudice* the silly mother, without calling parental authority into question. All young Werther's sorrows were no argument against Lotte's marriage and motherhood, let alone against the family overall, whether in young Werther's eyes or in young Goethe's own. Not easier divorce, but renunciation, was the lesson of Goethe's later *Elective Affinities* with its fateful adultery committed in the heart on both sides of the marital act. Dickens and Balzac painted bad families black-on-black only to paint good families white-on-white. Not only did European fiction first indict the family in 1879–1914; it did so then for a newly swollen mass market, with literacy rates surging and printing costs sinking.

That fictional indictment was no less powerful for being mostly implicit. A Henry James for one, though no family man himself, just might have arched an eyebrow if confronted with the implications of his storytelling against the regnant cult of Home, Sweet Home, but the implications would remain. Subversive messages get through best surreptitiously, which may be why Strindberg himself frequently denied being antifamily. In the nonfiction of this same period, a few autobiographers told of generational conflicts, mostly conflicts of outlook as in Turgenev's *Fathers and Sons:* thus Ibsen's disciple Edmund Gosse with novelistic flourish in his *Father and Son* (1907). Otherwise, though, the fictional strictures against the family found little echo in the explicit social criticism of the time. Previously, Europe had not wanted for straight-spoken, activist enemies of the hearth, from Dionysian revelers through Christian ascetics down to the numberless radicals and utopians who, in the long aftermath of 1789, had called for an end of marriage and the family in the name of human emancipation. By the 1880s, however, their most vocal survivors or descendants had put such drastic objectives on their programmatic back burners. Extremists now sought rather to reform the family, a few oddball diehards notwithstanding.[51] Witness Alfred Naquet, who in 1869 advocated universal free love on neo-Malthusian grounds and dismissed divorce as unavailing, then by 1876 was championing divorce in France as a means to preserve the family and boost fertility.[52] Even the boldest humanistic thinkers of the following decades, such as Nietzsche and Freud, did not quarrel with the family as an institution (Zarathustra's proud celibacy notwithstanding). Anthropologists stressed its universality while they inventoried its diverse forms. Sociologists upheld it as a vehicle of social cohesion and continuity—following Frédéric Le Play, who spent his career documenting and combatting an imaginary historic trend toward ever more "unstable" households with children moving out on their parents as soon as they were able.[53] Learned treatises on human degeneration did not discuss it as inherent in families;[54] only plays and novels did that. Public authorities, educators, religionists, hygienists, psychologists, criminologists: all saw in the family a bulwark of social salubrity, for that very reason to be protected, doctored, overhauled. Correspondingly, for over a century past the family had by all appearances been growing ever sturdier and homier, "closer and more affectionate," substituting conjugal and parental companionship for the old patriarchal norms, indeed reconstituting itself in fact and fancy as an intimate, privatized "retreat from the outside world" with its "crucial base" in this "sentimental bond" among its members.[55] The literary trend to the very contrary was, then, like the flip side of public consciousness—a latent countertendency at odds with the familial values entrenched in Europe's social instincts and attitudes, and outwardly flourishing as never before. This discordance, remarkable in itself, is doubly so in that the older, outright antifamilialism had been culturally marginal: the mainstream fictional campaign against the family that began around 1879 was new in being mainstream as well as in being fictional.

What gave rise to this mainstream fictional repudiation of the family throughout Europe that began around 1879? The first place to look for an answer is in the family itself, to see whether something there did not change radically in those same years. And something there did change radically. For those were the years when conjugal birth control first spread throughout the European population as a whole.

Traditionally, as Malthus originally saw or guessed, Europe's population had been self-regulating to obviate or, conversely, repair the ravages of famine and pestilence.[56] While illegitimacy was consistently discouraged, legitimate fertility rose or fell above all with bridal ages, also with marriage rates, and thirdly with breastfeeding practices. Marriage ages and rates adjusted to conditions of penury or plenty from time to time and from place to place on the quasi-invariable basis of so-called natural fertility within marriage, meaning no deliberate curtailments of conjugal reproduction. "Natural fertility" was a misnomer insofar as other species that pair off control their fertility by abstinence, fewer and smaller litters, abortion, neglect, and infanticide far more than by limiting their pairing rate. Legitimate fertility rates running slightly below those of the surrounding population over some generations have been found for certain well-to-do, educated, mostly urban groups in early modern Europe, affording presumptive evidence of birth control—the bourgeoisie of Geneva, Rouen, and Lyon; Tuscan Jews; Hungarian Calvinists; Venetian, Genoese, Florentine, Milanese, and Belgian aristocrats; and most strikingly French dukes and peers.[57] Other premodern instances of low-grade marital birth control have no doubt escaped detection, not to mention more assiduously contraceptive groups or families that would have eliminated themselves on short order. But the fact that all known deviations from natural fertility within marriage were isolated, sporadic, and moderate underscores the ground rule that Europe's premodern population tended spontaneously to constrict its high potential growth within feasible bounds by aggregate adjustments that excluded any intentional limitation of marital fertility. Indeed, these spontaneous accommodations served to protect and sustain natural fertility within marriage, so that natural fertility can be called the psychological sticking point of the premodern family. Even infanticide could be routine in marriages where birth control was unthinkable.

Marriage rates rose and marriage ages fell on balance in Europe as living conditions improved throughout the nineteenth century. Death rates meanwhile had begun plunging in the late eighteenth century, mainly from improved food supply and sanitation but also from a new concern with infant survival.[58] With ever higher proportions of offspring reaching childbearing age as a result, the problem arose for Europe to contain this huge human upsurge within manageable limits even despite the supermortality of marriageable males due to the wars of the French Revolution and Napoleon. Massive emigration ensued, with inadequate effects. At the same time Europe's richest and boldest nation, France, moved in another direction. Marital birth control, already known in France above all to the affluent and enlightened at least since the sixteenth century, began to spread significantly throughout the nation around the time of the Revolution. French marital issue fell off steadily thereafter until the 1840s, then leveled off for a generation or so before resuming its downward course in the late 1870s. And then it was, beginning in the mid-1870s, that the rest of Europe too took to deliberately limiting conceptions within marriage— the intelligentsia and the ruling classes first, the more northerly peoples first, as a rule the city folk also first, but in all national areas and all walks of life inside of a single generation, with revolutionary consequences for European society overall.

Europeans set their new course of generalized marital birth control collectively for want of a viable alternative in the face of a drastic existential threat. Why that course was set has long been a futile statistical guessing game in which one plausible hypothetical correlate of incipient marital birth control after another—industrialization, rising living standards, secularization, urbanism, feminism, the spread of contraceptive means or knowledge—has failed to check out causally.[59] The snag all along was conceptual. That European conjugal revolution of the late nineteenth century needs to be grasped as a collective doing, or group process, in line with Europe's age-old, inveterate demographic self-regulation. By the 1870s Europe faced an unprecedented, potentially devastating internal invasion. At the peak rate of increase it was then running, its population of some 330,000,000 in the 1870s was headed toward a couple of billion over the next century—a truly forbidding prospect. To have stemmed this human tidal wave in the traditional way, by juggling marriage rates and ages, to the extent that it actually did so by conjugal birth control would have called for condemning nearly two out of every three women to celibacy without issue or else forbidding all women to marry before their middle thirties—both options impracticable from the word go. *That* is why Europeans adopted marital birth control instead on top of their continuing large-scale emigration. And that radical emergency measure was too little too late at that: they topped it off with the positive check of massive self-slaughter beginning in 1914.

The incidence of birth control on family life was mainly of two sorts, both of critical psychological importance. First, with married couples having by design only just so many children—typically four or five among the first family planners, then three, then one or two, all of them expected to survive into adulthood—the parental investment in and concern over each child rose proportionally.[60] Earlier parents too might dote on their children, to be sure, but not even the Christian god could love each of his many creatures on a par with his only begotten son.[61] Through birth control the human family pushed to artificial lengths what biologists call the K-strategy of few, protected offspring as against the R-strategy of animals that scatter their seed in heedless abundance. Or again, to trespass on yet another discipline, the family developed the ultimate in a capital-intensive emotional economy. Familial intimacy soared, but at the same time it grew "explosive."[62] When the son exclaims in Ibsen's *Ghosts* (as quoted above): "Mother! How often I've almost wished and hoped you wouldn't care for me so deeply," the mother replies as if to bear him out: "Oh, Osvald, my only boy! You're all I have in this world and all I care about."[63] The parallel crucial effect of birth control on family life was that it created a generation gap within the family circle, and this even though the average parental age decreased. That is, the trend was for women to marry younger and, once married, to start childbearing promptly as before, then to stop earlier, so that parental ages fell by and large.[64] But formerly, with a wife normally bearing children until the end of her fertility span if she survived that long, her children's ages were correspondingly fanned out however many died along the way. Thus her first-born might already be having children of their own before she herself was done. As a result, each generation passed imperceptibly into the next. After the 1870s, by contrast, with a couple typically having four, three, or two children in its mid-twenties and then stopping, the generational divide was acute and conspicuous.[65]

These two phenomena together go a long way toward explaining the trouble that European fictionists all at once found with the family from 1879 forward—especially inasmuch as their grievances against it took shape fictionally, which is to say imaginatively rather than logically, or more in the way of dreams than of arguments. That families were against nature and inherently decadent; that their nexus was fleshly lust cloaked by false moralism; that their affective ties were dangerously ambivalent; that their built-in power struggles and claims on their members' loyalties were potentially destructive; that parents, for all their despotic or even tender authority over their children, were inaccessible to them: this whole fictional repertoire of charges against the family at large points to the small, tight-knit, birth-controlled family with its emotional involution and its generational divide. Tolstoy's protagonist in *The Kreutzer Sonata* actually drew this connection between conjugal birth control and the turn against the family in that he dated his own deadly struggle with his wife from her doctors' prescribing contraception when she fell sick after her fifth delivery—when her womb went on strike.[66] Likewise, sterilized sex is easy to recognize behind Strindberg's recurrent obverse symbol of filth and foulness clogging the hearth—and it is explicit in Strindberg's characterization of modern, unwholesome families where children are "nipped in the bud . . . in the bedroom" as a matter of course.[67] Zola's *Fertility* (1899) was a cautionary tale against marital contraception in which a fruitful family flourishes even as shrunken families come to grief. And Henry James set his grand little Maisie off against her parents' social set representing a contraceptive extreme: "There *are* no family women—hanged if there are!" declares Maisie's stepfather. "None of them want any children—hanged if they do!"[68] But birth control is written into the whole corpus of this antifamilial literature in that, after Nora's three children in *A Doll House,* the usual number for a fictional couple fast fell to two or more often one. Already in Turgenev's precursive *Fathers and Sons* each of the two sons was an only child. So were the children in Ibsen's *Ghosts* and *The Wild Duck,* in Jacobsen's *Niels Lynhe,* in Hermann Bang's *Hapless Breeds,* in Strindberg's *The Father* and again in his *Miss Julie,* and so on through the 1880s and beyond.[69]

The initial indication is, then, that Europeans, through their fiction of roughly 1879–1914 up and down the artistic scale, highlighted and drasticized the troubles they felt with their newly truncated families. That fiction tended to originate in the nations as in the milieux where birth control spread into the family earliest. But it was all-European in both inspiration and acceptance: nothing quite like it developed in contraceptive France alone before the 1870s, or for that matter in contraceptive America before the 1920s. Its authors were themselves of diverse familial circumstances. At the extremes among those cited above, Strindberg had seven and a half siblings to Zola's none and three marriages to none for Butler or Maupassant, while Tolstoy had thirteen children from his one marriage as against none for Zola or Shaw from theirs.[70] Each author was perforce sensitive to different problems with the birth-controlled family as a result of different personal experiences. What matters here, though, is only the vast resonance found by their works that add up to a horrified European shudder at the family itself.

Europe's dismal, depressive, mud-splattered fictional image of the family around 1879–1914 was mildly nightmarish—or rather, in a nonword, daymarish. It was the reverse, or the negative, of the exalted official image of the family that then held sway in Europe. It conveyed a deep undercover malaise felt inside the family and towards the family in Europe. And in its routine bleakness and catastrophism it was a guilty vision.

The source of the guilt infusing that vision is evident. Marital contraception crashed a huge moral barrier. Christianity had blessed the family down the centuries on the pagan premise that its purpose was to reproduce.[71] In the Christian perspective, God had designed sex for propagation, with marriage as its hallowed precinct. Christianly speaking, sex outside of marriage was naughty enough; unnatural sex within marriage, sex deflected from its reproductive end, was wickeder still—an obscene abuse of the marital sacrament.[72] That Europe's churchmen failed to inveigh much against gratifying the groin fruitlessly in holy wedlock until after massive contraception began in the 1870s suggests that they had little call to do so.[73] How those premodern Christian minorities that curtailed conjugal fertility here and there did so remains uncertain. But less marital sex is the safest bet, for there is no good reason why the strictures against defiling marriage with sex for its own sake should have gone unheeded in just those few instances and no others. Coitus interruptus made inroads into marriage from the late sixteenth century on,[74] but not distinctively among minorities with low fertility rates except French bluebloods, so it did not add up. In any case, the generalized adoption of contraceptive sex within marriage marked a daring and dizzying reversal of Europeans' basic attitudes toward their bodies and souls alike, a collective transgression of an age-old, Christianized taboo that had carried over intact even into post-Christian mind-sets. Wives often took the innovative lead, for it was they who had paid the stiff penalties of natural fertility all along while men had enjoyed easier premarital and extramarital sex. By contracepting within marriage, whether or not they thought it through in these terms, they in effect claimed their bodies as to be their own to use or enjoy as they pleased and not organic machines for reproducing as long as they could. Maupassant's "Useless Beauty" (1890) was like a manifesto for wives who had had it with reproducing: its thirty-year-old heroine feels she has paid her demographic dues in bearing her husband seven children, so she walks out on the lot of them by means of a lie and a ruse. Alternatively, walking out by mutual consent on reproduction *within* conjugality brought with it powerful latent shame and guilt—shame between spouses at copulating just for fun, as Tolstoy proclaimed, and guilt on each side first and foremost over the old taboo being broken.

Earlier I presented the factual family contraction and fictional family critique of 1879–1914 in Europe as cause and effect: smaller, tighter families, at closer emotional quarters but divided generationally, made for heightened domestic tensions that for the most part got spelled out or acted out only in novels or plays. But such fictional spelling out and acting out was largely ahead of its time. Europe's Sunday Children saw the crack in the house before it spread (to draw on Strindberg's self-version in *The Ghost Sonata*)—anticipated the full domestic incidence of a fertility revolution that had barely begun in the 1880s or even the 1890s. This anticipation came heavy with projective guilt from the broken taboo, over the contracepted children, toward nature itself. But much more to this same effect: in Europe at large, marital contraception was felt to be a first, decisive step away from the family. To call Tolstoy in *The Kreutzer Sonata* to witness again, with that step a wife and mother turned into a whore.[75] So indeed, to cite Henry James again now, did that wife and mother and that husband and father who called it quits after having just Maisie both promptly go promiscuous. Or to recur to the very point of departure for the fictional critique of the family: Ibsen's unpregnant Nora, eight years married, her three children all old enough to run on stage, had apparently put a halt to childbearing before the curtain rose. Hence this prototypical rebel against the family was also a prototypical contracepting wife. Her telling her husband on walking out: "Our home's been nothing but a playpen" is subtly evocative of a contraceptive ménage. Her declared position is that she will no longer be a mere wife and mother: if that is what marriage is for, then down with marriage. Once the natural family was on the line, so too was the family all in all.

Europe's fiction thereafter tended to justify and to punish the contraceptive revolt against the family at one and the same time by both blackening the family and visiting it with doom. The first generation of Europeans to practice sterile sex on top of baby-budgeting in marriage broke with the family as it had been known from time immemorial. If deep down that felt as though they were breaking with the family *tout court,* well might Europeans of 1879–1914 be haunted by visions of the seemingly snug and cosy birth-controlled family potentiating evils belonging to the family as such. And this was indeed the subtext of Europe's familial fiction in that great age of social realism.

CHAPTER TWO

Ideology in the Bedroom

When the material pressure of population growth forced a Europe-wide cutback in fertility beginning in the 1870s, France alone in Europe had already broken the moral barrier against marital birth control nearly a century earlier for no material reason. Historians of France have long puzzled over this aberrant national behavior. Their understanding has been impeded by their failure to see that the new departure in France was of a piece with one in America impelled by a revolutionary ideology that the two nations shared between them and that carried over from the public to the private sphere. That carryover is the focus of this second of the two chapters on group process in the adaptive mode.

Why did the French start cutting back on births nearly a century before any of their European neighbors? And why did that initial cutback coincide with the French Revolution of 1789, whereas fertility and politics do not ordinarily mix? These questions about the French have been raised as a rule in the French historic context alone, and they are as far as ever from being settled. I propose to address them comparatively instead, with due regard for a vital fact hitherto overlooked by researchers on France: the concurrent decline of American fertility. This latter decline took off from the American Revolution and actually outpaced its French counterpart. The comparison will reveal a causality that goes unnoticed when the French case is seen in isolation.

French historians agree about little else so strongly as that France's big jump on the rest of Europe in conjugal birth control was the most portentous, pernicious fact of modern French history. Toward the end of the Old

Regime, French fertility stood at .775 of the highest aggregate human fertility on record, that of the Hutterites in the United States.[1] This index had fallen to .471 by 1876, when the other European peoples began joining the French on the slippery slope of fertility decline. Was it not, then, in the marital chambers of France rather than on the battlefield of Waterloo that French power in Europe was broken? Fernand Braudel posed this loaded question about what he called "the identity of France" only to add, presuming on the answer: "It is therefore important to zero in on this French precocity and to search out its causes. . . . Obviously this is the major challenge facing the historian."[2]

By the latest reckoning, the French took the first, decisive step toward generalized birth control within marriage just as they were fighting their great Revolution. After having fluctuated with no clear direction before 1789, fertility fell off by more than 10 percent within the following decade and went on falling steadily for over a century and a half.[3] The initial falloff consisted primarily in a lowering of the average age of wives at last delivery and only secondarily in an extended spacing of successive pregnancies.[4]

These early stoppages of childbearing, given their large numbers, were evidently voluntary on the whole. How they were achieved is uncertain. Presumably wives' ploys for eluding intercourse led the way, backed up by makeshift contraception or timely withdrawal, with abortion as an option of last resort. Such at least is what can be read back into the French experience from accounts by working-class women in England a century later of how they got their baby counts down.[5] Birth control had been common practice since classical and even biblical antiquity not just in extramarital sex, but more modestly in marital sex as well: the differences in legitimate birth rates from one region to the next of prerevolutionary France speak clearly to this point. Such differences turned above all on the duration of breastfeeding, which could not be prolonged without some measure of preventive intent.[6] Accordingly, what varied most from one locale and one period to another before 1789 was the average interval between births rather than—as during the fertility decline that followed—the average age of mothers at their last delivery.[7] This variance leaves the bottom line intact: that in 1789 couples began making radically free use on a large scale of means as old as sin to reproduce less. With quantity thus becoming quality, the fertility transition was on.

"Its import can hardly be overstated," wrote Pierre Goubert in 1973 about the early French reproductive slowdown. Interpreting "this precocious adoption of birth control by the French" as a national cave-in of monumental historic proportions, Goubert pursued: "The diagnosis is clear, but the causality is elusive and has the historical demographers scrapping."[8] Three decades later they are still scrapping. Some seek that elusive causality in the means used to control births, though such means were no less available at other times and places. Others look to the motives for family limitation, though these too were hardly wanting earlier or else-where. Still others stress factors of so-called modernization, in particular the spread of secularism,[9] although the French had no monopoly on modernization in Europe when they were going it alone in fertility control. The falling death rate also has its advocates, who see in the national baby-budgeting a defensive reflex against the threat of overpopulation in France.[10] The trouble here is that in France the death rate originally fell not before the birth rate, as this causality would require, but along with it.[11] The regional approach has its adepts as well, who would substitute diverse local causes for a single national cause.[12] The statistical contours of the French fertility transition did indeed vary from region to region, from village to village, from family to family. Regardless: the impetus to family planning took off from broadly similar reproductive levels and attitudes throughout prerevolutionary France to sweep the entire nation inside of two or three generations without spilling over into neighboring countries at any point. A national phenomenon par excellence, the French fertility transition accordingly requires an explanation on the national level just as its local variants require explaining on the local level.

Let us approach that elusive national causality from another angle after first rectifying a huge misconception that the entire French historical establishment appears to share. Here is the offending error as formulated by Alfred Sauvy in 1960: "We know for certain that the birth rate declined in France long before it did in other countries."[13] In 1962 Sauvy saw in "this difference between France and the other countries . . . the most important fact of her entire history."[14] Pierre Goubert in turn stated in the early 1970s: "It is certain that France was the first birth-controlled nation in the world," and again: "France . . . was first in the world, and by far . . . to introduce systematic birth control."[15] In 1986 Fernand Braudel made the same mistake in discussing "the contraception epidemic" and with it the "revolution in behavior" that it entailed: "As for France," he wrote, "this revolution was more precocious there than anywhere else," indeed of "a clearcut and astounding precocity."[16] Pierre Chaunu joined the chorus in 1988 with the laconic formula: "In France and nowhere else."[17] More graphically, the cover of volume three of the paperback edition of Jacques Dupâquier's *Histoire de la population française* shows the author pondering "France's solitary entry upon the demographic transition."[18] This repeated misstatement hints at national pride in a national first, however deleterious. Foreign scholars appear to indulge their French colleagues, tolerating the running error ever so tactfully or else correcting it ever so discreetly. Thus Étienne Van de Walle affirmed that "the decline took place in France much earlier than anywhere else"[19]—he who had earlier found a formula at once precise and nuanced for contraceptive France: "alone in Europe."[20] A demographer long established in America, Van de Walle must have known that the fertility transition in the American colonies that broke

Total fertility rate, United States and France, 1800–1940
(number of children per woman)

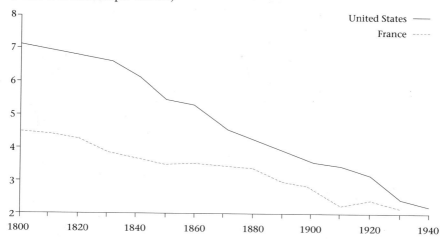

This diagram shows clearly that the fertility decline, originating in the revolutionary period in both America and France, progressed faster in America despite continual immigration from higher fertility nations.

Sources: Jean-Claude Chesnaise, *La transition démographique* (Paris: Presses Universitaires de France, 1986), table 11.1, for France; Ansley J. Coale and Melvin Zelnik, *New Estimates of Fertility and Population in the United States* (Princeton, NJ: Princeton University Press, 1963), table 2, for the United States.

away from the English crown accompanied or even preceded the one in France. To the same effect, the American who in 1982 examined the American fertility transition in the journal of the official French demographic institute obligingly did so only from 1800 on and without mentioning the parallel French development.[21] Shortly after his article appeared, moreover, some twenty French historical demographers blithely contributed to a volume entitled *Dénatalité: L'antériorité française 1800–1914,* which its joint editors, Jean-Pierre Bardet and Jacques Dupâquier, presented as an attempt to determine "how and why contraception was so widely practiced in France during the nineteenth century more than a hundred years in advance of all other countries."[22]

That other, concurrent fertility transition unnoticed by French observers came into American historiography with a bang in the 1970s on the strength of mutually reinforcing archival findings indicating that in revolutionary America, just as in revolutionary France, marital fertility entered upon a decline that continued without a letup until after World War II. To be sure, fertility was much higher at the outset in America than in France,[23] and it long stayed higher to boot, largely because of a continual influx of immigrants more fertile than their hosts. This disparity aside, the similarity of the two curves of fertility decline is striking, with the two ultimately hitting rock bottom together in the depths of the world depression of the 1930s. Even though the use of different statistical categories from one American monograph to the next precludes any rigorous synthesis of the diverse findings, the decisive demographic turning point in America can be situated in the revolutionary period itself or shortly thereafter for the principal communities studied—all of Rhode Island; Hampton in New Hampshire; Andover, Hingham, Sturbridge, three farming villages, and Nantucket Island in Massachusetts; and Quakers wherever they were.[24] Furthermore, a comparative study of twenty-odd towns in colonial New England revealed the wide variety of their demographic structures:[25] like the French transition, the American was therefore fundamentally national. The biggest difference that I can make out between the two transitions is what looks like somewhat more spacing of pregnancies in America than in France before the average cut-off age of childbearing fell.[26]

Was the near parallel between the two transitions a mere transatlantic coincidence? Hardly. Two huge new historic departures roughly equivalent and roughly simultaneous, or more exactly two radical breaks with age-old behavioral norms by the two revolutionary nations of the period stirred by the same spirit of enlightenment and sharing the same faith in a humanity capable of casting off the servitudes of the past and adopting the pursuit of happiness as its guiding purpose: these twin vital developments, born of the same innovative impulse, were one and the same at bottom, only configured slightly differently from the one national context to the other. So the question is not why French couples, or American couples, began to limit their progeny at that historic juncture, but why French *and* American couples began to limit their progeny at that historic juncture.

Historians all revere Marc Bloch, and ever so rightly. It were high time, then, that they heeded his teachings on the comparative approach to developments occurring close together in time and place. He once lectured medievalists on the subject and chose his examples accordingly: the counterpart in Provence to the English enclosures, the rise of the provincial estates and of the Estates General, the formation of feudal principalities, the growth of the seigniory, the rise of villenage as against serfdom. He sprinkled his lecture with warnings against "local pseudo-causes" and with proclamations of "the need for comparative studies, which alone can dispel the mirage of false local causes." Some of his utterances were lapidary: "A general development can only have equally general causes." Others were at once pointed and incisive: "To attempt to explain the formation of *Gutsherrschaft* [manorial domain] in Mecklenburg or Pomerania, or the amassing of land by the English squire, solely on the basis of facts gleaned in Mecklenburg, or Pomerania, or England, would be to waste one's time on a sterile guessing game." Or again: "Only one thing is certain. There can be no accounting for the English openfield, the German *Gewanndorf,* the French *champs ouverts,* by looking only at England, at Germany, or at France." And as if anticipating the controversy over the French fertility transition, he even specified: "The authors of monographs must be told again and again that they have a duty to read what has been published on subjects close to their own not just in the same region, as they all do, nor even in immediately adjacent regions, as most of them do, but also, as is all too rarely done, in more remote societies separated by political conditions or by nationality from the ones they are studying." He concluded with a resounding appeal: "Let us stop . . . talking forever from national history to national history without understanding one another."[27]

So let us stop talking national history and instead try to account for the French and American fertility transitions both together, excluding not only any explanation suited to only one and not the other of the two countries where fertility fell in unison, but also any explanation that could apply just as well to third countries where fertility did not fall. Or in brief, let us seek an origin at once common to, and exclusive to, these two transitions. Origins are easier to rule out on these terms than to rule in. Consider the decline of religion, urged as a cause in the French case above all by Pierre Goubert:[28] we can eliminate it twice over, for the English (to take just them) were fully as freethinking as the French at the time, whereas their American contemporaries were on the contrary experiencing a religious revival.[29] A prior fall of the death rate in France, real or not, does not pass the comparative test either, since "mortality was, if anything, increasing" during the American transition.[30] The widespread thesis of the elites' having set the contraceptive fashion in France cancels against the elites' having been the last to follow that fashion in America.[31] And neither the long-term influence of courtly love invoked by Jean-Louis Flandrin nor that of Jansenist asceticism invoked by Pierre Chaunu makes it across the Atlantic, so they too get washed away.[32] Indeed, as far as the going causal explanations of the French transition are known to me, none of them passes the comparative test. On the other hand, the causal explanation most often advanced in America for the American transition fits the French transition fully as well, as I shall show. But first I must prepare the ground.

The French and American peoples were alone in conducting not just two unprecedented reproductive revolutions in the eighteenth century, but along with them two unprecedented political revolutions as well. That a demographic dip should have gone with a political upheaval challenged the French historiographical orthodoxy of the heroic days of family reconstitution out of the parish registers of the old regime, when researchers strained on the contrary to hold politics and ideology at a radical remove from those historic depths where the likes of fertility transitions were thought to germinate, snugly sheltered from the play of mere surface events and transient opinions—the stuff of politics. The numerical data drawn from church archives tended accordingly to get lumped into chronological segments that submerged the year 1789 as if in a slow and steady stream of collective life. This was in particular the effect conveyed by the study that the French Institut National d'Études Démographiques conducted in the 1970s on marital fertility in the four quarters of France at the end of the old regime: its apparent finding was of a fitful, diffuse flow along a self-given course of decline with something of a speedup toward 1800.[33] David R. Weir situated the French transition on the contrary squarely in the revolutionary decade that began in 1789 on the strength of a reprocessing of the data yielded by this monumental inquiry, yet he still respected its spirit so far as to stress rightly that "the fertility transition did not occur overnight in response to a specific event like the storming of the Bastille, the nationalization of the Church, or the promulgation of the Napoleonic Code."[34] Weir thus rejected any direct causal link of the political revolution to the demographic transition without denying that the two were related. Meanwhile in 1988 Pierre Chaunu, a staunch believer in the immanent, gradual change of such human basics as fertility, was calling for "an end of the false debate over the Revolution"[35]—just before that debate, true or false, rebounded with the advent of the bicentenary of 1789.

A few partial dissenters had kept the French debate from dying out altogether before it rebounded. Thus a 1958 study by Étienne Gautier and Louis Henry evidenced "an abrupt fall in fertility due to the limitation of births within marriage" in the Norman parish of Crulai at the very time of the Revolution. Rightly seeing behind this fall a "major modification of behavior," the authors commented: "The fact that this modification came about very quickly, under the shock effect of the Revolution, suggests that minds were prepared to accept it."[36] As against this logic, however, a shock effect accepted in advance would no longer be a shock effect. In 1963 a study of three villages in Île-de-France revealed the sudden onset of a fertility decline there "around 1785 or 1790," and the author inquired ever so cautiously: "Is this to be seen as a consequence of the revolutionary legislation on inheritance?"[37] But such a consequence would incongruously have preceded the legislation behind it, which in any case had no equivalent across the Atlantic. A 1969 analysis of the "fertility revolution" in Meulan stated flatly, though with no further elaboration, that "its decisive stage coincided with the political Revolution."[38] One of its authors, Jacques Dupâquier, seeing these coincidences multiply from one monograph to the next, eventually concluded that the Revolution had somehow acted on the birth rate, though without ever quite saying how.[39] And in 1988 Alain Blum wondered in passing about a possible "primacy of the event": "The French Revolution exists in and of itself, through its shock effect, the mobility and spread of behaviors due, for instance, to conscription for the army of Year II; legal changes such as the adoption of the Code Civil—which, as is well known, introduced equal inheritance—gave the impetus to a transformation of family relations, or at the very least of the links between population and the agrarian system, the mode of exploitation."[40] The one clear causal factor to emerge from this opaque conjunction of the fall of fertility with the Revolution in France is the very French fear of a fragmentation of land holdings; this fear had no counterpart, however, in that country across the Atlantic with frontiers wide open to all comers where fertility nonetheless took the same steep turn downwards.

"Primacy of the event," immateriality of the event: both are equally unfit to account for two interconnected effects of a single radical ferment that was at once defiant and creative—to account, that is, for the political and familial revolutions that issued together from the same spirit of rejection and renewal in both France and America. An Edmund Burke or a Friedrich von Gentz, observing the two political revolutions from the outside, could contrast the one with the other all the way down the line without departing too far from the facts; it remains that the two revolutionary peoples felt a close solidarity centered in a shared refusal of any servitude not freely consented. Adolphe Landry, decades before the detailed statistical study of what he christened the "demographic revolution" began in France, recognized its kinship with the political revolution there: "A great advance took place in people's minds," Landry wrote in 1934, "freeing them from an age-old submission . . . to established authority. . . . There was a tendency to revise the ideas governing both individual and family life. Men were in particular no longer inclined to let nature multiply their progeny without limits, but on the contrary wanted to decide for themselves how much to multiply according to their personal preferences."[41] The spirit of the age that rejected ancestral patriarchal authority in the political sphere also rejected it in the domestic sphere by the same token. The two revolutions appear to have gone together even regionally in France— witness neighboring Normandy and Brittany, the first markedly more revolutionary both politically and demographically than the second—but strictly comparable quantitative data on the regional level are lacking.[42]

Landry wrote according to the old masculine-unisex convention that "men" of revolutionary persuasion sought to regulate their reproduction as they saw fit. His use of this generic term was especially inept in this context. For is not reproduction more women's business than men's? This rhetorical question takes me back to the theory about the American transition that, with some minor qualifications, has won at least tacit acceptance from most American historians. Formulated in 1973 by Daniel Scott Smith under the name of "domestic feminism,"[43] backed up then and since by a wealth of extracts from letters, diaries, and manuals for married couples, this explanation has it that American women who espoused the liberal, egalitarian, and individualist values of the Revolution, only to find themselves excluded from public life despite those very values, reacted by taking control of their family life, and in particular of their own bodies, inasmuch as they refused to accept unrestrained childbearing against their will. Not that they necessarily exerted pressure for this purpose:[44] a wife could not impose contraception or even abstinence on her husband without at least some modicum of cooperation on his part any more than she could compel a reluctant husband to conceive with her. According to Smith, what American women presumably obtained from their husbands at the time of the transition was not interrupted intercourse ("the male contraceptive par excellence") so much as less intercourse.[45] The supposed predilection for withdrawal in France may be an artifact of the French sources most widely consulted, novelists being little concerned with marital abstinence and priests being less exercised by that sin of omission than by the "sin of Onan."[46] In any event, the revolutionary ideology emboldened American women domestically: in growing numbers they put their husbands on the defensive wherever they did not win them over straight off. Mary Beth Norton nicely demonstrated this "indelible effect" of the Revolution on women as wives.[47] Carl N. Degler defined the effect psychologically: "Women have always had a reason for limiting children that men have not, but that reason could motivate behavior on a large scale when women became self-conscious about themselves as individuals—that is, when they began to see themselves as beings separate from their husbands and their families."[48] None of these newly self-conscious American women was more eloquent on this score than the old-fashioned mother who noted in her diary of the 1790s that one of her daughters who had just borne a dead son "may pass through, if she lives, the same excruciating trouble a year the sooner for this loss," then recorded concerning another daughter exhausted after a sixth birth: "This day is 38 years since I was in agonies bringing her into this world of troubles: she told me with tears that this was her birth day, I endeavour'd to talk her into better spirits, told her that, the time of her birth was over by some hours, she was now in her 39th year, and that this might possibly be the last trial of this sort, if she would suckle her baby for 2 years to come as she had several times heretofore &c."[49]

The fact that the first two demographic revolutions were concurrent with the first two democratic revolutions suggests that the causal link found to hold in the one case should be found to hold in the other as well. A 1978 study of the role of abortion in the French fertility decline did show how French women, having failed to gain the same civic rights as men because of their failure to organize, "simply took matters into their own hands" and "set out to play an active role, by whatever means, to control their fertility."[50] In 1793 the French National Convention prohibited women from forming public associations lest as a result they neglect the familial duties "to which nature summons them."[51] Some made bold to protest, whereupon the Municipal Council of Paris outdid the Convention by reminding them of "brazen Olympe de Gouges . . . who abandoned the care of her home to mess with the Republic and whose head fell

to the avenging blade of the law."[52] Thus in France as in America "the Revolution reinforced the separation of the public and private spheres,
boosted the family, and differentiated gender roles as between political
men and domestic women."[53] Put back in their old place, French women
could at least assert themselves fully there even if the revolutionary legislation dismantling the patriarchal family did prove short-lived.

Such self-assertion was long overdue. At the close of a pioneering study
on the origins of contraception in France, Philippe Ariès asked "whether
the revulsion at continual childbearing did not originate with women, and
with women exclusively, as a feeling unknown to men and ignored by
them."[54] "The study of memoirs and letters from the seventeenth century
lends decisive support to . . . this important hypothesis," affirmed Hélène
Bergues,[55] who assembled a vast array of French source material on the
matter from the eighteenth as well as the seventeenth century. In France,
however, the Age of Enlightenment was also the age of alcove secrets:
spontaneous personal accounts of married life were lacking right through
the revolutionary decade inclusive,[56] so that in France the fertility transition is not recorded in correspondence and diaries as it is in America.
Nonetheless, from the material assembled by Bergues, as also from the
naughty novels that Bergues disregarded, it emerges clearly that in both
the seventeenth and the eighteenth centuries it was the women who
mainly imposed birth control or urged its adoption in France.[57] Of the father confessors cited by Bergues, the one closest to the lower social orders
was Père Féline, who in his *Catéchisme des gens mariés* [catechism for married couples] of 1782 denounced "husbands' excessive indulgence of their
wives" and specified with a clean canonical conscience: "They have sensi-
tized themselves all too much to complaints from their wives about how
hard childbearing is on them."[58] Other testimony by priests spread the
blame equally between husbands and wives for damnable efforts to cheat
nature.[59] But no matter: the bottom line was that for the Church "submission was required of wives in all circumstances."[60] Add to that the monarchy's persistent push for population growth, and a wife wishing to resist
an insensitive husband before 1789 could find precious little moral support anywhere.

I may have implied inadvertently that the new view of reproduction
within marriage as a matter of free choice won over most French wives
and, only a little less readily, husbands in the 1790s. In fact it was linked
to a revolutionary outlook that never commanded universal allegiance in
France any more than in America and that suffered a severe setback in
France during the Reign of Terror. In fact baby budgeting was never advocated openly at the time; in public, on the contrary, revolutionary women
would routinely extol motherhood in the service of the nation.[61] But it
took relatively few refusals of another pregnancy to trigger the process of
progressive fertility retrenchment within the relatively self-enclosed

French breeding pool. A comparative study conducted at Princeton of the fertility transition throughout Europe since the mid-1870s established its automatic character once a national birth rate fell by more than 10 percent.[62] Accordingly, with an average of around six births apiece for French wives at the end of the old regime, it took only one out of five French wives in the 1790s refusing to bear children beyond the third for the decline to set in irreversibly. It is indicative of this process that, as compared with French women married before 1770, fully a fifth more of those married from 1790 to 1819 left off childbearing by age thirty-five in the northeast quarter and even a good fourth more in the northwest quarter of France.[63] Again, by David R. Weir's calculations, "at least a third of the first post-1790 marriage cohort stopped having children younger and ended up with fewer children than under the regime of natural fertility at the beginning of the eighteenth century."[64]

That critical threshold was a moral sticking point. From time immemorial, Western morality had sought to confine procreation to marriage. In return, the price of marriage was the duty to produce children, and to produce them dutifully rather than voluptuously. Erotic fun was reserved for extramarital relations—fornication, adultery, prostitution—the choice province for contraceptive tools and techniques. Voluntarily sterile sex within marriage put even libertinage to shame. Behind the conjugal imperative prevailing in old France to be fruitful and multiply—partly carnal piety, wholly carnal servitude—one might incline to see the combined influence of Church and State, which were emphatically at one in the matter. Such a view would be myopic, however, for the selfsame marital duty was incumbent on spouses in colonial America with no pressure from either the civil authorities or the Puritan church.[65] Clearly, then, it was grounded in a subjective constraint deeply ingrained throughout the West. The fertility transition meant that married couples were violating that constraint not only more frequently, but deliberately. Before, they could space pregnancies with no clearcut, considered intent, mainly by breastfeeding often combined with abstinence;[66] after, they could not cut their childbearing short without conscious design. To be sure, there had always been some couples, however few in relative terms, who deliberately cut down on births but not on sex. Salacious literature confined the "fatal secrets for cheating nature" to amorous adventures outside of marriage; in reality, such sly skills were fully capable nonetheless of subverting conjugal duty now and again, only to be absolved in the confessional afterwards.[67] They smacked of the illicit, of the forbidden, of transgression, which suited them to dalliance but which spoiled more than it spiced the marital act. No matter, the moral barrier was equally in place for those who observed it and for those who sneaked around it. Only the revolutionary spirit would eventually bring that barrier down.

The transition was, then, not a matter of new means or new motives. Rather it was—as Pierre Goubert put it, using quotation marks to distance himself from his own troubling insight—"a certain sort of 'liberation' from ancient 'taboos.'"[68] He might perhaps better have said from a double taboo inherent in marriage since time out of mind: against both its hedonistic abuse and its intentional sterility. The transmission of a new "family planning" mentality from parents to children, the boost it got from living examples of less burdensome motherhood, the higher odds of child survival in smaller families, women's growing sense of rightful autonomy and equality at least in the private sphere, husbands' increasing considerateness of their wives even when reluctantly conceded, the gradual erosion of the stigma of infertility: nothing about this process is problematic except that France was the only nation in Europe to experience it before the 1870s whereas it spread rapidly across the whole continent thereafter. This singularity of the French experience in Europe argues an extraordinary tenacity of the old, inveterate taboo: breaking it required either a genuinely revolutionary audacity or—as was the case with Europe continent-wide in the 1870s—an imminent threat of massive overpopulation.[69]

Breaking a taboo is, though, a far cry from lifting it. A whole nation cannot shed a taboo overnight; it does so only gradually from one generation to the next. Today the conjugal taboo is done and over with, but the generation that first infringed it in Europe beginning in the 1870s paid the penalty in the classic form of a guilt crisis clearly inscribed in the creative literature of the time, which smeared the new-style, contraceptive family all up and down. This smear has been examined in the last chapter. Now, though, the question perforce arises whether France should not have felt this same guilt already in the postrevolutionary period, when in fact no trace of it showed in literature or elsewhere. The question is crucial for anyone concerned to dip down into the vital sources of history. It arises moreover as much for America as for France—and once again it is an American study of America that supplies an answer equally applicable to France. I am referring to a key study by John Demos distinguishing two systems of morality that prevailed by turns in New England. By Demos's account, the first of the two, founded on shame, ruled the consciences of the Puritan colonists until about 1750, and the second, founded on guilt, took over around 1800. The period in between, which Demos describes as "largely obscure,"[70] exactly encompasses the American fertility transition. Under the primacy of shame, the supreme moral sanction was the reproving gaze of others, internalized as the all-seeing eye of God relentlessly ferreting out even the slightest secret sins.[71] The successor system substituted the individual's own inner eye, the personal conscience: one saw oneself as guilty, one might even be devoured by inner remorse, while paying no heed to the surrounding world. Or rather, since 1800 guilt has performed only "the heavy work of morality,"[72] with the two moral regimes interpenetrating right down to date. At first sight, the abundant documentation that Demos provides for colonial New England seems to come out of an austere moral universe poles apart from that of worldlier prerevolutionary France. However, the moral discourse of the French old regime affords no more evidence of an inner sense of guilt than does that of Demos's American colonists, but only fully as frequent allusions to shame itself or else to immodesty, disrepute, disgrace, opprobrium, sin before God. The concept of guilt still applied only to the outer fact without denoting the—often unwarranted—inner feeling of having lapsed or transgressed. This dominion of shame in old-regime France elucidates the tacit preference then given to spacing pregnancies, as against stopping them early, wherever birth rates ran relatively low: spacing was less self-exposing, less suggestive of secret intent. As much as the fertile woman was held in honor by a Greuze or a Diderot, that much was the barren woman held in contempt.[73] The first French women to cut down perceptibly on childbearing for reasons of principle in the course of the Revolution had to answer for it to their fellow citizens more urgently than to their own consciences. But morality was even then being internalized, and more rapidly than the taboo on the contraceptive abuse of marriage could be lifted.[74] Indeed, this taboo was still being felt in France when, in the 1870s, the rest of Europe in turn began to challenge it.

To talk about a taboo being broken before being lifted is to talk psychohistory again. And talking psychohistory takes us back to Marc Bloch, who stipulated at the end of his *Apologie pour l'histoire:* "Historical facts are, in essence, psychological facts. Hence they normally find their antecedents in other psychological facts." Concerning such psychological facts Bloch hastened to specify that "there can be no psychology of clear consciousness alone" and accordingly to call for penetrating the mental life of the past way down into "its obscure depths."[75] In this psychohistorical perspective proposed by Bloch, let us cast a quick second glance at the egalitarian and antipatriarchal spirit that took hold from wife to husband during the two great political revolutions that ushered in the contemporary era. Was that spirit sufficient cause for the fertility plunge that ensued? Yes, if we confine ourselves to that fertility plunge alone, isolated from what came with it and after it. However, the penetration of this revolutionary spirit into the home marked the start of a major upheaval and turnabout in relations between the sexes which has since spread throughout the West and, intensifying from year to year, has tended not only to undermine the time-honored male primacy in the public sphere, but also to break down all the long-established differences between the sexes in domestic and professional walks of life—in dress, in hairstyle, in ornamentation, even in ways of making love. A century ago theorists were still seeking to pin down what was inherently masculine or inherently feminine; now this notion of anything intrinsically masculine or feminine is out of season.[76] To see women assuming control of their own fertility in the home as the point of departure for this whole revolution in progress is to raise the question whether what I posited as cause was not really effect: whether the egalitarian and antipatriarchal spirit introduced into the home by revolutionary American and French wives who claimed decisive power over their own reproductive function was only the first surface sign of a slow transformation of human sexuality, of a biological revolution only gradually unfolding. To track that group process down into "its obscure depths" calls for an approach no longer primarily, let alone exclusively, demographic but above all, as Marc Bloch would have wanted, psychohistorical.

Our inquiry on the parallel American and French fertility transitions has thus come to a halt before the need for a whole new departure in demographic research. It is evident from that inquiry that, with the human breed as with all other species, the statistics of sexuality and reproduction reflect group dynamics operating at a deeper level than that of individual choice. For all its science, demography will be wanting in explanatory value unless and until such collective determinants are identified—until the mechanics of adaptive group process have been sorted out for humans as perceptively as for insects or rodents.

CHAPTER THREE

A Community of Fate

With groups as with individuals, adaptation may fail in cases of overwhelming shock, upset, or distress, especially of a deathly variety. Of the possible maladaptive reactions, by far the most productive, or more often destructive, historically is for the afflicted group to work through its trauma anew and unawares in circumstances contrived to mirror, or often magnify, the original traumatic setup, sometimes recasting it backwards or lopsided the better to deny the equivalence. Such traumatic reliving may be facilitated by a leader responsive to the group's traumatic need; in that case the reliving and, behind it, the trauma itself is best approached through the leader responding. This first of two chapters illustrating traumatic reliving *en groupe* deals with a massive replay led by a dictator empowered for that very purpose: the replay of the German trauma of defeat dated 1918.

To an uncanny degree Adolf Hitler shared in his own person the shock and pain felt by Germans collectively after their 1918 defeat. This was the source of both his rapport with them and his ascendancy over them. By 1930 Germans as a whole began to feel increasingly powerless against him and empowered by him. After 1945, when they were called to account for the Nazi past, their sense of fatedness on the national level, of having been swept along by Hitlerism regardless of personal consent or dissent, was largely disallowed inside as well as outside of Germany. Since then the Hitlerite groundswell has been explained instead on the basis of concurrent individual judgments and special interests within the body politic. Such explanations slight the core fact that, from the time the dictatorship was established, potential German opposition was not so much blocked or repressed from on high as inwardly inhibited or paralyzed. Hitler's will was not merely defined as law; it was felt as law. Hitler himself explained why when, just before his sudden, swift rise to power, he claimed to be obeying a popular will deeper than mere public opinion.[1] For once he told the truth.

It was in calling outright for ruthless German expansion to the east that Hitler, until then only a fringe agitator in Munich, began to build up a mass following all across Germany. He first proclaimed that predatory eastern aim outright in volume one of *Mein Kampf,* which he wrote during his thirteen-month incarceration for his abortive putsch of November 1923. There he considered three other hypothetical remedies for an alleged German land shortage, only to find them wanting and to settle instead on a land grab along Germany's path of least resistance.[2] He repeated this argument of the "four ways" tirelessly thereafter as long as he openly advocated eastward conquest: until November 1930.

Some three years earlier Hitler had already advanced this same line of argument short of the expansionist conclusion to which he took it in *Mein Kampf.* At a Nazi meeting on 31 May 1921 he dismissed three false ways out of a supposed national land squeeze before claiming that the Treaty of Brest-Litovsk, imposed by Germany on Russia in early 1918, had brought Germany a fleeting prospect of true deliverance: "By the peace with Russia," he declared, "Germany's nourishment as well as the existence of work were to be supplied through the acquisition of land and soil, through raw materials imports and friendly relations between the two countries."[3] He recapped this lost gain to Germany in an outline for a similar, undated speech: "Brest-Litovsk was to assure German people's nourishment through: I. soil, [and] II. securing raw materials by industry and trade."[4] This fanciful tribute to brutal Brest-Litovsk resonated with a key point of the Nazi Party program issued on 24 February 1920 with strong input from young Hitler: "We demand land and soil for our people's nourishment." Such an unfocused demand might have looked like a mere ritual protest over Germany's lost overseas colonies, but Hitler gave it a bellicose continental twist within another nine months if, as the Munich police noted, he stated in a speech of 19 November 1920: "Once we are inwardly strengthened we can turn to the east."[5] At all odds he was manifestly looking to the east for that lost "land and soil" when on 31 May 1921 he celebrated Brest-Litovsk in language resonant with that of Erich Ludendorff, Germany's de facto military dictator in the late stages of the lost war of 1914–1918 and latterly a mascot of Munich's right-wing radicals. At the close of 1915 Ludendorff had written about Poland in that same rapacious vein: "Here we shall win ground to breed the men needed for further battles to the east."[6] And Ludendorff's instructions of December 1917 for the negotiations in Brest-Litovsk had specified: "Annexation of Lithuania and the Courland, including Riga and the islands, as we need more land for our people's nourishment."[7]

After 31 May 1921 Hitler never again recurred to that "existence of work" (a courtesy to his nominal topic, "Versailles and the German Worker") or to those "raw materials imports and friendly relations" (which he nonetheless actualized for a brief spell under the Germano-Soviet Pact of 1939). On the other hand, Germany's need for more "land and soil" in the east was a fixed talking point with him from then on. In the outline for his undated speech like the one of 31 May 1921 he all but reached his later expansionist conclusion: "German colonization: 8th–13th century. First the eastern march, then the northeastern march. Is our people fit for that? Prerequisite: power."[8] He reached that expansionist conclusion off the podium by the end of 1922, when he expounded his program for a future German dictatorship to a confidant of the then Chancellor:

> Abroad, Germany would have to go over to a purely continental policy, avoiding any damage to English interests. The breakup of Russia with England's help should be attempted. Russia would provide enough land for German settlers and a broad field of activity for German industry. Then England would not butt in when we settle with France.[9]

A jotting for a speech of April 1923 reads: "*Overall aim:* land and soil for the nation."[10] A half year later Hitler again specified behind the scenes that "we must expand eastward."[11] But not until after his failed putsch did he go public with his projected eastern land grab, and then he did so guilefully as if he were reasoning his way to it from scratch, step by step, from his putsch trial through a magazine article to *Mein Kampf*.[12]

By the time Hitler's eastern policy emerged behind the scenes at the end of 1922, its derivation from Brest-Litovsk and Ludendorff's eastern imperium of 1917–1918 was no longer in evidence. Yet not just the concepts and terms, but the same "four ways" argument that he had used to deplore the loss of the eastern conquest of 1917–1918 reappeared intact in his public pitches for eastward expansion. Hence at bottom the land grab from the USSR that he urged in private as of late 1922 and in public beginning with *Mein Kampf* was for him Ludendorff's land grab from the USSR all over again. Accordingly, in urging the conquest of Soviet Russia he was in effect urging a repeat of Ludendorff's brief conquest of Soviet Russia. Consciously, though, he was already passing over this 1917–1918 referent for his eastern aim by late 1922. At the point where in *Mein Kampf* he set forth the need to expand the "motherland" to the east so that the "Germanic mother" might nourish her offspring sufficiently, he declared: "In this we National Socialists consciously put an end to the course of Germany's prewar foreign policy. We pick up where Germany left off six centuries ago."[13] Unconsciously it was more like six years.

How did Hitler come to his basic purpose of repeating Ludendorff's lost victory of 1917–1918? The process began when to a stock subject of his earliest oratory, the Versailles *Diktat,* he added Brest-Litovsk by audience demand. As he related in *Mein Kampf:* "At the very first sentence containing a criticism of Versailles you had the stereotyped cry flung at you: 'And Brest-Litovsk?' 'Brest-Litovsk?' . . . I set the two treaties side by side, compared them point by point, showed the truly boundless humanity of the one as against the inhuman cruelty of the other." He added that he "repeated and repeated" this demonstration "dozens of times in ever varied form"[14] at the prompting of his public. For, as he put it, "the orator receives a continual correction of his speech from the crowd he is addressing inasmuch as he can see from the faces of his listeners how far they are able to follow his presentation and take it in, and whether by the impact and effect of his words he is attaining the desired end. . . . A popular orator of genius," he concluded,

> will always let himself be carried along by the great masses so that instinctively the very words flow from him which he needs to speak to the hearts of his listeners. But should he err ever so slightly, he has the living correction before him all the time. As stated above, he is able to read from his listeners' facial expressions whether, first, they comprehend what he is saying, second, whether they can follow it all the way through, and third, to what extent his presentation has carried conviction.[15]

This account is borne out by numberless army, police, newspaper, and Party reports of early Hitler speeches. Hitler did indeed adapt his set piece on Brest-Litovsk to his audiences while striving to put his message across. But his intense rapport with his audiences suggests, beyond mere adaptation, counterinfluence, especially as his nominal point, the "boundless humanity" of Brest-Litovsk, was mere polemical sham (he had little use otherwise for "boundless humanity"). Indeed, it was in the very heat of contrasting humane Brest-Litovsk with inhumane Versailles that, on 31 May 1921, he deplored Germany's loss of the land and soil wrested from Russia at gunpoint. He never repeated that set piece on Brest-Litovsk thereafter.

The indication is, then, that Hitler picked up from his public the purpose latent in his policy of "land and soil": to repeat Ludendorff's short-lived eastern conquest. That indication is supported independently by the fact that the particulars of his "land and soil" policy can be traced to no personal determinants such as underlay his other, older, anti-Jewish policy in its entirety.[16] His failure to cast his eastward aim in his prior anti-Jewish terms points that same way. From the start of his political career in September 1919 Hitler saw the supposed Jewish menace as international[17] and Bolshevism as Jewry triumphant. Hence Russia was for him the power center of the international Jewish menace. It was also the chief breeding ground of the Jewish race. Accordingly, obvious premises lay ready to hand when, after 31 May 1921, he slowly turned a regret over the loss of land conquered from Soviet Russia into a call for a future conquest of land from Soviet Russia. More, those ready premises even entailed that foregone conclusion. If the Jews were a deadly international danger with their power base and their vast breeding ground in Russia, then that deadly international danger needed to be met not just within Germany's borders, but above all in Russia as well. Destroying Jewish power in Germany alone would only incite world Jewry to revenge.[18] "To grasp the evil by the root and eradicate it root and branch," as Hitler proposed to do,[19] necessarily meant to conquer Soviet Russia.

Hitler moved around and around this clear connection without ever drawing it over the nineteen months he took to turn his look back at Brest-Litovsk into a look forward. On 12 April 1922 he declared after an hour's raging against the Jewish-democratic-plutocratic-Bolshevistic world peril: "There are only two possibilities in Germany! . . . Either victory of the Aryan side, or its destruction and victory of the Jews."[20] He developed the ideological aspect of this theme in a memorandum of 22 October 1922 on building up the Party:

> What is at stake here is not winning a majority or even winning so-called political power. What is involved is a life-and-death struggle between two world views that cannot coexist. Their clash will leave only victors and victims. This conception has become second nature to Marxism (witness Russia). A victory of the Marxist idea means the total extermination of its opponents.[21]

This claim against Marxism, alias Judeo-Marxism, was styled as if to ground Hitler's scheme to destroy Soviet Russia with England's help. Indeed, logic pushed hard for carrying the deadly domestic showdown between two worldviews into Russia itself. The anti-Bolshevik rationale for invading Russia lay ready to hand when Hitler prefaced his confidential maiden mention of the scheme in December 1922 by declaring: "With the suppression of Bolshevism in Germany, iron-fisted dictatorship must rule."[22] He then nonetheless ignored that ready rationale and reverted instead to his problematical premises of nineteen months earlier—to the Germans' right to grow at others' expense and to secure their food and raw materials on the European continent, meaning through its subjugation. It was likewise on this basis alone that, beginning with *Mein Kampf*, he promoted the eastern conquest with the German public—openly until shortly after the Nazis' great leap forward in the national elections of 1930, then only deviously with the ears of the world tuned in to him.

On a theoretical plane Hitler meanwhile synthesized his expansionist with his anti-Semitic policy by way of the alleged historic law that peoples all struggle among themselves for living space—all except the Jews, that is, who live off other peoples as parasites and thus threaten the human breed with extinction by their growing ascendancy.[23] No more in his theorizing than in his speechifying, however, was the one world-historical imperative, killing Jews, the logical ground for the other, conquering land. Even so, he kept his completed theoretical integration of these two intellectually and psychologically distinct policies under wraps by secreting his 1928 manuscript that contained its final formulation.[24] For long years meanwhile he also kept his racial-ideological grounds for the proposed eastern conquest to himself while continuing to advocate it in the Ludendorffian language of soil and nourishment and raw materials and a blockade-proof continental sphere.

While he promoted the proposed eastern conquest in these terms only guardedly in public after the Nazis' electoral upsurge of September 1930, he did so quite starkly behind closed doors in his political and military councils following his accession as Chancellor. To Reichswehr commanders on 3 February 1933, after four days in office, he foretold "the conquest of new living space in the east and its ruthless Germanization."[25] Before roughly the same group enlarged by SA and SS leaders on 28 February 1934 he again pointed ahead to "creating living space" for Germany in the east.[26] On 5 November 1937 he briefed his five top political and military aides on his contingency planning "to solve the German space question."[27] In a military conference of 23 May 1939 he held forth on "expanding our living space in the east and securing our nourishment."[28] As for Judeo-Bolshevism's mortal designs on Germany, he cited and slighted them in *Mein Kampf* as only the last of many reasons for Germany not to ally with Soviet Russia.[29] In his secret sequel of 1928 to *Mein Kampf* he merely observed in an improbable context that, populous as it was, the Soviet Union was no military, but only an ideological, menace.[30] In his memorandum of August 1936 on the Four Year Plan to initiate economic mobilization he did note the threat from international Jewry based in Russia, but altogether separately from Germany's need for more living space as a "definitive solution" to German economic problems.[31] The Anti-Comintern Pact, which Germany concluded with Japan in November 1936 and with Italy a year later, carried a hint of secret aggressive designs in its sham defensiveness against Bolshevik expansion.[32] This propaganda ploy of the red menace prompted Hitler to remark to the Japanese negotiators in June 1936 that he had "always seen Europe's sole salvation in the uncompromising fight against Communism" and in July 1936 that the Bolshevik threat could be met only by a dismemberment of the Soviet Union.[33] Here then, in these talks with Japanese negotiators behind closed doors, Hitler for the first time derived his eastern aim explicitly from his anti-Bolshevism, hence from his anti-Semitism once removed. Two years later his henchman Heydrich told a confidant: "It is the Führer's will to liberate Russia from the Communist yoke. The war with Soviet Russia is a settled matter."[34] And on 2 June 1940, as France was falling, Hitler put it to an army headquarters group in Belgium that he expected a "reasonable peace settlement" with Great Britain that would free him "at last" for his "great and proper task: the showdown with Bolshevism."[35] But only when the invasion of the USSR was mounted did he open in full the parenthesis— "(witness Russia)"—that he had tacked onto his assertion of 22 October 1922 that the fight against Bolshevism was a "life-and-death struggle between two world views." On 30 March 1941, in handing down the eastern operational plan "Barbarossa" to 200–250 assembled army commanders, he announced an impending "struggle of two world views against each other," adding: "What is involved is a struggle of annihilation."[36] He therewith ordered the army to kill captured Communist officials (the "Commissar Order"), and Heydrich instructed his SS henchmen that "eastern Jewry is the reservoir of Bolshevism and therefore, in the Führer's view, is to be annihilated."[37] With the start of the invasion, secret instructions went out to the press to switch its tack to "the annihilation of Bolshevism," then some days later to the link between Bolshevism and Jewry.[38] Living space had taken second place.

Now to pull the threads tighter together. In the latter 1920s Hitler the aspirant German dictator advocated eastward expansion on power-political grounds that had originated with Hitler the Bavarian agitator in early 1921 as reasons for deploring Germany's loss of Ludendorff's eastern imperium. Between times Hitler worked out other, anti-Semitic grounds for that same eastward thrust, but these he kept to himself, or almost, until at long last the attack on Soviet Russia was mounted. Then he brought the anti-Semitic grounds out into the open and put them before the power-political ones. It follows that the anti-Semitic grounds were *his own* grounds for his eastern policy. They were also the simpler and more logical grounds for it. If Hitler nonetheless kept them to himself, or almost, and argued from the other, power-political grounds exclusively as he solicited and achieved dictatorial power for the express purpose of waging that eastern war, the clear indication is that these were *the Germans'* grounds for a policy addressed to *them*. Indeed, Hitler worked up the latent sense of his eastward expansionism, which was to relaunch Ludendorff's lost eastern conquest, into a power-political program derived in its entirety from the disastrous national experience of World War I and tending to repeat that experience as a whole.

Beginning in *Mein Kampf,* Hitler programmed German expansion in three stages. First, Germany would colonize the European continent with England's support or at least compliance. Next, either peaceably or through a regretful showdown Germany would supplant England as the dominant power in the eastern hemisphere. Finally, in the fullness of time Germany would fight the United States for world dominion. The Empire's fatal mistake, he argued, had been to conflate these three stages in its thrust for world power. He, by serializing the three stages, would succeed where the Empire had failed. Even within the first stage he would proceed serially and defeat France before engaging Russia. This first sequence threw back to the strategy with which the Empire had entered World War I—to the failed Schlieffen Plan for defeating France before confronting Russia all-out. To the same effect, Hitler in his power-political planning never mentioned the East Central European "successor states" carved out of the defeated German, Austrian, and Turkish empires even though he slated them as well to be absorbed or neutralized serially for starters preliminary to stage one: this omission too threw back to Europe before World War I. The built-in weakness of his stage one was that its success turned on England's acquiescence in a German conquest of the continent. He planned to bring England around by renouncing German overseas ambitions until stage two. But this purported trade-off was none, for Germany would pose no threat to England overseas unless and until Germany *first* colonized the continent. Hitler tardily faced up to this telltale snag in his planning only when England failed to come around even when his pact of August 1939 with Stalin sealed Poland's fate. He then upped his offer to a guarantee of the British Empire—a siren's song that duly fell on deaf ears.

In sum, Hitler's expansionist program, which he derived from his German public and its painful experience of World War I, set Germany up to repeat that experience in all essentials as if with the aim of rectifying its outcome. Such intricate, unknowing repetition of a painful experience marks that experience as traumatic. Wherein had World War I been traumatic for the Germans?

The answer takes us still farther back historically. Throughout the nineteenth century, while nationalism was destabilizing Europe, German identity had remained unsettled. Varieties of German were spoken across the continent from the Atlantic to the Volga and from the Baltic to the Adriatic. The Germany that Bismarck forged through battle in 1870–1871 was an empire of Germanic peoples whose primary loyalties were largely dynastic and regional. It included many non-Germans, especially Poles and Danes, and excluded many professed Germans, beginning with the seven million Austrians who headed a heterogeneous empire of their own. There could be no uniting all the Germans of Europe on their native soil without subjugating non-Germans out of all proportion. Hence German nationalism under the empire was of necessity expansionist and imperialist. For that very reason Bismarck would have none of it. Bismarck was first and last a Prussian who established Prussian hegemony over the states of the German Empire that he forged. From the moment of its creation, as he saw it, his empire was already too strong in Europe for its own good, so that its sole chance of survival was to avoid at all costs inciting a combination of powers against it. In this perspective, German nationalism was dangerously provocative, on a par with German colonial or maritime expansion.

On the other hand, in order to consolidate his empire Bismarck had to win popular support for it over and above all the provincial, social, and ideological divisions tending to rend it asunder. He found no more felicitous a device than to combat Catholics and Socialists because their group identities reached beyond its borders—a fateful precedent. Young William II, less fretful if no more secure, dismissed Bismarck in 1890 and rallied his imperial subjects by practicing *Weltpolitik,* or throwing Germany's weight around in the world. The result was heightened tensions in Europe that exploded into World War I.

When they exploded, all the Emperor's men fell into martial array at the bugle's sound and burst into a jubilant battle cry of unison. Theirs was no predatory blood lust, for their mood was defensive, as in a fortress besieged. Rather, it was a joy of new-found oneness within a professed "community of fate" fusing Rhinelander and Silesian, Junker and worker, Conservative and Socialist. In those legendary "August Days" of 1914, the approximate Germany that Bismarck had created was inwardly unified at last even as the losing battle was joined outwardly against a world of enemies. For over three years thereafter, against all odds, the German Empire withstood a tight blockade and a hopeless two-front war at fearful cost. Then suddenly in 1917 it toppled the Russian Empire with Lenin's help, and vast vistas of conquest opened up before it to the east. The following spring warlord Ludendorff mounted a massive victory offensive in the west. The offensive ground to a halt that summer, whereupon the High Command, seeing its reserves in manpower and materiel depleted, called for an armistice.

This unforeseen turnabout caught the nation traumatically short. In the shock of defeat the empire fell back into its old regional, social, and ideological divisions, now escalated with a vengeance as internecine strife raged at fever pitch. In the rump Germany that emerged from the Armistice and the peace treaty, stripped of a tenth of its prewar territory and population and hemmed in by the Allies' exactions, it was Hitler who spoke straightest and loudest to the submerged memory of oneness in battle array against a world of enemies. His magic formula for undoing the defeat bore his galvanized listeners back to the crest of the illusory victory wave of 1918 just before it broke. His rhetoric of "land and soil" to be regained in the east pinpointed just why the military collapse had caught the public so far off guard. "We stood deep in enemy soil," ran the bemused refrain of a people unable to assimilate the sudden, drastic reversal of its fortunes. Hitler was acutely and uniquely sensitive to this traumatic sore spot behind the German postwar political turmoil. As he spoke, the old mood of jubilant unity within a "community of fate" revived until the fatal power-political adventure was relaunched.

How did a scantily educated Austrian underling come to sense and supply the felt need of a Germany overwhelmed by defeat in 1918 to relive that defeat with grim finality and as a penalty due? To begin with, Hitler experienced the traumatic 1918 defeat in his own flesh.[39] It found him, a front-lines soldier since 1914, in a military hospital convalescing from gas poisoning and resultant temporary blindness. At the news of the Armistice he blacked out again in deathly despair and was cured by hypnotic suggestion to the effect that Germany needed him to redress her loss. A complex of personal referents underlay that blackout and cure. He associated the gas that hit him with a toxic iodoform treatment of his mother for terminal breast cancer that he had urged on her Jewish doctor eleven years before.[40] After her death he had recreated with the "motherland" (as he called Germany) his deep affective tie to his mother. She had borne him to make good her loss of her three previous children to a diphtheria epidemic and, while overly nursing and coddling him, had suspended her fertility for the exact duration of her earlier experience of motherhood, from first conception to third death, thereby reliving her maternal trauma unconsciously. In formulating his doctrine of feeding ground, Hitler harked back to his formative experience at his traumatized mother's breast. A nursling's oral aggression sounded shrilly through his talk of "land and soil," as in this formulation of 23 March 1927:

> How can we feed the nation? Either we export people or goods, or we strive to adjust land and soil to population. Nature lays this possibility at every living creature's cradle. That is the self-preservative instinct. The child does not ask, when it drinks, whether the mother's breast is being tortured. Hunger and love are healthy instincts.[41]

But this infantile fixation beneath Hitler's doctrine of land and soil must not be mistaken for its point of departure. Its point of departure was Germany's traumatic need, to which Hitler was uniquely attuned from the first. The basic constitutive experience that fitted him to pick up that need from his public entered into his articulation of it. So did, from his public's side, the starvation that had accompanied the German experience of the war and defeat. Of itself, an oral-aggressive fixation would never have led him to replace a revisionistic demand for the return of Germany's colonies with a continental expansionist aim going back to 1917–1918.

And how did Hitler integrate that eastern aim, which he brought out only gradually following his putsch fiasco, with his anti-Jewish aim, which was his controlling political purpose? The psychological sources of the two policies differed: Germany's 1918 trauma of defeat on the one side as against his mother's death at a Jewish doctor's hands on the other. So did their respective premises differ: inadequate land and soil versus the parasitic, poisonous, profiteering Jew. To integrate them he needed to surmount a radical disconnect between his basic arguments on either side: if the 1918 defeat was due to a fatal strategic mistake, then it was not due to any treachery by the Jews. He met the rhetorical challenge as he had met the theoretical challenge: with aplomb. His integrative formula, which he elaborated in countless speeches of the late 1920s as he built up his mass following, ran: removing the Jews will ensure national unity, which in turn will ensure the conquest of feeding ground. At times it came out only: removing the Jews is the precondition for national unity, itself the precondition for the conquest of feeding ground. But even then the context ordinarily left no possible doubt that he saw the preconditions as sufficient of themselves to generate the necessary means.

Jews alone, then, sow disunity among Germans; through unity alone will Germans be victorious—the particulars will take care of themselves. This victory formula can best be grasped schematically:

REMOVAL OF JEWS → NATIONAL UNITY → CONQUEST OF LAND

Such was indeed Hitler's message already in his political beginnings except that then its end term was still only the repudiation of the Versailles Treaty. Here, in chronological order, are a few of his typical early utterances to this effect:

> Against all divisions, for a single Germany! Out with the Jew band![42]
>
> We knew and know that the German nation alone can help itself and that it will do so if the national will is joined to that end.[43]
>
> We want to shake off the oppressive yoke imposed on us, but first we must have the will to do so. . . . After the will, [the] deed.[44]
>
> Unity! If we stop fighting among ourselves we shall achieve the position that is rightly ours.[45]
>
> Do we want to restore Germany's freedom and power? Then let us first rescue Germany from her spoilers.[46]
>
> Cowards cry: But we have no weapons!—Weapons here, weapons there! If the whole German nation has but the will to fight for its freedom, the instruments we need will come to hand! . . . The inner struggle must precede the outer![47]
>
> Our aspirations abroad can be imposed only through a prior inner cleansing![48]
>
> If 60 million people had the single will to be fanatically national, the weapons would spring from their fists![49]

This takes us up to the putsch of November 1923. After his ensuing jail term Hitler declared upon refounding the Party: "From this day forth we shall work together again to steel the German people's will to freedom until someday no power will any longer be able to bend that will, which instead will meet Germany's need."[50] As here already, so afterwards, in calling for eastern expansion Hitler newly stressed the middle term of his formula above the first and last. Two further examples should suffice:

To conquer land and soil, strength is needed. It lies in unity. . . . And the people should not be diverted by other problems. It must have a single goal.[51]

There is but one goal: honor, freedom, and bread for the German people, and the way to it is called struggle. That is why the German people should close ranks to become a power factor in world history capable of obtaining the feeding ground for its natural increase.[52]

So spoke Hitler—on and on.[53] None of these quotations from his speeches of the 1920s is exceptional; any one of them can be matched dozens of times over. That whole decade, plus a little before and after, he reworded the same message continually without ever changing it. Undoubtedly none of his listeners grasped in all its primitive simplicity this hocus-pocus-like formula on which his political rhetoric turned. It was no less bound to register with Germans somewhere short of clear consciousness as the basic sense of his politics.

The first thing to be said about this basic sense of Hitler's politics is that it was nonsense. The disunity among Germans was not the Jews' doing. More, closed ranks will not ensure victory if the material means are lacking. Inherent in Hitler's victory formula was, then, a double insurance that it would miscarry: the removal of the Jews together with their influence would hardly produce national unity, which would not suffice anyhow for victory. To be sure, no reasonable person would have expected Hitler to rely on his magic formula alone to conquer Europe however insistently and fanatically he recited it, but reasonable expectations play no role unconsciously. A second crucial point about Hitler's magic formula is that it drew on a popular legend about Germany's war experience of 1914–1918: that the Germans had been united and victorious at the outset, but then nonpatriots had sown disunity among them so as to snatch defeat from victory. Here is how he himself put it early along:

As long as the people, in inner awareness of the national imperative, still stood squarely behind the German armies, these remained victorious. The progressive stifling of this elemental involvement of the entire people in its history sapped the vitality of the fighting front. . . . The condition for rebirth consists, therefore, first and foremost in the removal of whatever can affect our people divisively in any way—namely the Jews.[54]

This legend remained constant through all Hitler's variations on it as he invoked it ever and again with an anti-Semitic spin to validate his formula.[55] Widespread as it was, it was purely a legend, and it so took in no one unconsciously. Even the paranoiac does not fool himself unconsciously with his delusions. A third notable fact about Hitler's victory formula is that it provided no cause, on the contrary, to go after Jews outside Germany as he was dying to do and as his case against the Jews required.[56] Hence it was for him a mere device for use with his public. Finally, national unity was, by the terms of the formula, no aim in its own right, but only a means to an end: the conquest of land. Nor did the "national community" interest Hitler outside the formula even as a euphemism for dictatorship.

The observation that, by the terms of Hitler's rhetorical formula, the "national community" was a mere means to the end of conquering land in the east leads me to the subtlest point of all about Hitler's communication with his public. This is that systematically beginning in November 1930, but quite frequently already in the late 1920s, Hitler toned down or even muted the first and third terms of that formula (removal of the Jews, conquest of feeding ground) until the second term (national unity) sufficed to recall the hushed first and third to his audiences. No doubt he muted the first and third terms out of prudence toward foreign listeners. In any case the ticklish concepts "removal of the Jews" and "conquest of land" came through to the Germans undiminished, especially as he often expressed them through mild substitutes notoriously equivalent in his usage, such as "Marxism" for Jewry or national "freedom" for foreign aggression. Already before 1930 he made increasing use of such soft synonyms along with the two ticklish concepts and then gradually in place of them. Thus once in November 1928, even as he was calling outright for a racial purge and a land grab, he stated in passing that the treble aim of his movement was "to steel the body politic, to give it faith again, and one day to stand up for freedom."[57] In context, this was transparently his old, fixed formula without seeming euphemistic. Another two years and he was expressing himself in this way only, as on 7 November 1930: "The key to foreign markets and supplies is named not diligence, but concerted force. . . . If a great people is determined to sacrifice everything in the service of the nation, then a power so compelling emerges that it can transform the image of the world and the age. . . . If the entire nation had the spirit of the SA and SS, we would already be out of our servitude by now."[58] And the next day: "We . . . are convinced that the time will pass when the German people dissipated its strength internally. Then the hour will strike for which millions are longing. So let us fight for our children's bread."[59] Then a few days later: "I have the firm conviction that, the moment the German people . . . turns its whole strength outward again, the yoke of servitude will be broken."[60]

Thereafter he also strongly accentuated the middle, or connective, term of his magic formula. The modified oratorical patern is best visualized schematically somewhat like this:

[REMOVAL OF JEWS] → **NATIONAL UNITY** → [CONQUEST OF LAND]

In his famous speech of 27 January 1932 to industrialists in Düsseldorf the stress fell heavily on national unity, though the two associated concepts did find some muffled expression. "Forming the will of the nation as a whole is essential," he declared;

it is the point of departure for political operations [abroad]. . . . If we want to develop a new domestic market or solve the problem of [living] space: ever and again we shall need the concerted political strength of the nation. . . . With today's body politic, no active foreign policy can be conducted any longer. . . . If from the tiniest cell [the Party in 1919] a new body politic does not form to vanquish the "ferments of decomposition," then the nation as a whole will be unable to rise again. . . . We are inexorably resolved to exterminate Marxism in Germany root and branch.[61]

From just about any of his further public utterances of 1932 can be seen how skillfully Hitler intimated the first and third terms of his magic formula while outwardly putting the whole stress on the second. Here is a random example from the electoral campaign of July 1932: "Is that German if our people is torn into thirty parties? . . . Our aim is to do away with those thirty parties and restore unity and order in Germany in the awareness that national greatness depends . . . above all else on the strength of a united people."[62] "Is that German . . . ?" was necessarily answered "No, Jewish" in the back of every listener's mind, where similarly "national greatness" could not fail to assume spatial contours bulging eastwards.

Not only did Hitler's cover terms connote the real terms of his formula. As a rule they also denoted the first practical measures to be taken toward either extreme: the removal of the Jews or the conquest of living space. Statements from around the time he took power are particularly instructive. On 4 December 1932 he spelled out those first practical measures to a Reichswehr colonel:

1. Repression of Marxism and its effects unto complete extinction. Preparation for a new national unity of mind and will.
2. General spiritual and ethical rearmament of the nation on the basis of this new unity.
3. Technical rearmament.
4. Organization of national strength for national defense.
5. Attainment of formal recognition from the rest of the world for the new situation already brought about.[63]

Four days after taking office he extended this short list in a talk to Germany's top brass (as noted by one of the generals present):

Overall political goal solely the recovery of political power. Here the entire state apparatus (every agency!) must be brought to bear.
1. Internally. Complete reversal of present domestic situation in Germany. No tolerance for any show of sentiments (pacifism!) opposed to the goal. He who won't bow must be bent. Extermination of Marxism root and branch. Youth and entire nation must be attuned to the idea that only

> struggle can save us, and everything must yield to this idea. . . . Toughen-
> ing of youth and strengthening of will to defense by any and all means.
> Strictest authoritarian rule. Removal of the cancer of democracy!
> . . . .
> 4. Buildup of the armed forces most important requirement for reaching goal
> of winning back political power. . . .[64]

Here the emphasis on national defense over the expansionist war meant only that the expansionist war was for later.[65] Likewise, the displacement from the Jews themselves to their institutional and intellectual mischief meant only that the Jews' own turn for "removal" would come later. And now Hitler's cover theme of ending divisions among Germans—that intoned hyphen between the muted end terms of his politics—sounded shriller behind the scenes of the incipient dictatorship.

The middle term of Hitler's formula, while linking his two policies logically, separated them psychologically. It also subordinated the anti-Jewish to the expansionist policy by making them means and ends respectively. This too is a sign that Hitler was pitching his expansionist policy to German priorities—that through it he was acting out a national determination. All indications are, moreover, that his sensing and serving the national pathology that issued from the 1918 defeat was the root of his political appeal. His anti-Semitic track did not run beyond fringe agitation in and around Munich—not even to a proper putsch there, but only as far as the Odeonsplatz and the Landsberg jail. But then in the late 1920s, as soon as the regional bans on his public speaking were lifted, he preached the eastern land grab far and wide. In so doing, he rapidly built up a national following to work through the 1918 disaster anew. That following simply took his anti-Jewish aim into the bargain. Germans were hardly surprised when Jews later disappeared from Germany and German-controlled Europe. They rather looked the other way if they could. But those who didn't made little fuss as a rule, and some could not even remember afterwards. The bond between Hitler and the Germans was his replay of their 1914–1918 catastrophe. The project was theirs, the agency his.

To relive trauma is routine in the emotional life of individuals. It is no less so in the emotional life of peoples. The war Hitler promised and delivered for his own traumatic purposes is a clearcut case in point. Once it is seen that way it can no longer be seen otherwise.

CHAPTER FOUR

The Sublime and the Grotesque

A group even larger and looser than a nation-state may be traumatized by a shock less sudden and less menacing than the German military defeat of 1918. More, a group may relive such a slow shock spontaneously, with no dictator leading or prophet pointing the way. Romanticism wherever it spread was just such a reliving of a mass trauma, more mental than material, that had hit home only gradually. This second of two chapters on traumatic reliving will discover what that mass trauma was and how creatively it was relived through the Romantic repertoire.

What was Romanticism? This for a start: a cultural movement that flourished in Europe from the 1790s through the 1840s at the outside. Some aspects of it can be traced farther back or forward, but not the movement as a whole. And it is this historic movement that will be considered here rather than its ageless, recurrent features called romantic with a small *r*.

Its chief traits are familiar enough. At least those are that have been taken to set it apart, to define its special nature. Cultural historians will each play different ones up or down, add or delete some, distinguish nationally and circumscribe temporally in new ways, as learning and understanding grow overall. Even so, the common ground from one account of Romanticism to the next has by now come to form a distinctive historic landscape that we all recognize whatever passages of it we may focus on—Wordsworth's cheery daffodils, or Friedrich's eerie mists, or Lamartine's memory-haunted woodlands. So a few stock props should suffice to set that familiar historic scene.

Romanticism was a revolt, indeed a double revolt: against rationalism with its primacy of the head over the heart, and against classicism with its hierarchies of style and subject matter, its formalizing and normalizing. Romantic thought dealt in consciousness more than reason, process rather than causation, the organic by preference to the mechanistic. Romantics upgraded the everyday and the lowly while also putting a premium on the singular and the surpassing. They exalted genius, prized individuality and originality, strove after the spontaneous and the authentic. They rated creative spurts above workmanlike accomplishment, grand failure above petty success, self-searching above self-seeking. They eschewed routine, compromise, and complacency, middle age and everything else middle except the Middle Ages. The extremes of political revolution and political reaction were equally Romantic. So were community *and* inwardness, the folk *and* the loner, the common path *and* the rare destiny. Romanticism featured precise observers and visionaries both; self-display and self-concealment; bursts of energy and spells of torpor. It was hospitable to forbidden passions, to extreme states of soul, to mysterious cosmic forces, to the exotic and the marvelous, the fantastic and the nightmarish, the morbid and the macabre. Its salient aberrations included wallowing in sentiment, yearning for the infinite, reveling and languishing by quick turns, and cultivating melancholy and malaise for display. These trends and fashions, and many more like them, swept Europe to its farthest reaches. Probably no single Romantic fell in with them all. Yet they went together, or at all odds go together in our established sense of what *Romantic* meant.

Where shall we plug into this Romantic complex psychohistorically? Nowhere. An established sense of things is suspicious just because the evidence for it will leap to mind. A pack of truths is always harder to see through than a pack of lies. Our best bet is to sidestep the scholarly consensus and probe the Romantics in the raw.

A promising spot to probe them first is their soft underbelly: sex. Genital sex is fairly barren historically in that it does not differentiate cultures any too sharply. What, then, was the Romantics' pet erotic vice? It emphatically was not so-called romantic love—inflammatory, ungovernable, all-consuming. Crazed amorous thralldom belonged to the Age of Reason— literarily to a play by Racine, say, or to a novel by Abbé Prévost. Proto-Romantic in other ways, Goethe's Young Werther and Mackenzie's Man of Feeling were sentimentally of the old order in succumbing to their fevered affections. The Romantic love story came into its own with the passion outlived of Benjamin Constant's *Adolphe*. Nor was a preference for desire over fulfillment much of a Romantic ailment. Keats professed it, but only to bail out a Grecian youth stuck panting on an urn. Nonetheless the Romantics' *péché mignon* did stop short of outright practice as far as the records show except in a single notorious half instance. I mean sibling incest and Byron's amour with his half sister. This amour went first into *The

Bride of Abydos by Byron and, at friends' bidding, out again.[1] Then it was elevated to Manfred's amour with Astarte, and again Cain's with Adah, being spared Don Juan in his wanderings only because ". . . he never had a sister: / Ah! if he had—how much he would have missed her!"[2]

Shelley did not go the whole hog like Byron, but did elope with his sister's closest friend first, then with his foster father's daughter. His child lovers Laon and Cyntha in *The Revolt of Islam* were brother and sister until his publisher intervened. He did penance twice over in *Rosiland and Helen:* Rosiland picks a spot where sibling lovers of yore came to grief to recount her own brother-romance cut short at the altar. Then, doubling back, he gave his Prometheus unbound a sister as "insatiate bride"[3]—even after his foster-sister-bride had contrived a dire fate for a foster-sister-bride in her thriller *Frankenstein.* Young Wordsworth for his part left a mistress pregnant in France and set up back home with his sister (who called him "my Beloved" in her notebook) until, after ten years, he married her best friend. Coleridge, more devious, was smitten with Wordsworth's wife's sister while married to Southey's wife's sister (Sara and Sarah respectively). And Keats's unrequited, demeaning, unshakable love was for his sister's namesake, Fanny. Quite unremarkably, Macaulay wrote home to his sister Hannah: "my darling . . . I pine . . . for your caresses."[4] Every degree of incest had flourished in British letters with the Gothic drama (thus Horace Walpole's *The Mysterious Mother*) and the Gothic novel (thus Lewis's *The Monk*), but then sibling incest swept the field with the Romantics. Even Jane Austen, little touched by Romanticism otherwise, produced a multiple brother-sister intrigue in *Mansfield Park.* Of Britain's big Romantics only Scott held off, or nearly: in *The Antiquary* a mother tells her son just for spite that his wife is his half sister. The frenzied, forbidden love beyond life itself between Cathy and her foster brother, Heathcliff, in Emily Brontë's *Wuthering Heights* was the grand culmination of a stereotype. Some maudlin brother-sister erotism persisted into the murky realism of Dickens's *Hard Times.*

Bernardin de Saint-Pierre launched the theme of sibling incest sentimentally in thin disguise among the French with his best-selling *Paul and Virginie* about two fatherless children who grow up together in savage, loving innocence, only to perish as if in atonement; the disguise was so thin, and the disguised motive so strong, that French brothers and sisters were named Paul and Virginie almost routinely throughout the Romantic period. Romanticism in person, Chateaubriand, mourned his sister Lucile through his Atala, who poisons herself to keep from breaking a chastity vow for love of her virtual brother. That virtual promptly went actual with Chateaubriand's alter ego René, who shares with his sister a "guilty passion"[5] that drives her to a convent and him to the wilds of America. "Be mine, be my sister," Vigny's sly Satan whispers by way of seducing Eloa.[6] The Marquis de Sade and Restif de la Bretonne had touted sex with any and all relatives interchangeably, but pornography's family circle narrowed to siblings (or cousins) in Romantic France. The rare exception that proved the rule was the same as in polite literature: the lewd rogue who fouls his demure daughter. And in high and low letters alike, nuns shared honors, or dishonors, with fleshly sisters.

Young Goethe brought the brother-sister romance to Germany out of his own childhood, with the heroine of his playlet *The Siblings* declaring her love for her supposed brother. In his later *Wilhelm Meister's Apprenticeship*, enchanting Mignon is the child of a brother and sister whom the world's persecution cannot tear asunder but does destroy. Lessing meanwhile had his Nathan the Wise get a brother and sister to sublimate their mutual passion. Young Goethe's friend Friedrich Klinger novelized Oriental princeling Giafar's dynastic severance from his soul mate of a sister. Ludwig Tieck's *Peter Lebrecht* told of a couple separated at their very wedding only to learn after years of cooling off apart that they are siblings. And Tieck's *Blond Eckbert* in turn had a hero hexed a whole life long until a witch tells him why: his wife had been his half sister. Schiller upped the incestuous ante with twin brothers competing tragically for a sister in *The Bride from Messina*, but then Schiller's planned sequel to *The Robbers* centering in sibling incest never came off. Clemens Brentano in *The Rosenkranz Romances* took epic pains to avert unsuspecting incest between a painter's three sons by his wife and three daughters by her sister (a nun). In Achim von Arnim's *Ariel's Disclosures* a father can break up an incestuous triangle only by taking his relentless daughter and two rival sons to hell to repent. But then in Arnim's *Halle and Jerusalem* fate intervenes to spoil an unwitting brother-sister courtship. Adolf Müllner's one-act tragedy *The Twenty-Ninth of February* reworked Tieck's *Blond Eckbert*. In Kotzebue's comedy *The Buck, or the Innocent Culprits* a lord and his lady fall for their disguised sister and brother respectively. In *The Devil's Elixir,* a tale of Hoffmann, a monk goes to unspeakable lengths in hot pursuit of his half sister after sipping an infernal potion. In Grillparzer's *The Ancestress,* a lost son returns to kill his father and, updating Oedipus, wins his sister unawares. When it all hits home, he groans: "True, the will is mine, / Yet the deed is Fate's."[7] The hero of Immermann's *The Epigones* goes nearly mad from mistaking a one-night bedmate for his half sister. In clearer southerly climes, Espronceda's Sancho Saldaña and his sister are childhood sweethearts, as are symmetrically Sancho's later lady love and her brother. At the other end of the continent, Pushkin named the fatal flirt in *Eugene Onegin* after his sister Olga. Balzac melodramatized a half-brother-sister liaison in *The Girl with the Golden Eyes.* In other tales Balzac promoted his beloved sister Laure, trusty confidante of his wickedest intrigues, to a trusting, adoring sister back home milked by an arriviste brother in the capital. Felix Mendelssohn, less fanciful, simply died of mourning his sister. From life to art and back, the variants were numberless.

On from sex to death, specifically the Romantic death par excellence: Romantic suicide. Romantic suicide goes back to one factual and one fictional precedent set respectively by young Thomas Chatterton, a poet-genius-outcast, and Goethe's Young Werther, an ungratified lover and superior misfit. With suicide even more than with incest, this confluence of fact and fiction was typical for Romanticism. So was their interplay: Goethe committed Werther's suicide in lieu of his own, yet it set off an epidemic; Chatterton's in return was repeatedly poetized, dramatized, and painted. The Romantic was the first Western school of suicide since the Roman. Roman suicide was deliberate, dispassionate, civic-minded. By contrast, Romantic suicide was egoistic and, while not normally impassioned or impulsive, nonetheless grounded in intense feeling. Far from being the wages of dishonor or disgrace—these called for counteraction from Romantics—it was the full price of a deeply reflective and sentient estrangement from the world that redounded to the world's discredit. No mere pathetic dropouts from life like our modern-day, post-Romantic breed, Romantic suicides were lofty souls, sublime specimens too good for mean human circumstances and arrangements. Their act epitomized the Romantics' scorn for adjustment. Much more, it was the limiting, or perfected, expression of the Romantic cult of the extraordinary individual standing apart from society, over against it, incompatible with it. At the opposite pole was the mystique of the community or nation submerging all personal identity: here too the individual perished.

Beddoes and Raimund, Nerval and Larra, Franz von Sonnenberg and Caroline von Günderode, Edward Raczyński and Alphonse Rabbe, all killed themselves. So did Baron Gros and Léopold Robert and Benjamin Robert Haydon. And so did Kleist with a death partner. Second-tier Romantic suicides included, to take France alone, neglected penmen Imbert Galois and Léon Laya; failing tenor Alphonse Nourrit and declining traveler Charles Didier; publisher Auguste Sautelet, who left a death note on *Werther,* and litterateur Servan de Sugny, who left a book in press on suicide condemning it as cowardly; world-weary dramatists Victor Escousse and Auguste Lebras, aged nineteen and sixteen respectively, who explained themselves in one angry and one stoical letter, and whose fate Béranger sang. In 1852 the polygraph Bourg Saint-Edme closed out this line with a chillingly positivistic account of his last hours before hanging himself. Romantic suicide scored meanwhile in prose and poetry, what with Foscolo's Jacopo Ortis, E. T. A. Hoffmann's mad Nathaniel in *The Sandman,* Byron's Sardanapalus, Musset's Rolla, Lenau's Faust, Mickiewicz's Konrad Wallenrod, Vigny's lovers of Montmorency, and Balzac's painter of the unknown masterpiece. "It would be pointless to name the works having a suicide or a discussion of suicide in them," wrote one historian of Romanticism; "such an enumeration would encompass nearly the entire literature of the time."[8] In the preceding era, only ethical suicides had been depicted, and then sparingly, as in Racine's theater, or more prominently in Baroque and Neo-classical painting—Lucretia dishonored, Sophonisba escaping dishonor, Cleopatra in defeat, Saul avoiding capture. Romantics by contrast painted suicides generated from within and psychologically colored: perennial favorites were Chatterton and Atala, Ophelia and creepy Sardanapalus destroying his whole entourage for a warmup.

Celebrated and emulated on a par with actual suicides among the Romantics were virtual suicides by men of genius unrecognized or unfulfilled, persecuted or ostracized, consumed or driven, who coveted or courted death and met it young as a rule and suspiciously apropos: Nicolas Gilbert and André Chénier, Büchner and Grabbe, Espronceda and the poet of suicide Juan Antonio Pagés; Miskiewicz and Leopardi, Novalis and Keats, Shelley and Byron; Géricault and Chassériau; Schubert and the starved poetic purist Émile Roulland; Pushkin and Lermontov, Charles Dovalles and Armand Carrel and Évariste Galois—the last five in duels that Pushkin for his part anticipated as Lensky's in *Eugene Onegin* and Lermontov as his own in *A Dream*. Fictionally, René goes off to a living death in America while his sister succumbs nursing the plague-stricken; dolor undoes Achim von Arnim's Dolores; Byron's Manfred meets a dark, dire fate by pre-appointment; Vigny's Moses implores the Lord for "the sleep of the earth";[9] Stendhal's Julien and Büchner's Danton comply with their own executions in the offing. Gautier conjoined actual with virtual Romantic suicide when in *The Comedy of Death* he put Werther and René down together as "true poisoners of the heart."[10] Kleist demonstrated the continuity from virtual to actual Romantic suicide in that the one was the central theme of the works he left behind when committing the other.[11] Lamartine's Raphaël clinched that continuity. The mournful youngster contrived to die of a wasting disease. Yet at least one authority on Romanticism has him down for an actual suicide.[12] And Durkheim in *Suicide* quoted him to exemplify "egoistic suicide" (essentially the Romantic kind):

> I plunged into the depths of sadness. But this sadness was vibrant, and it contained enough thoughts, impressions, and intimate communing with the infinite and with the penumbra in my soul for me never to want to come back out of it. A human sickness! but a sickness that felt enticing rather than painful, with death resembling a voluptuous absorption into the infinite. I was determined to abandon myself to it altogether.[13]

These Romantic demi-suicides form an unbroken series with other Romantics who attempted or contemplated suicide—Goethe, Saint-Simon, Chateaubriand, Friedrich Schlegel, Carlyle, Schumann, Lenau; with Romantic apologists for suicide—Rousseau precursively, Chénier again, Senancour, Vigny, Sainte-Beuve, Pétrus Borel; with partway apologists

Germaine de Staël and Schopenhauer; with death-ridden Michelet, who at eighteen fell head over heels in love with his aging landlady when her daughter committed suicide; with, finally, at the outside, Wordsworth, Manzoni, and Schopenhauer again, who were self-contentedly burnt out early along.

But suicide was not just the extreme expression of the Romantic agony; it was the final consequence of the Romantic attitude even if some Romantics, like Peacock's Scythrop or Carlyle's Diogenes Teufelsdröckh, excused themselves from drawing it. As Achim von Arnim, who knew his Romantic casualties, put it: "Our miserable age leads to suicide; most follow and succumb even without lifting a hand against themselves."[14] In the last resort, the Romantic vocation for death was a protest against the human condition—a defiant refusal to be trapped by mortality or frailty or banality, or to be caught up in ephemeral joys. For the Romantics, life unenchanted or disenchanted, hence all life sooner or later, was not worth living. This Romantic quarrel with life carried over into the aesthetic revenge taken on an inaesthetic reality by a Baudelaire or a Flaubert—into their perfected renditions of existence in all its ugliness or emptiness. For these fugitives from Romanticism, art became what suicide had been for the Romantics before them: an escape from, and triumph over, life seen as both intolerable and irremediable.

Romantic sibling incest, Romantic suicide: these were, then, the ultimates in Romantic loving and living. So they call for a switch to an everyman's everyday item from the Romantic repertory. A striking one that historians have unaccountably overlooked is the Romantic's conflictual tendency to involvement in, and retreat from, the world—the tension, in confronting the world with all its faults, between participation and withdrawal, engagement and disengagement, opting in and opting out. Anyone and everyone finds the world flawed as against his ideal demands on it. Short of renouncing his ideals, his choice is to do battle for them within the world or to back away from the world. The Romantic does both. That is, whichever way the Romantic goes at a given moment or over a lifetime, his choice is open, or reopened, continually. In the phantasmagoric perspective of *The Night Watches* signed Bonaventura, poets are a harmless lot "with their dreams and raptures" until "they make bold to hold up their ideals to reality": then they "turn nasty" and "hack away angrily."[15] Oscillations between fight and flight were common, but so were long vacillations and midway courses, and one-sided commitments that left the soul troubled. Other ages have known this conflict as well, and even have felt it acutely in particular cases; at no other time, however, was it an ongoing shared preoccupation or an issue so problematic and dramatic. This two-sidedness of Romanticism has been noted over and again, and each side has been observed in detail. But the fact of a duality, or double direction, within all Romantics individually has gone unnoticed.

The height of activist Romanticism was political: such causes as Greek or Polish independence, such movements as monarchism or nationalism or socialism, such personalities as a Chateaubriand or a Benjamin Constant or a Lamartine, spring to mind. Preferred channels of Romantic escape were aestheticism and exoticism, dreams and visions, Weltschmerz and ennui. But again, no Romantic was a full-time activist or permanent escapist; what was Romantic was precisely the unresolved conflict. Just this was for Goethe the tug-of-war between the two souls in Faust's breast, one lustily embracing this world and the other soaring out of range. A familiar variant of the Romantic polarity was the sense of dissolving into the sea of Being or any of its estuaries on the one side and, on the other, of absorbing all Being into the self as, in Michelet's words, "that false little universality confronts the grand and devouring universality of the all."[16] Romantic nature poetry well exemplifies this variant, what with the poet merging into autumn or the west wind at the one extreme (Keats and Shelley) and autumn or the sedge's song resonating with the poet's soul at the other (Lamartine and Lenau). "I live not in myself, but I become / Portion of that around me . . .": thus Byron,[17] who, rugged ego and all, was as sensitive to ". . . the feeling infinite, so felt / In solitude, when we are least alone,"[18] as was fragile Leopardi gazing and listening from a hillside: ". . . Thus my thoughts / Drown in this immensity, and sweet / It is to drift in this sea."[19]

As to human society, a common Romantic pattern was the pendulous one of plunging in and pulling out by turns. A hallmark of the Romantic age was the intimate, introspective diaries kept by writers, artists, and composers to offset their worldly activities. Diarist Jules Michelet once noted: "On 14 November: τα εχτος [exterior things]. On 19 November: τα εντος [interior things]."[20] Historicism à la Michelet or Ranke was a neat Romantic meld of immersion in and removal from reality, past and present respectively. Young Chateaubriand overindulged his penchant for emigrating from the world, so his Father Souël rebuked his René: "I see a youngster with a head full of vain fancies, whom everything else displeases, and who shuns the burdens of society to lose himself in idle dreaming."[21] Shelley wound up an outcast and exile because of his preaching and practicing social radicalism; Mary Shelley's narrator in *Frankenstein,* reversing this sequence, sets out alone for the North Pole for the sake of "the inestimable benefit which I shall confer on all mankind."[22] Eugène Sue balanced off dandyism and socialism, snobbery and slumming. Balzac frequented all walks of Restoration society while rejecting it as a historic disaster and novelizing it between times in monkish retreats. More, a recurrent theme of Balzac's was that of the idealist corrupted by the world's values while struggling to impose his own. Thus in *Lost Illusions* the young poet Lucien quits and at length betrays his closed circle of purists, the Cénacle, as he takes up the good fight within the enemy ranks of journalism only to succumb to its evil devices. Better the pure vision however futile, Balzac argued, half meaning it.

Romantic cénacles of the 1820s in France—the first was the royalist literary one of Hugo and Sainte-Beuve, Nodier and Vigny—were vehicles for opting both in and out *en groupe,* for applying unworldly values internally and promoting them outside. Their equivalents in other Romantic lines were socialist societies and *kruzhki,* Tugendbunde and Burschenschaften, Carbonari and Young Italy. The danger inherent in these little counterworlds was not worldly corruption as with Balzac's youngsters on the make, but—for all their combativeness—self-involved remoteness from the world proper. Witness Mazzini animating Young Italy down the decades mostly from abroad and at length mistaking his ideal Italy for the real one: his undeceiving after Italian unification drove him into bitter reclusion. Of a kind with these select or secret societies was, in Romantic letters, the outlaw band formed to redress or avenge lawful injustices, beginning with those suffered by its leader. Robin Hood, Goethe's Goetz von Berlichingen, Schiller's Karl Moor, Pushkin's Dubrovsky, Kleist's Michael Kohlhaas, Grillparzer's Jaromir, Hugo's Hernani, Balzac's Ferragus: all act out the Romantic defiance of the world as it is, with occasional surrenders on the one side or irremediable estrangements on the other.

The Romantic artist per se, in rejecting patronage and academic standards in favor of an anonymous public and a self-created aesthetic, was entering the fray at the accepted risk of thereby exiting into a closed artistic world all his own, misunderstood and misesteemed. Indeed, the Romantic opted out in his heart whenever he opted in. Uhland rhymed this compromise: "The world is murk and mire. / But if you want to show / That you deserve one higher, / Then plunge in here below."[23] Byron was haughtier to the same effect when he affirmed of "the crowd" of his contemporaries: ". . . I stood / Among them, but not of them . . ."[24] Benjamin Constant spoke to himself this same way through his Ellénore's dying words to ambitious young Adolphe: "You will walk alone amidst the crowd that you are so impatient to join."[25] Distinctively Romantic too was Balzac's Rastignac in *Old Goriot* challenging Paris in outrage from the heights of Père Lachaise: "Now it's between the two of us!" while pursuing his fatal social climbing.[26] Sublimely Romantic was Vigny's Moses, "sad and alone" even in leading his people.[27] Büchner's Danton also craves release as his own revolutionary principles triumph all too bloodily. Young Manzoni withdrew from worldliness all at once at the pop of a firecracker, rushing from a festive Paris crowd into lifelong solitary piety. To other Romantic converts, religion meant on the contrary a communal bond to counteract aloneness: same difference!

A favorite Romantic way of turning to and from the world by turns was the dialectic of immediacy versus anticipation or recollection. Especially recollection: Romantics were high on self-accounting, which even when most searching and scrupulous, as with Stendhal, was a departure from raw experience. A Stendhal's happiness lay mostly in reminiscence; a

Leopardi's refuge from a painful present was the still beauty of remembrance; a Wordsworth's preferred use for emotion was to recollect it in tranquillity. Yet another Romantic retreat from hard outer reality led into the fantastic and, beyond that, madness, which for the Romantics was continuous with sanity. Poe called it an open question "whether madness is or is not the loftiest intelligence."[28] Mackenzie's proto-Romantic Man of Feeling, a contemporary of Young Werther, drew hilarity from fellow tourists in London when he empathized with inmates of Bedlam. But it was Rousseau who, by his own example, launched the Romantic concept of genius bordering on insanity. Some Romantics who crossed that border were Lenz and Hölderlin, Lenau and Schumann, Nerval and perhaps Friedrich. Romantics who depicted insanity as of a piece with sanity included Goya in his fearful *The Sleep of Reason*, Géricault in his touching portraits of mental patients, Wilhelm Kaulbach a trifle satirically in *The Madhouse*, Ludwig Tieck and E. T. A. Hoffmann and Vladimir Odoevski in their fanciful tales, Büchner in his placid and penetrating *Lenz*, Gogol seriocomically in *The Memoirs of a Madman*, Pushkin in every which way in one story or poem after another—*The Queen of Spades, The Bronze Horseman, Poltava, God Keep Me from Going Mad*. Just because Romantics saw the irrational as a soul-baring extension of the rational and felt its lure, raving madness was for them a fringe effect and not over the brink—not pure opting out.

Pure opting out, or in, was indeed impossible for a Romantic pulled both ways, meaning a Romantic as such. As Blake said of his visions: "I . . . take the world with me in my flights."[29] Romantic composers attained the ultimate in otherworldliness, as in Schubert's "Great" C-Major Symphony, even while dignifying folk music and developing program music. Romantic painters fled social reality—Friedrich into misty landscapes, Danby into apocalyptic imaginings, Turner into light and air, Géricault into horsemanship and horrors, Delacroix into colorful carnage. Yet all could be documentarists too: witness Friedrich's chilling *The Wreck of the "Hope" in the Polar Sea;* Danby's *The Shipwreck,* also depicting the wrecked "Hope"; Turner's testament to human cruelty, *The Slave Ship;* Géricault's monumental reconstruction of an official outrage, *The Raft of the "Medusa";* Delacroix's *Liberty Leading the People* with its spectrum of insurgents out of 1830, bosomy Liberty herself excepted. Lamartine's perpetual poetic refrain: "Flee, my soul, to depths of solitude, / Flee this world, unfaithful or perverse . . ." rejoined his Raphaël's resolve to plunge into his melancholy at full time, "to cut myself off from all human society that might distract me from it, and to cloak myself in silence, solitude, and coldness amid whatever people I should meet; my mental isolation was a shroud through which I no longer wished to see men, but only nature and God." Surely *that* spelled total withdrawal? Yes, except that its author also led the French Revolution of 1848. Musset's Lorenzaccio was Lamartine's fictional counterpart of sorts: he appears to be lost in debauchery even as he plots revolution in secret.

THE SUBLIME AND THE GROTESQUE 71

The root formula of so-called Romantic Idealism was to look away from all externality and into one's own mind, but only in order then to construct the universe subjectively. Here too Young Werther was precursive: "I draw back into myself and find a world." Irregularly in this same line, Novalis opted out straightaway in his first Hymn to the Night: "Downward I turn to the holy, inexpressible, mysterious night. / Far below lies the world, sunk into a deep chasm, bare and lonely . . ." only to come back out of himself into history and society in the fifth. Possibly, though, he came full circle in the sixth because of lassitude or fright; the fragmentary text is inconclusive. His message in any case was the Romantic one of a need to search through one's inner night before one might redeem the daylight world outside. Akin to Novalis in this was Senancour's Oberman, ordinarily taken for an oracle of alienation from the world:

> One must get away from human affairs not just to see how they might be changed, but to dare believe it. One needs isolation not to work out the means one would employ, but to hope for their success. One enters into a retreat and lives in it; the habit of established things weakens; the extraordinary is judged impartially, it ceases to be far-fetched, one believes in it. One returns and succeeds.[30]

Hugo said as much with a democratic twist: "Only in solitude can one work for the masses"[31] and again: "The prophet . . . goes into the desert to think of—whom? Of the multitude."[32] A reveler in the multitude, Hugo also had a vocation for exile: "I am the outlaw fled afar / Who dreams and sings in his flight / Together with the owl and the star / The somber song of the night."[33] And Vigny wanted in as much as out when he noted: "Oh! to flee! to flee people and withdraw among a chosen few drawn from a thousand thousands of thousands!" Nerval assuredly went the limit opting out—into exotic travels and mystery cults, dreams ("Dreaming is a second life," his *Aurélia* begins) and fantasy love, elusive prose about dreams and fantasy love, stark verses all in obscure symbols, at length madness and suicide. His was even the last word on this very subject: "God seems to want to tell my soul in its despair: / Leave the impure world, the crowd that does not care."[34] Yet Nerval too was involved with his times all the way, however tenuously. Well may he have dreamed in the grotto where the siren swims, as he put it in his poetry; so long as he published that poetry, his self-distancing from the earthier world was incomplete. Besides, his outbound paths were all beaten Romantic trails, beginning with his Oriental itinerary: thus a historian of Romantic letters has shown the striking parallels between his *Aurélia* and Novalis's much earlier *Hymns*.[35] His suicide itself was not just in the Romantic line like his madness; it was no exit for him either inasmuch as he imagined every passing experience to survive somewhere indestructibly. And this too was, from Goethe to

Gautier, a widespread Romantic notion sprung from the quintessential Romantic creed voiced by Grabbe's Hannibal before his suicide: "Out of this world we shall not fall."[36]

As between outward attachment and outward detachment, between opting in and opting out, Romantic love occupied the ambiguous position of an opting out à deux, or equally of a total, drastically local opting in. For pre-Romantics, all-out, exclusive love was inherently either tragic or comic. And in either case it was all-out only within its own erotic province; it did not possess, but at most only perturbed, the entire personality; its victims could run their affairs, even their kingdoms, on the side, however badly. Normal preferential love meanwhile—say, Jane Austen's kind even in the Romantic age—integrates the loving couple into society through marriage and children. But the *specificum* of Romantic love is precisely to occupy a lover altogether, to the exclusion of everything else, and this in and of itself neither tragically nor comically. Full absorption in a beloved is no cinch for the egocentric Romantic: René, Adolphe, Childe Harold, and Musset's Octave fall back on themselves emotionally again and again. If it does come, though, Romantic love is a cutoff from society, a pullout from the world, on a par with an opium trip or solitary moping. And, when mutual, such love will lock the lovers into its chambers even while their vital business goes to ruin outside—while a Stendhal hero's death warrant is drawn up or a Balzac hero's creditors close in for the kill. Even one-sided, such love carried a death penalty for Kleist's Prince Friedrich caught up in amorous reverie while waging war. Adolphe's consuming liaison holds him back from his career even after it goes stale; Don Juan's idyll with Haidée is a dalliance that proves fatal. Both are fittingly set. Don Juan's commences in a cave: "Their priest was solitude, and they were wed."[37] And Adolphe's runs aground in the Polish provinces. This opting out à deux, when followed by a return to the world, has a clear referent in the sex act itself—that total immersion in the other and withdrawal from the rest of existence, followed by a withdrawal from the other and refocus outside. And opting out à deux was perfected on its antisocial side if, like the sex act vis-à-vis polite society, it required to be hidden. A forbidden, illicit love was accordingly the Romantic love par excellence.

Sibling incest, suicide, opting in and out: what next? Nothing. Three new inside lines on a subject should suffice for fresh insight. Do the three connect? A first, partial linkage is obvious: if forbidden love was Romantic love par excellence, the forbidden love par excellence was brother-sister incest. Parent-child incest, while equally illicit, is less idyllic on the face of it when the parties to it are in the dark. Sibling incest (to quote a pioneer study of it in Romantic letters) "can change, in a moment of blinding recognition, from a blessing to a curse, from a socially sanctioned love which unites the lover with his beloved and with the community to a lust which alienates him from all society . . . and makes him an outcast."[38] But such a turnabout was only a middle term between two equally usual Romantic depictions of sibling incest, one tabooed-explicit, the other titillating-inexplicit. That is, a brother-sister pair in Romantic fiction might be a knowing one that grows more and more affectionate until tragedy ensues; or unknowing siblings might love unsuspectingly until the truth emerges; or else foster siblings might love under a curse that the public unconsciously understands. The tension between social sanction and social outrage, between falling in and falling out with the world's ways, is inherent in all three situations, above all in the first and most lifelike. Romantic suicide also mixed opting in and opting out in equal overdoses. For in suicide the Romantic self rejoined the elements, dissolved into the cosmos, at the same time that it cut itself off from them with radical finality. Even the most intense Romantic craving for death—the urge to "fade far away" with Keats's nightingale,[39] or the cosmic nihilism of Büchner's Danton—was a yearning for integration as well as disintegration, for the departing self's absorption into the all. Self-destruction (actual or virtual) followed on sibling incest (actual or virtual), as in *Paul and Virginie* or *Manfred,* the more readily since both bespoke the same duality of opting in and opting out. And this duality was at the heart of Romanticism.

But what can account for such an odd conflict informing a whole age? A Freudian might reduce its two terms, opting in and opting out, to object-love and self-love respectively, with Romantic love proper betwixt and between; that would hardly help to explain it, though, let alone suggest why one and only one cultural movement built up around it. A trickier counterpart in common experience has already been cited: the sex act, an opting out of the world and into the partner that goes into reverse when completed. Likewise of all eras, but structurally a neater fit, are sleeping and waking, hyphenated by lovers' sleeping together. We opt out of reality when we sleep and back into reality when we wake: it's as simple as that, and the more compelling given the Romantics' unexampled concern with sleeping and waking—including the interplay between the two and counting the sleep-related phenomena of trance and reverie, of visions and dreams and nightmares. The dialectic of dream and reality pervaded Romanticism, often in derivative or figurative form, more often outright as with Jean Paul and E. T. A. Hoffmann, Coleridge and De Quincey, Fuseli and Runge, Hölderlin and Kleist, Leopardi and Musset, Nodier and Nerval and Gautier. The Romantic accent fell on the ambiguity rather than the continuity as between sleeping and waking. "World becomes dream, dream becomes world," was a Novalis motto.[40] *Der Traum ein Leben* was an untranslatably ambiguous Grillparzer title for his play about dreamed living or lived dreaming, whichever. "Was it a vision or a waking dream?" and "Do I wake or sleep?" were questions that Keats left dangling in *Ode to a Nightingale.*[41] Wordsworth had earlier pulled a Platonic switch in *Intimations of Immortality:* "Our birth is but a sleep and a forgetting."[42] Shelley followed Wordsworth's lead when he mused wide-eyed atop Mont Blanc: ". . . do I lie / In dream, and does the mightier world of sleep / Spread far around and inaccessibly / Its circles?"[43] and again when he affirmed in *Prometheus Unbound:* "Death is the veil which those who live call life: / They sleep, and it is lifted . . ."[44] In a ghostly nighttime soliloquy, Büchner's Robespierre in *Danton's Death* likens waking life to sleepwalking.[45] Poe even gave an epistemological edge to sleep: "They who dream by day are cognizant of many things which escape those who dream only by night."[46]

This perpetual Romantic blurring of the boundaries between dreaming and waking, or interchange between the two, suggests a shock effect of some Europe-wide awakening from some European dream. And indeed, one rude awakening from an exalted dream did haunt the Romantic consciousness, the one involved in the example from Büchner: when the French Revolution passed over into the Reign of Terror. In sentiment, the young of heart all over Europe opted into the grand French enterprise of rebuilding the world ideally from below in 1789, of launching a rule of reason and love, of justice and brotherhood. Then, as the ever-so-promising new order turned chaotic and threatening, and the prospect of human emancipation faded into the fact of inhuman tyranny, the revolutionary enthusiasts of the first hour in France opted out, disheartened, into exile or counterrevolution or apoliticism, and hearts sank everywhere abroad. Was *this* the origin of the Romantics' contradictory drives to worldly engagement and worldly disengagement?

The indications are that it was. There is no end of direct testimony to the powerful impact of the sequence Revolution→Terror outside France as well as inside. The Revolution, Southey recollected, opened up a "visionary world. Old things seemed passing away, and nothing was dreamt of but the regeneration of the human race."[47] "It was a glorious dawn," Hegel told his students. "All thinking beings joined in rejoicing. A lofty excitement carried the day, a spiritual enthusiasm thrilled through creation, as if God's reconciliation with the world were at hand."[48] In Wordsworth's familiar verses on 1789 in *The Prelude:* ". . . a shock had then been given / To old opinions; and the minds of all men / Had felt it." And again: ". . . Europe at that time was thrilled with joy, / France standing on the top of golden hours, / And human nature seeming born again."

More to my point are Wordsworth's less familiar lines on the sequel:

> . . .—my nights were miserable;
> Through months, through years, long after the last beat
> Of those atrocities, the hour of sleep
> To me came rarely charged with natural gifts,
> Such ghastly visions had I of despair,
> And tyranny, and implements of death.[49]

Friedrich von Gentz put it that the French had tantalized sick mankind with a dream of cure only to redouble human suffering.[50] Friedrich Schlegel recounted that the Terror "awakened the deeper-searching political theorists and observers of the world from their illusion."[51] At the time of his own awakening, Schlegel recoiled from the Revolution as from "a nearly worldwide cataclysm, an unfathomable inundation of the political world," and "a frightful tragicomedy of humanity." In 1800 he poetized: "Europe's spirit went out,"[52] and in 1827 in still vivid recall: "Thunderously the earth quakes in cavernous abysses."[53] For Coleridge in 1794: "Creation's eyeless drudge, black Ruin, sits / Nursing the impatient earthquake."[54] Coleridge later fell back on Scripture to express his view of the Revolution degenerating: "A great and strong wind rent the mountains, and brake in pieces the rocks before the Lord; but the Lord was not in the wind; and after the wind an earthquake; and after the earthquake a fire; and the Lord was not in the fire."[55] Hölderlin invoked the god of the times: "You in the dark cloud . . . / It is too wild, scary all around, and it / Crumbles and totters wherever I look."[56] Looking back, Tieck saw "the old chaos" looming,[57] Görres "a raging typhoon,"[58] Adam Müller "a glimmer of the dawn of hell,"[59] Kleist a train of wreckage across Europe.[60] Hazlitt, though a mere child when the Revolution began, called it the crucial event for his generation in England.[61] The later-born also spoke this same language. Shelley termed the failed Revolution "the master theme of the epoch in which we live" and asserted: "The sympathies connected with that event extended to every bosom. . . . The revulsion occasioned by the atrocities of the demagogues and the re-establishment of successive tyrannies in France was terrible, and felt in the remotest corners of the civilized world."[62] Byron was pithier: "France got drunk with blood to vomit crime."[63]

Romanticism was the response of Europeans to their shattered revolutionary dream—"or, rather," in Hugh Honour's formulation, "the diversity of individual responses to it, united only at their point of departure and constantly subject to revision in a constantly changing world."[64] To be sure, Romantic suicide went back to Chatterton and Werther in the early 1770s, sibling incest to *Paul and Virginie* of 1787. More, the dual impulse to remake and to reject the world, the two-way direction of Romanticism, manifestly threw back to Rousseau with his lifelong split into worldly activist and unworldly self-outcast, and especially his two-way message about society as both our source of corruption and our means of regeneration. As at any other traumatic juncture, so when the Revolution went from dream to nightmare: those thrown by the event reached back into the past for the stuff of their reaction out of a natural desire to have been through it before—in an instinctive effort to familiarize the unfamiliar. And like many another happening that hits too hard to be absorbed, this one was relived, more or less disguised, in countless variants on a few basic themes. Through cultural transmission it was relived by individual Romantics of the last hour as of the first. Romanticism was just that reliving.

Initially the most pronounced mode of reliving was a retreat into fantastic visions derived from the traumatic Revolutionary sequence of enchantment and disenchantment. As against a Chénier who mounted the scaffold or a Wordsworth who espoused rusticity, a Blake and a Coleridge, a Hölderlin and a Novalis, waged private symbolic struggles between life and death, heaven and hell, day and night, without identifying the historic referent outright. "The sleep of reason produces monsters" was Goya's caption for a key one of his *Caprichos,* a repertory of horrors natural and supernatural. These were published even as the Swiss painter Jean-Pierre Saint-Ours produced the first of his several versions of *The Greek Earthquake,* which shows an imaginary cataclysm overwhelming mankind and its greatest monuments. Hugh Honour, citing this instance of obsessive disillusionment with events in France, comments that "the excesses of the Revolution under the Terror . . . overturned belief in the possibility of establishing an ideal society, or art, based on human reason."[65] Saint-Ours's earthquake was of a piece with a vast Romantic catastrophism in painting—plagues, deluges, shipwrecks, other earthquakes—that matched the Romantics' catastrophist rhetoric on the Revolution point for point. Recurrent Romantic nightmares of beloveds turning into devils or of the world disintegrating fill this same bill. Still closer to the traumatic source was the Romantic decapitation dream, which Hoffmann in *The Magnetizer* called the typical dream: it came into Arnim's *The Guardians of the Crown* and Hugo's *The Condemned Man's Last Day,* into two of Nodier's *Fantastic Tales,* two *Brown Tales* by Philacrète Chasles, two of *The Thousand and One Ghosts* by Dumas.[66] More subtly, Kleist's Prince Friedrich is condemned to death when he exceeds his battle orders because he is distracted by an enchanted dream: thus his dream takes him *away from* public life, *to* which he is rudely awakened—a reversal of 1789–1794 that is unreversed in the end in that his dream proves to have been a waking experience after all. Mary Shelley's *Frankenstein* told of hopes for human betterment through human wizardry issuing in a man-made monster's uncontrollable crimes. Here the specter of the French Revolution looms behind line after line: "Mingled with this horror, I felt the bitterness of disappointment . . . and the change was so rapid, the overthrow so complete!" or: "Alas, I had turned loose into the world a depraved wretch whose delight was in carnage and misery," or again: "So frightful an event is single in the history of man," or yet again: "I often sat for hours motionless and speechless, wishing for some mighty revolution that might bury me and my destroyer in its ruins," or finally when, with Frankenstein's bride murdered, their wedding bed becomes a "bridal bier."[67] Keats gave the passage from enchantment to disenchantment an ambiguous twist in *La Belle Dame Sans Merci* as the enchantress lulls to sleep a knight-at-arms who then awakens from fearful dreams to find himself alone in a desolate world. Keats's *Lamia,* which followed, was unambiguous: there a wedding gown turns into a winding sheet. Byron's Haidée has a nightmare amidst a dreamlike idyll with Don Juan that thereupon turns into a waking nightmare.[68] Büchner's lusty, exuberant Danton has nightmares that hark back to the September Massacres.[69] Nerval's *Aurélia* alternates luminous dream with stark reality and, on the dream side, silver and gold with orgy and carnage. John William Polidori, Byron's physician for a season, did his dissertation on the nightmare—and, just to close our thematic circle, hastened to commit fictional sibling incest in his *Ernestus Berchtold, or The Modern Oedipus,* and then factual suicide.

Politically, meanwhile, the cause of human emancipation from below flared up again and again in countless forms among Europeans—national wars, liberal conspiracies, social movements, socialist experiments—pending the climactic Romantic uprisings of 1848, when in concert with Lamartine's France nearly all of Europe relaunched the old, shattered Revolutionary enterprise, updated. The dreamer-doers were duly shot down here, starved out there, washed away elsewhere, often horrifyingly, always with memories of 1789–1794 and gloomy forebodings intermingled. France led the way in historic replay to the bitter last with a bloody repression of insurgent workingmen in June 1848 and with Louis-Napoleon elected president of the Republic the following December—by a 325-to-1 margin over Lamartine, who had cautioned himself in 1839: "There, seek your peace at last in your own self; / Your happiness has come off short in dreams.[70]

Mazzini brought up the rear in 1849, resuming his accustomed exile as his glorious Roman Republic succumbed to French artillery and bayonets. This reexperience at first hand by French and non-French alike of the wreck of the Revolutionary hope (the pun on Friedrich's painting is called for) was a last Romantic fling. Romanticism thereupon split up between its two components of dream and reality—into upbeat Symbolism and downbeat Realism—which went their separate ways in the arts until the next century. (This split was already impending as between a Gautier and a Balzac, or a Nerval and a Stendhal.) With this breakup of Romanticism, the experience of the Revolution engendering the Terror did not cease to haunt history. How deep that trauma cut shows at a glance in the consecrated century-old European pattern of revolutions passing over into systems of terror. But since 1848 too many other determinants have intermixed with that one for its workings to be sorted out with much clarity.

Lots of familiar facts of Romanticism will now be recognizable as shock effects of the Revolution-run-amuck. Indeed, Romanticism showed surprisingly few other derivations from first to last. To illustrate at random, the eruption of lowly personages and problems into serious art with the Romantics mirrored the plebeian upsurge of 1789. The collapsing of the hierarchy of styles and subjects in art and letters recapitulated the destruction of the old estates and privileges in 1789. Romantic dramatists repudiated the three unities, and Romantic painters rejected academicism, like the Revolutionaries throwing out the old order: with noisy ado and quiet carryovers. The Romantics' intensified emotional highs and lows recalled the buildup and letdown of idealistic enthusiasm between 1789 and 1794. The brother-sister romance ran the same disaster course each time through, and with the same pretensions to universality, as the Revolutionary mystique—which fittingly turned all sex into sibling incest by its Fraternity clause. The fairy tale and the horror story, two Romantic specialties, recast the end terms of the historic original of 1789–1794. So did Hugo's Romantic aesthetic that coupled the sublime and the grotesque, and Balzac's Romantic underworld "with its abrupt transitions from the pleasant to the ghastly."[71] The graveyard Romanticism of Géricault or Michelet, Tieck or Jean Paul, was the Terrorists' *Guillotinenromantik* (Büchner's apt word[72]) once removed. Organicism began with the Romantics as a way to explain political society in opposition to social contract theory, which was blamed for the Revolutionary fiasco. And the Romantic concept of a logic of events was originally, with Hegel, a rationalization of the Terror. Effects could also be quite indirect and still unmistakable: thus the Romantics' notorious alternation of bursts of energy with spells of torpor was a spinoff from the waking-sleeping syndrome. Effects were each overdetermined besides, but the cluster of them called Romanticism was not. Take once again the boom in sibling incest real or imaginary. It went with Romanticism, but may well have been further a release of naughtiness once the royal lid was blown, or a retreat into the family once the mob and then the guillotine ruled outdoors, or lots else. Historians have long recognized the Revolution as the point of departure for one Romantic theme after another,[73] even for Romanticism itself. But they have not recognized Romanticism as an unconscious reexperiencing of the Revolution that drew on cultural motifs of an earlier vintage before fashioning additional motifs of its own. In brief, they have seen the fact of a connection but not its nature.

That nature was no quirk. Unconscious reliving is the truth to the old adage that history repeats itself. But this truth goes well beyond what just Romanticism alongside of Hitlerism can disclose. Nor can a mere two historic cases together speak to the multifarious hows and whys of traumatic reliving. I shall probe these hows and whys on a broader basis later. But before moving on I see a need to explain that it was not contradictory for the Romantics to have relived the failed Revolution unconsciously with that Revolution consciously in mind: in traumatic reliving it is the fact of reliving, and not the thing relived, that is unconscious. Also, reliving apart, Romanticism was no less an effect of the Revolution for being a compound of older elements; to analogize, the ingredients of a cake all preexist too. One big evidential shortcoming of my presentation bears mentioning: of the French incessantly refighting their Revolution I cited only 1848 and Lamartine, minus Lamartine's best-selling history of the Girondins at that. Finally, I left America largely out of account because Romanticism ran late there. But there too it ran to form: witness Melville's *Pierre* with its half-brother-sister couple confronting the world fitfully until their double suicide caps a climax fraught with nightmare and madness.

CHAPTER FIVE

Being, Doing, Having

Adaptation to pressure (material or ideological), trauma relived (material or ideological): these two forms of group process are both reactive. By contrast, the third form of group process proposed here is the spontaneous symbolic projection of fundamentals of human consciousness as they evolve historically. Such running projections are best called "cultural" in the broad sense of the word that covers manners and morals as well as the arts and sciences. The cultural development to be considered in this chapter with respect to the evolving human condition it expresses is that of the highest personal values held by Europeans since the Middle Ages.

This chapter concerns the personal ideals that have prevailed by turns in Christendom since the moral hold of Christianity itself began to loosen in the Renaissance. Being, Doing, and Having are my generic terms for the three forms taken by what people have most valued in themselves and others over the past few centuries. Moral analysts have often used these three terms before, though for the most part nonhistorically and to denote basic orientations toward life rather than ideals.[1] I claim no originality either in defining any one of the three kinds of value that I call by those names or even in associating any one of them primarily with a particular period of history. But my big point is, I believe, new: that those three varieties of supreme personal value shaped up successively in the West as cultural norms beginning in the Renaissance, each predominating in turn without wholly eliminating its predecessors.

These three generic modern ideals succeeded, without entirely supplanting, the medieval Christian ideal of sanctity. This prior Christian ideal for its part did not sweep the field quite clean of pagan ideals, which indeed regained a certain currency in the Renaissance. But residual pagan ideals are no part of my subject. Nor again is the ideal of sanctity except to the extent that the three worldly modern ideals of Being, Doing, and Having developed in reaction against it. Medievals were mostly sinners, yet whatever survives of their culture suggests that they would rather have been saints. Sin could be fun, but hell loomed so scary that it spoiled the fun. The seven deadly sins cannot have flourished more than did the conviction that they were deadly. The *vanitas* and the *memento mori,* grim reminders that the things of this world are ephemeral, belong to a later age; medievals needed no such reminding. To luxuriate in one's earthly person, accomplishments, or estate—in one's Being, Doing, or Having—spelled pride, the sin of sins. Even if medievals did commit that sin of the spirit continually, their aspirations ran the other way. And aspirations, alias ideals, are my subject.

The first great personal ideal to supplant Christian saintliness, the one I call Being, emerged in the Italian Renaissance (with input from an upgraded pagan antiquity). It is the easiest of the three great modern ideals to characterize, having been defined and redefined throughout the Renaissance in theory and practice alike. Vittorino da Feltre promoted it in his highly influential academy, as did Giovanni della Casa in his popular manual of breeding.[2] It found authoritative expression in that bible of Being, *The Book of the Courtier* by Castiglione, published in 1528. Not that Castiglione prescribed which qualities the perfect courtier, or gentleman, should cultivate. Instead he purported to record, somewhat freely, a running debate on that very subject by a select company at the model court of Urbino. The debaters reach no hard and fast conclusions, but a consensus does inform their discussion to the effect that the most estimable, enviable human being is the one who masters the broadest range of choice capabilities as if effortlessly, without ostentation or insecurity. The pick of those capabilities, which so exercised Castiglione's courtly set, is beside my own point, which is only that the highest human value in Castiglione's model court lay in being visibly up to whatever showing was held in honor. Feats of sonneteering or swordsmanship, say, were not ends in themselves, nor did the issue of enjoying them ever arise. They mattered to Castiglione's cultured party only as signs of a superior self-styling designed to draw recognition unobtrusively. Castiglione's urbane Urbinians' concern amounted to the very worldly one of how the perfect courtier should come across—what, and again what, he should appear to be without trying. The margin between real and perceived attributes, which here signals the shift from Christian to worldly perspectives, gave Castiglione's party no pause. Perception was the payoff, and besides, whoever got to be *seen as* unruffled no matter what would soon enough really *be* unflappable. Nor does it make any substantive difference that Castiglione's courtier, that paragon of Being, can be described in terms evocative of Doing or Having—as capable of *doing* this or that, or as *having* this or that quality. For Castiglione's courtier was valued not for what he accomplished or acquired, but for what he appeared to *be* in and of himself. From his perfected person, deeds in kind would flow; to his perfected person, possessions in kind would accrue; deeds and possessions were, however, equally immaterial to his perfected person—or indeed to hers, for while the feminine differed from the masculine ideal in specifics, it too was defined by core attributes. For both sexes, moreover, the topmost attribute was discretion, and the clincher (oddly analogous to Luther's "one thing needful" in the spiritual realm) was an inherent, constitutive grace without which no performance or possession availed. In all-sided Alberti's earlier view, even that grace might be acquired, but then it was to be passed off as a natural gift. Alternatively, monkish Erasmus argued Christian as against courtly civility: the core inner self was to be schooled as the source of all outer behavior.[3] But Castiglione's was most nearly the prescriptive Renaissance conception of self-contained Being. And Castiglione's master or mistress of social skills was not only what those courtly discussants in Urbino, but what his whole huge readership and discipleship, would ideally have liked to *be*.[4]

Urbino's native son Raphael painted a portrait of Castiglione in 1516 that is a perfect visual counterpart to Castiglione's Urbino-based treatise on the self as a work of art.[5] Casually yet faultlessly clothed, his bearing both sturdy and placid, his features manly though also delicately refined, Raphael Castiglione conveys mature wisdom and gentle authority through blue eyes gazing straight at us out of rich inner resources. No viewer wonders what such a human specimen has done or enjoyed in its day; its whole reason for existing is that image it projects of dignity, equipoise, compact strength of character, and cultivation of every proper sort. No other late Renaissance or especially Mannerist portraits quite manage to render the same courtly ideal without some touch of the haughty, showy air to which it was prone in practice.[6] Shadowy, ponderous Rembrandt himself modeled a self-portrait of 1640 on Raphael's suave and soft-glowing *Castiglione,* with even a hint of Titian's self-glorying *Man with the Blue Sleeve* of 1511–1512 thrown in.[7] The portraiture most prized in the Baroque, such as Van Dyck's, routinely lent its subjects the look of aloof detachment and easy elegance that was by then the consecrated mark of Being.

Like Mannerist *poseurs* in paint, the perfected selves of later prescriptive works on Being lacked the serenity of Castiglione's courtier. In the Castiglione vein, Baltasar Gracián's writings were also largely recipes for "man at his peak"—for improving oneself day by day "until reaching the point of consummate being."[8] But Gracián's hero, out to cut a great figure, was craftier in this than ever Castiglione's courtier was. He cultivated the more noticeable qualities by preference[9] and contrived to appear to harbor

Raphael, *Baldassare Castiglione,* 1516
(Musée du Louvre, Paris). (Erich Lessing / Art Resource, NY)

more of them than he actually did.[10] He even rationed their display so that they would serve as reminders of his greatness and not be taken for granted.[11] His premise was nonetheless Castiglione's, also expressed in a Spanish saying that dates from this time: *"No basta ser bueno, sino parecerlo"*—it's no use being good unless it shows.[12] The ideal of Being, made in Italy, traveled north as well along with the rest of the Renaissance: thus Montaigne scorned his own times for lacking men of "fine parts" like the finest of the ancients,[13] while Spenser's knight Calidore declared that it lay "in each mans self" to fashion his person howsoever he chose.[14]

Pascal in his pious jottings of the mid-seventeenth century deprecated the idealized self on display: "it wants to be perfect and sees itself full of imperfections; it wants to gain men's love and esteem and sees that its faults deserve only their aversion and contempt . . . it takes every care to cover up its defects both toward itself and toward others, and cannot bear to have them pointed out or noticed."[15] But hardly was Pascal dead when the ideal of Being went on to attain its apogee in the stagy Grand Monarchy of Louis XIV. The Sun King himself radiated *"ma dignité"* for all the King's men to ape. The reigning standard for Being in his realm was endowment, not achievement. In Molière's mocking formulation, "Persons of quality know everything without ever having learned anything."[16] Molière's were the didactics of Being in the negative vein: what not to be. His comic theater made fun of departures from the standard of civility and sagacity set in Versailles and Paris. Preciosity, sanctimony, miserliness, hypochondria, amorism: these were laughable to Molière's public because they went too far in the right direction. The art of Being was one of dosage: just so much refinement or piety or thrift or hygiene or gallantry and no more. Equally funny to Molière's audiences was the clash between the real and the ideal in self-styling, as when a glutton and lecher professed spirituality. Offstage that clash was an issue by no means distinctively French: thus Rembrandt, his self-images cast in unworldly inwardness, was cynically suspected of bidding them up at auction on the sly. To put an obvious point on it, the ideal of an age will not be its common practice any more than its common practice need reflect its ideal. Nor by the same token were self-cultivation, performance, and possession each peculiar to a single age as pursuits even if as supreme values they were.

The preferred recipes for Being varied and evolved over the centuries incalculably more than a passing mention of the pose struck by Rembrandt or the posture preferred by Molière may suggest. Even so, a near consensus did emerge among the philosophes of the eighteenth century on virtue as the ornamental attribute of choice even while they undercut that consensus with relish in their daily lives. At the same time, suavity yielded to snobbery in straight line of descent from Castiglione's noble courtier. At the perverse end of that line was Beau Brummell, George IV's parvenu arbiter of fashion in England: aspirants to royal recognition knew they came short at Hampton Court when Brummell cut them dead.

By the time of the French Revolution, the ideal of the superior self had begun giving way to a new highest ideal of surpassing oneself through great deeds. Already the Calvinistic pursuit of prosperity as a token of inner grace had rivaled locally with the ideal of Being. Now a stress on accomplishment for its own sake swept the moral field. Carlyle put it pithily that "the done Work" was "the epitome of the man."[17] No longer did virtue signify a shiny air of well-meaning; henceforth virtue was as virtue did.[18] The glamor of this new ideal of Doing lay in boldness, daring, audacity: these were the catchwords that now stirred youth. For the Romantics, the paradigmatic doers were Faust in legend and Napoleon in fact. True, the ancients had had their Prometheus and their Alexander—not, though, as role models for everyone and anyone to emulate. Byron's restless alter egos—Childe Harold, Don Juan, Cain, Manfred—vied with Byron himself for far-flung ventures. Stendhal's Julien Sorel, though tender of heart, construed love itself as a Napoleonic campaign. Tennyson's Ulysses gave the age its energetic motto: "To strive, to seek, to find, and not to yield." Romantic heroes were either Promethean doers (in the subtitle to *Frankenstein* Mary Shelley's hapless heroic wizard is a "modern Prometheus") or else languished for want of an opportunity to act on a grand scale.[19]

More prosaic were the post-Romantics, for whom the ideal of Doing was defined by Samuel Smiles in his *Self-Help* before being novelized a hundredfold by Horatio Alger: to make one's own opportunities. For Smiles as for his times, the self-made man upstaged the self-fashioned gentleman. Like Alger after him, Smiles did also stress the virtue of character, even insistently, yet only as a springboard to success rather than as a showpiece in itself. And he equated success with achievement, never with enjoyment. The best seller of the nineteenth century after the Bible, *Self-Help* abounds in vignettes of inventors, industrialists, colonizers, statesmen, and creative artists surmounting early failures by dint of character. By character Smiles meant not the grand manner, let alone mannerliness, as in the old moral regime, but above all rectitude, resolve, and forbearance, accessible to all. His numberless concordant quotations on the instrumentality of character are of a kind with this one from Canning in 1801: "My road must be through character to power."[20] Money was for Smiles a means not of gratification, but to pursue worthy aims. The tombstone inscription he willed for himself speaks straight to the ideal of Doing: "Samuel Smiles, author of Self-Help."

The Romantic portrait nicely reflects the change from Being to Doing. Earlier portraiture had aimed to fix its subjects in a privileged posture (typically seen a bit from below), with their distinctive functions, activities, and possessions intimated alongside. Personal qualities too, besides being conveyed through demeanor and attitude, might be symbolized for good measure: thus Judith Leyster depicted herself making music in concert to signify her inner and outer harmony (c. 1633) but inactive beside an easel painting, brush and palette in hand, to show her profession (1635).[21] Even Velazquez in turn, in his celebration of himself as painter, *Las meninas* (1656), did not show himself actually painting, while Vermeer's artist at the easel in *The Art of Painting* (c. 1670), though quite possibly Vermeer himself, is seen facelessly from behind.[22]

François-André Vincent, *Mademoiselle Duplant*, 1793

(Calouste Gulbenkian Foundation Museum, Lisbon)

A century later Gainsborough's musicians were still only holding their instruments or scores, not playing them. A transitional mode developed roughly from Hogarth's David Garrick playing Richard III (1745) to Vincent's Mademoiselle Duplant at the piano (1793),[23] with subjects doing, or nearly doing, what defines them but also dominating it, fully self-possessed. Witness Quentin de La Tour's opulent Madame de Pompadour, patroness of the arts, fingering a manuscript with one hand and a musical score with the other while gazing aside in dreamy detachment (1755).[24] The transition to Doing was complete by the time of Delacroix's Paganini lost in a virtuoso performance, a mere shadowy appendage to his violin

(1831), or of Ingres's restless press tycoon Monsieur Bertin, his vitality bursting nervously out of his ill-suited salon attire (1832). Consider the transition closely. Vincent's Mademoiselle Duplant has turned to face the viewer, one hand still on the keyboard. Devoted to her music she emphatically is, but her center of gravity lies outside of it. She is a person first and last, and that person is musical. By contrast, Delacroix's Paganini is an unseemly runt transfixed by his own playing: it possesses and consumes him while his sinewy hands and feverish eyes glow demonically out of the darkness enfolding the rest of him.

Eugène Delacroix, *Paganini*, 1831.
(The Phillips Collection, Washington, D.C.)

Religifying Doing, Goethe decreed in his *Faust:* "In the beginning was the *deed.*" Hegel declared it the essence of Spirit "to *act.*" Auguste Comte went the length of devising a new religion with benefactors of humanity as its saints of Doing. Karl Marx reduced all value to labor. Tennyson immortalized sheer Doing as the ultimate: "Theirs not to reason why, / Theirs but to do and die."[25] Schoolboys learned to admire feats of courage, endurance, ingenuity. At Rugby under the foremost schoolmaster of the age, Thomas Arnold, "Every pupil was made to feel that there was work for him to do—that his happiness as well as his duty lay in doing that work well."[26] The public applauded, and obituaries recorded, realization. Feminism protested women's enforced idleness within the leisured set: "They have nothing to do," Florence Nightingale complained, so that their "heroisms" were rusting.[27] As against this complaint, for the lady of a novelistic portrait by Henry James "to be rich was a virtue because it was to be able to *do.*"[28] The *mal du siècle* was neurasthenia, a sit-down or indeed liedown strike against the ethic of Doing; its locus classicus was Goncharov's cautionary tale *Oblomov.* Workaday toil was dignified, and not just by socialists: never until the nineteenth century did novels or paintings dwell on men or women laboring[29]—titanically in the Romantic decades, then more as drudges later along. At midcentury Courbet celebrated the dignity of labor in *The Stone-Breakers,* Millet its sanctity in *The Gleaners,* Ford Madox Brown its manifold varieties in *Work.*[30] England set the industrial stan-

Gustave Courbet, *The Stone-Breakers*, 1849

(destroyed; formerly Zwinger, Dresden). (Foto Marburg / Art Resource, NY)

dard of Doing: "Industry is, in a word, *the* distinguishing quality of our nation," boasted Edward Bulwer-Lytton.[31] America reset the standard at the
start of the twentieth century as that American apotheosis of dehumanized
Doing, Taylorism, quickened individual output in factory production to
the breaking point.

Fichte launched Doing philosophically in 1800 on the ground of the
human "drive to absolute, independent activity [*Selbstthätigkeit*]."[32] In
1843 Moses Hess, correcting Descartes's *cogito ergo sum,* declared: "I know
. . . that I am *active,* not that I *am.* Not *being,* but *doing,* comes first and
last."[33] In 1887 Nietzsche clinched the philosophic shift from Being to Doing. "There is no 'being' behind doing, effecting, becoming," he proclaimed; "'the doer' is merely superadded to the doing—the doing is everything."[34] The philosopher's defining purpose, according to Nietzsche, was to
"*do* something for the truth," so that a philosopher instinctively avoids having "to think *about himself*"—and has small use for possessions, Nietzsche
added, considering that "he who possesses is possessed."[35] At the century's
end, pragmatism spoke straight to this philosophic spirit of the age and,
by making practicality the warrant even for truth, lent Doing its aptest
philosophic sanction.

Ibsen created a veritable poet of the entrepreneurial deed in John
Gabriel Borkman. John Gabriel has served a jail term for swindling in-
vestors in order to develop mines. Unchastened, he plans to take up again
where he left off: by great work alone can one atone for one's misdeeds, he
tells his son.[36] Oblivious of the two women who have spoiled their lives
for him, he cries out his passionate love for the imprisoned treasures that,
by hook and crook alike, he has freed from the dark bowels of the earth.[37]
An idealism no less virile has brought celebrity and high esteem to
Thomas Mann's overwrought prose artist Aschenbach. This tireless toiler
with words has long spoken to the temper of the times as a champion of
the suffering-active virtue that overrides inner inadequacy by force of will,
as when his hero Frederick the Great battled on and on to victory against
hopeless odds.[38] At length Aschenbach's own soldierly will cracks from his
straining beyond his creative strength, and he plunges into unmanly de-
pravity in Venice, marking an inglorious end of this whole strenuous
moral regimen.

Sometime early in the twentieth century the active ideal of making
one's mark by Doing yielded its primacy to the passive ideal of gaining fulfillment through Having. Having encompasses first and foremost having
goods, and having them as a matter of course, even by rights. But this possessiveness extends into less tangible realms as well. As early as 1881 a
woman of the world imagined by Henry James defined the incipient
ideal of Having when she declared: "What shall we call our 'self'?
Where does it begin? where does it end? It overflows into everything that

belongs to us—and then it flows back again. I know a large part of my-self is in the clothes I choose to wear. I've a great respect for *things*! One's self—for other people—is one's expression of one's self; and one's house, one's furniture, one's garments, the books one reads, the company one keeps—these things are all expressive.'"[39] Henry's brother William, the theorist of pragmatism, elaborated in 1890: "*In its widest possible sense . . . a man's self is the sum-total of all that he* CAN *call his,* not only his body and his psychic powers, but his clothes and his house, his wife and his children, his ancestors and friends, his reputation and works, his lands and horses and yacht, and bank-account."[40] Georg Simmel in 1900 saw this last item fast displacing all the rest as the measure of the modern self.[41] Yet the list was growing. Thorstein Veblen in *The Theory of the Leisure Class* of 1899 added conspicuous leisure, conspicuous consumption, and conspicuous waste to what he called the pecuniary standard of self-esteem. In 1908 H. G. Wells described shopping by "economically ascendant people" (alias yuppies): "They plunge into it as one plunges into a career; as a class they talk, think, and dream possessions. . . . Acquisition becomes the substance of their lives." Of that class Wells remarked that "it includes nearly all America as one sees it from the European stage."[42] Fittingly, the personalities featured in two of America's favorite magazines *(The Saturday Evening Post* and *Collier's)* went from "idols of production" before World War I to "idols of consumption" shortly afterwards.[43] But America had no patent on the new ideal. José Ortega y Gasset in *The Revolt of the Masses* of 1930 saw demandingness as endemic to the "mass man," who had overrun all walks of Western life since the late nineteenth century. "The world that surrounds the new man from birth," Ortega observed, "does not induce him to limit himself in any sense; it sets up no veto or barrier against him; on the contrary, it stirs his appetite, which in principle can grow indefinitely."[44] Wanting more and ever more was for Ortega no artifact of salesmanship but inherent in the mindset of the ascendant masses.

Later social critics, American and then also especially French, blamed the market economy. In 1957 Vance Packard in his best-selling *The Hidden Persuaders* denounced the "penetrating pervasive techniques" of marketers intent on creating new wants,[45] and in 1960 Packard expanded on the human hazards of our systemic stress on ever more production and consumption, each spurring the other on.[46] In *The Affluent Society* of 1958 John Kenneth Galbraith likewise argued against "our single-minded commitment to production,"[47] against "production as an all-embracing goal,"[48] against "a production-oriented society,"[49] against "a culture that accords consumption great social value" and "in which consumption is an end in itself,"[50] and most particularly against "the powerful and very visible tendency of the modern economic system to cultivate or create the wants that it satisfies."[51]

August Macke, *Large Lighted Shop Window*, 1912 (Sprengel Museum, Hannover)

The ideal of Having was novelized to perfection in Georges Perec's *Les choses* (Things) of 1965. With Flaubertian irony Perec told of a young couple's yearning to *have* as it expands from mere things to embrace a vast range of nebulous, costly delectations:

> They would have liked to be rich. They believed they would have known how to dress, to look, to smile like rich people. They would have had the needful tact and discretion. They would have forgotten about their wealth, known not to show it off. They would not have gloried in it. They would have breathed it. Their pleasures would have been intense. They would have loved to walk, to stroll, to choose, to value. They would have loved to live. Their life would have been an art of living.[52]

Their ideal, though immaterial around the edges, nonetheless has its hard core in owning. "The world, things ever since, would have had to belong to them, and they would have multiplied the signs of their possession," for "they loved riches before loving life."[53] Nourished by middle-brow magazines, their consumerist daydreams fill out graphically: "studding them like so many promises were marvelous luminous images of immaculate fields of snow streaked with ski tracks, of blue seas, of sun, of green hills, of fires crackling in stone fireplaces, of bold highways, of sleeping cars, of grand hotels."[54] Though their fancies acquire ever more discriminating precision, the bottom line remains: "They wanted superabundance."[55] An attempt to flee their sense of constriction within their middling lifestyle leads them to a dead end in the Tunisian desert: "It seemed to them now that earlier they had at least had the craving to have."[56] Their sentimental education complete, they reintegrate into postindustrial society with its permanent frustration amid finite plenty. Fact imitated Perec's fiction. The clearest demonstration of the ubiquity of this ideal of Having in postindustrial society was the failed revolt against it launched by junior intellectuals worldwide in 1968: they too duly reintegrated like Perec's fugitives, except only the few diehards who went underground or over the brink.

Increased availability of goods and services does not temper the craving to *have,* that perpetual aching for more and still more which, to quote Jean Fourastié, "turns children's playrooms into storage rooms for toys. Clearly," Fourastié pursued, "the dreams-desires-needs sequence is limitless. To snap the chain calls for strict taboos. The thrust of advertising and of the consumerist society is, on the contrary, to keep going one better. Thence dissatisfaction springs eternal."[57] Jean Baudrillard gave that thrust a Freudian twist: "For the mechanism of buying (already invested with a libidinal charge) is substituted a whole eroticization of choosing and spending."[58] And, addressing my very point, Baudrillard added that, "if consumption seems irrepressible, that is because it is the acting out of a total ideal [*une pratique idéaliste totale*] which, beyond a certain threshold, has nothing more to do with the satisfaction of needs or the reality principle"; rather, it is in and of itself "a reason for living."[59] Commercial advertising speaks the language of Having in its purest form. As François de Closets observed, advertising does not so much display products as it does people consuming those products[60]—*havers* reveling in this or that clothing, furniture, luggage, whisky. By implication, "it turns the consumer into a reflection of what he consumes. He does not create his own happiness; he receives it from the material world."[61] In coaxing the consumer's interest away from inner to outer resources, Closets noted, advertising imposes "the predominance of having over being"[62] even as, "in this dialectic of desire and satisfaction, frustration keeps beating out contentment."[63]

The ideal of Having has drawn far more criticism in its own time than did the ideals of Being or Doing in theirs—perhaps unjustly, for affluent frustration frustrates less than does real want. In the aggregate, like it or not, the more we earn or own, the happier we feel: it's as simple as that.[64] That the market economy creates, or at least promotes, the needs it falsely claims to fill, with the prospect of satiety ever receding, is nonetheless a commonplace by now. Its simple corollary should be a commonplace too: that consumers today crave, over and beyond satiety itself, ever new felt needs, ever new ways of *having*,[65] even illusory ones. Science fiction, virtual reality, drugs: all cater to the fantasy of comandeering thrills beyond the pale.

In the perspective of Having, knowledge is cultural capital. Similarly, experience is an asset not just for job applicants. Experiences add up: where one has been, what one has seen, whom one has known, are social credentials. The glamor of the jet set is habitual costly travel: the world is its oyster. Like ad models, role models are depicted as savvy about living and enjoying.[66] Life is all theirs: such is the tacit text of portraits by "photographer to the stars" Herb Ritts.

Heading the vast philosophical backdrop to the twentieth century's ideal of Having, Bergson conceived of time itself as cumulative. Heading the even vaster literary backdrop, Rilke and Proust conceived of memories as possessions. For Camus in *The Fall*, the paradise lost by his modernday John the Baptist was, most expressively, "life grasped directly" [*la vie en prise directe*]. Comparably, William Golding's "pincher" Martin clutched crablike at life. As soon as tapes were available, Beckett's Krapp stored his past on them. Today's Krapps store TV shows instead—stock experiences to be had or rehad at will.

The tragic twentieth century's loftiest values came down in the end to earthly indulgence. Happiness meant getting the most out of life, and equity meant getting yours while others got theirs. Communist militants fought and died for a future society of all-around Having. Then at the first opportunity, in the late 1980s, Sovietized Europe jumped at the market economy because it promised everyone a quicker crack at plenty. At the opposite ideological pole, Harold Macmillan won an electoral landslide telling the British in 1959: "You've never had it so good," and when a television reporter asked an usherette at the 1996 Republican Convention to define the American dream, the right answer came off the tip of her tongue: "Having more than your parents had."

I observed at the outset that old ideals linger on even after losing their preeminence. I should add that the three modern ideals of Being, Doing, and Having put in many an isolated showing even as ideals before they came to predominate each in turn. Thus a precursive devotee of daredevil Doing was Benvenuto Cellini, who gloried in his exploits (real or imaginary) even above his proud person—an exception that proves the rule in that Cellini's autobiography found its first public among the Romantics. And a forerunner of *Self-Help* by Samuel Smiles was *Poor Richard's Almanack* by Benjamin Franklin, who, however, was most recognizably himself in the familiar pose of an idle sage.

According to *The Communist Manifesto,* the ruling ideas of any age are the ideas of its ruling classes. This dictum is arresting for the ideas of freedom and property put forth as universals by the rising bourgeoisie. Beyond that double case in point, however, it applies to few ideas that have exercised mankind. Yet the ideals of Being, Doing, and Having do match up loosely with dominant social groups in their respective heydays. The ideal of Being reflects the patrician cult of breeding (if with a touch of Platonist and Christian otherworldliness). Its exemplars were called "noble," and Castiglione's discussants considered that, whereas one did not need blue blood to be noble, it helped. Similarly, the ideal of Doing, together with its correlate that mere personal value in itself was sterile, like inactive capital, was bourgeois—or perhaps more nearly entrepreneurial, for aristocrats might share it and functionaries might scorn it. In Goethe's view of it, whereas the nobleman "may and should appear," the bourgeois "must perform and produce."[67] The covetous ideal of Having, finally, is plebeian in origin, however much it now pervades the upper reaches of society. Have-nots first hoisted it high. In Ortega's analysis, it is the ideal of the "mass-man," who, though classless, arose out of the populace in our democratic age.[68] These social-historical correlates of the three ideals are inescapable. But the question remains why society at large adopted the ideals of those groups as they won political control. The answer looks obvious at first blush for Being and Doing. When patricians ran the show, the regnant ideal amounted to being a patrician. Later, even patricians aspired to be enterprising when business venturers' stock rose above theirs. Having, though, spoils this simplistic scheme, for in adopting that low-level popular ideal we would all be aspiring *down* the social scale.

Now to conclude psychohistorically. Half a millennium of change in personal ideals, glimpsed from the cultural top down: this overview, if it is roughly accurate for all its broad sweep and sharp contrasts, tells of ever greater personal impoverishment. For whoever wants to *be* feels deficient, yet close enough to a self-ideal to imagine attaining it. Whoever aspires instead to *do* would supply that same felt deficiency once removed, through his or her deeds, like a parent seeking fulfillment through a child. Whoever, finally, aspires to *have* seeks completion entirely from the outside, for Having precludes absorbing what one has. Let me take that again for clarity. If I want to be defined, known, and judged first by what I manage to *be*, then by what I manage to *do*, and finally by what I manage to *have*—if, say, I want to *be* impressive or seductive, then to *do* record-setting stunts, then to *have* a rich, full life—these successive ideals betoken a progressively more impoverished self-seeking to fill itself out farther and farther afield.

In sum, selves have felt increasingly inadequate and deficient in modern times. Thence the tyranny of secondary, or group, identities, mainly ethnic and ideological. And this mounting tyranny of secondary, group identities throws the problem of diminishing selfhood into starkest relief.

CHAPTER SIX

Three Mourning Mothers

This second of two European cultural developments to be defined and deciphered will be followed over a longer stretch than was the evolution of the highest Western value—over a whole as against a half millennium. But its subject is as narrow in scope as the first was vast: the motif of the Massacre of the Innocents in Christian iconography considered up to the point at which another Christian motif, that of the Pietà, emerged out of it. This emergence will be seen to have culminated a corresponding development in the Christian cast of thought and outlook on human history.

Over the course of historic time, meanings and connections that were once self-evident may come to look strange and strained. The Christian Middle Ages in particular left behind a trail of statements both verbal and visual that were straight and clear in their time but now strike us as twisted and obscure. Conspicuous along that trail are the texts and images spawned by the twin concept of prefiguration and fulfillment. Not only are such texts and images bewildering to noninitiates today; they are barely accessible any longer even to scholars steeped in the culture of the period.

The twin concept of prefiguration and fulfillment was at the core of the whole new perception of the human lot that the apostle Paul and the evangelists propagated on Jesus' messianic account.[1] It served in the first instance to authenticate Jesus' messiahship on the ground that every step along his way from the manger to the cross had been taken once already, albeit in an outwardly different form, and had been registered precursorily in his people's sacred texts pending his advent. Thus for the evangelist

Matthew, when wicked Herod had all the baby boys in Bethlehem slain upon learning that the Messiah was among them, the bereaved mothers' lament that ensued threw back some six centuries to Jeremiah's vision of the tribal matriarch Rachel lamenting in Ramah for her children who "were no more,"[2] meaning the children of Israel then held captive abroad in Babylon. On Matthew's construction, the later wailing in Bethlehem "fulfilled" the wailing in Ramah heard by Jeremiah,[3] as when a harmony is resolved, and with that fulfillment the prophetic circle linking Ramah to Bethlehem closed. To sophisticated pagans confronted with this Christian figural construction, the equivalence between live deportees to Babylon and, long ages later, baby boys massacred in Bethlehem was no more compelling at first blush than it is now again in modern times. Yet not only did the figural view of sacred history as in Matthew penetrate the topmost reaches of pagan learning along with Christianity itself; once that approach to the scriptures was assimilated throughout Christendom it began to evolve, acquiring ever new latitude and fluidity over the centuries.

The earliest church fathers from Tertullian to Augustine already construed the Judeo-Christian holy writ imaginatively to the effect that a figure (Latin: *figura*) or type (Greek: τυπος) and its fulfillment or antitype, though separate in worldly time and space, were yet wholly at one in the eternal, absolute order of things. They thereby spun out the concept metaphysically, that is, though without actually extending its use. Of greater practical moment was a later, creeping development, in full swing by the second Christian millennium, whereby a figure and its fulfillment might be drawn not just from the Old and the New Testament respectively, but both at once from Christ's life alone. Thus in art and letters equally, Mary holding the infant Savior might look ahead to Mary holding the crucified Savior,[4] just as Mary holding the crucified Savior might look back to Mary cradling the infant Savior, with the one Mary reflecting on the other in both cases alike;[5] or again, circumventing Mary to the same final effect, the dead Christ might be "stretched out on the altar in the form of a child."[6] This slow turn in creative fancy to the possible interplay of prefiguration and fulfillment within the New Testament alone was quickened during the twelfth and thirteenth centuries by a mounting concern among Europe's faithful for the earthly, human experience of Mary and her son culminating in the Passion: their holy sufferings loom at once gigantic and intimate in Bernard of Clairvaux, in popular Franciscan sermons, in the best-selling anonymous *Meditations on the Life of Christ,* and in numberless devout poetic effusions such as then proliferated throughout Christendom.

In a further undatable innovation both conceptual and practical within the Christian figural scheme, not merely two but thenceforth three biblical persons, places, and events, as a rule one from the Old Testament and two from the New, might compose a single figural continuum while retaining their three distinct identities. In such cases of a figure fulfilled cumulatively in two stages instead of one, the terminal stage was invariably Christ's death and resurrection. These sets of three were of a kind with those in the highly influential late-twelfth-century teaching of Joachim of Floris that earthly events of divine import all came in threes: an Old Testament original would recur twice in new guises during the Christian era before achieving closure.[7] And not just arithmetically was Joachim's unitary tripling akin to the twelfth- and thirteenth-century scholastic definitions and mystical visions of God as three distinct persons composed of a single substance.

Only on these gradually expanding and loosening figural terms of reference are the iconography of the Massacre of the Innocents and its eventual input into the Lamentation of Christ and, later, the Pietà intelligible. That iconography and that input are my subject here.

Depictions of the Massacre of the Innocents began where Christian art did: in the catacombs of Rome.[8] The earliest extant Massacre scenes might show only fierce Herod handing down the grim order or only his henchmen doing his fearful bidding. More typically, though, Bethlehemite mothers also appeared in Massacre scenes from the first, either grieving in unison or else, increasingly over the centuries, clinging to innocent little victims before, during, or after the bloody deed. Also from the first, one of those mothers would stand out from the assemblage by dint of her raised arms. This stereotypical figure, full-fledged already on a surviving fifth-century ivory, held her ground in subsequent miniatures, ivories, mosaics, paintings, and sculptures of the Massacre well into the Renaissance, her arms ever distinctively aloft. Outside of Byzantium, her specific Oriental-style gesture of grief and despair alluded to wailing Rachel.[9] So too did an occasional halo on a mourning Massacre mother allude to Rachel as the mourning matriarch of Israel.[10] For good measure, this figural referent for the Massacre scene was often spelled out in Greek or Latin in the form of Matthew's quotation from Jeremiah about Rachel weeping for her children who "were no more." Today such allusions or inscriptions are commonly held to have identified the gesturing mother or the haloed mother as Rachel herself physically present in Bethlehem, an impossibility in material fact that was just as impossible in the mode of figure and fulfillment. What they did was rather to affirm the Rachel original for the bereavement and lamenting in Bethlehem. That Rachel original was further implicated in the pictorial convention that only mothers ever came into Massacre scenes bereaved and lamenting, with no matching fathers or other relatives ever in sight.

While Rachel's wailing in Ramah resounded in Bethlehem from Matthew onward, only toward AD 855 did Rachel herself, without budging from Ramah in the days of the patriarchs, figurally fuse with those later mothers wailing in Bethlehem. She did so in an arresting adornment of a

Ivory carving, c. 430, detail

(Staatliche Museen, Berlin). (Foto Marburg / Art Resource, NY)

monogrammatic "D" that flanked the text for Innocents Day in the sacramentary of Drogo, archbishop of Metz.[11] Drogo, an illegitimate son of
Charlemagne, was a leading European patron of the arts as well as a powerful conciliatory figure in the bloody disputes over the Carolingian suc-
cession. The indications are that he personally shaped and styled the
sumptuous sacramentary prepared for him.[12] In that case he was the immediate source of the two big iconographic innovations wrought inside
that historiated "D." Much the simpler of the two for all its huge signifi-
cance was the reintroduction into Western art of the figure of a mourner
holding or embracing a corpse. Lest that reintroduction pass unnoticed in
Drogo's miniature, three aggrieved mothers each hold two dead sons at
once across their knees. The earliest clear-cut precedents in art that I know
for this intimate mourning are some clumsy archaic Sardinian statuettes of

a hefty matron, perhaps a goddess, holding a small dead warrior on her lap;[13] the closest such precedent in date is a graceful archaic Attic tazza decorated with Eos holding her slain son Memnon.[14] Ancient painting and sculpture shied away from any and all macabre pathos even though many potential subjects for it other than just Eos with dead Memnon abounded in antiquity: Thisbe with dead Pyramus, Hero with dead Leander, Thetis with dead Achilles, Hecuba with dead Hector, and Aphrodite with dead Adonis all qualified equally.[15] Ancient letters were less restrained than ancient art: witness the curtain-ringer in Euripides' morbid masterpiece *The Bacchae,* with unsuspecting Agave sporting her son's bloody head as a trophy of her Dionysian revels until her tragic undeceiving. So were early Christian letters less reticent than early Christian art: thus in the fifth century of our era Basil of Seleucia, in a gripping sermon much imitated thereafter, related in graphic, gory detail how after Herod's massacre each weeping mother gath-

Drogo Sacramentary, Metz, c. 850, detail (Bibliothèque Nationale, Paris)

ered the scattered remnants of her son to her bosom for a farewell kiss.[16] Four centuries passed after that virtuoso pulpit performance by Basil before Drogo brought up the rear in art with his triplicate mother not even kissing her two undismembered dead sons, but at least holding them both on her lap.

Drogo's innovative miniature of the Massacre was even more of a significant first in assimilating not merely the lament in Ramah into the lament in Bethlehem as Matthew had done, but also Rachel herself figuratively or spiritually into the assemblage of lamenting mothers in Bethlehem. All three bereaved mothers in Drogo's mournful "D" are as if poured out of the same mold and then displayed at different angles. The three together stand for the totality of the Bethlehemite mothers, three being as many as a marginal "D" could accommodate in the mutual isolation that Drogo clearly intended for them. One of the three holds a single arm straight up, signaling a conjunction with Rachel. Further, the two dead baby boys draped side by side over each mother's knees betoken Rachel's own two sons. To be sure, Rachel died bearing her second son, and the children of Israel lamented by her in Jeremiah's prophetic vision were mostly grownups. More, the two dead boys trebled in Drogo's "D" are roughly identical in each case, which in good logic would make them either twins three times over or else not both the same mother's. The clear point, however elusive in retrospect, is that the two are no more literally Rachel's sons than that grieving mother with one arm raised is herself literally half Rachel. Rather, their twoness is an additional sign of Rachel's figural convergence with the bereaved mothers of Bethlehem. That convergence transcending geography and history lasted as long as the figural perspective itself did even though the aggrieved mothers, initially a uniform lot, were increasingly individualized in Gothic depictions of the Massacre beginning some three centuries after Drogo commissioned his seminal "D."

In conjoining Rachel herself figurally with her Bethlehemite successors, Drogo's miniaturist lifted their common spiritual posture out of its two narrative contexts and suspended it in the middle of nowhere. This transpersonal fusion of those distinct identities across time and space, thenceforth a settled iconographic fact, was strikingly pronounced in Drogo's dreamlike surrealism. Rarely again did Rachel appear so integrally fused with the bereaved mothers in Bethlehem. Nor for another few centuries did that resultant composite of maternal grief again loom so nearly solitary or self-enclosed as, despite her triplication, she managed to do even in Drogo's tiny "D."

That looming was her delayed legacy. For, just as Drogo's bold composition marked a gigantic figural stride forward, so did it foreshadow further developments down that same figural path running from Ramah to Bethlehem and eventually beyond. The most conspicuous of these developments that ensued was the gradual emergence within full Massacre scenes of just such a distinctive, commanding, monumental figure as Drogo's of a mother self-isolated in her grief over the dead son she holds, emotionally alone even inside or alongside a Massacre crowd that would grow ever more tempestuous and diversified over the centuries ahead. Her aloneness amid that agitated company was in the nature of maternal grief as it is in fact experienced. But her detachment also went with her figural transcendence of the maternal grief specific to Bethlehem. Being emblematic of a composite lament common to Ramah and Bethlehem, that matronly mourner was no more the bodily Rachel translocated from Ramah to Bethlehem than was the older stereotypical lamenter with arms aloft, who indeed might henceforth conjoin with her or else appear beside her. Like that arms-up icon of raging grief before her, this singularized figure of self-enclosed desolation in its turn upstaged the rest of the doleful maternal chorus in Bethlehem. By the eleventh century its pictorial ascendancy over the Massacre scene was pronounced and definitive from one end of Europe to the other.

That commanding figure of bereavement came in two basic postures. One, which took off from the Drogo model itself, was at its simplest a seated mother holding a dead son across her lap. This lap-type model promptly swept Europe in every visual medium from pictorial miniatures to giant frescoes and from fine carvings to monumental sculpture. Here for a change letters followed instead of leading art: a twelfth-century Italian preacher cited a panel painting of Herod's butchery of the babes of Bethlehem as a basis for his horrific account of the event culminating in his pathetic evocation of a mother who "held her newly slain infant on her knees and bitterly wept."[17] Intact, impressive early specimens of the Drogo model adorn an eleventh-century ivory plaque from Lorraine, an early-twelfth-century mural in the village church of Saint-Jacques-des-Guérets, a later twelfth-century one in the abbey of San Pietro in Valle in Ferentino, a still later twelfth-century stone cathedral façade in Soria,[18] and a metal cathedral door of about 1200 in Benevento.[19] Some naïve eleventh-century depictions piled three or more sons at once onto that single, doleful maternal lap.[20] Byzantine miniaturists took up the model only tardily and artlessly despite its remote derivation from that fifth-century Greek sermon by Basil of Seleucia: it first appears in Byzantine manuscripts of about 1100 in a simplistically stylized version recopied time and again thereafter.[21] But even this inglorious tardy appropriation from western Christendom suffices to disprove the received view of Byzantine art as fairly impervious to outside influence.[22]

In her other, later basic posture, that mother who stole the bloody scene in Bethlehem grieves over a tiny son stretched out dead before her. This alternative, ground-type pose occurs in romanesque and especially Gothic France, with crowning examples on a wall and a window of the cathedral in Chartres.[23] Its earliest showings beyond the French heartland date only from the early 1300s.[24] In a ghastly subform of it, which spilled over from

Ivory plaque, Lorraine, late eleventh century, detail
(Victoria and Albert Museum, London)

Bronze cathedral door, Benevento, twelfth century, detail.
(Hirmer Fotoarchiv)

Embrasures, Portail Royal, Cathedral, Chartres, 1145–1155, detail. (Albert Schmidt)

French churches into French miniatures, a kneeling mother cradles or kisses a little head severed from a body seen somewhere nearby.[25]

Unlike the first, lap-type model of the emblematic Massacre mother with her dead son, this second, ground-type model did not penetrate Byzantium in its own right. There instead, inspired with some lag by sermons of George of Nicomedia in the ninth and Symeon Metaphrastes in the tenth century,[26] a scene of Mary caressing the dead Christ emerged out of the traditional Entombment[27] to parallel that ground-type Bethlehemite posture then germinating in France. Possible influences either way are hard to explore with any precision because the record is so spotty and the datings mostly uncertain on both sides of the east-west split within Christendom. Nor does it help that on either side of that split only the blurriest of lines separated the evolving Entombment from the emergent Lamentation with its sharper focus on Mary cradling a dead Christ recumbent before her: in both funerary scenes alike Mary is simply the chief one of her martyred son's intimates preparing his body for burial.[28] But the trickiest complication is that the Lamentation developed in Italy with a visible Byzantine impress from the late eleventh well into the thirteenth century even as midway its two central figures overlapped with the ground-type Massacre mother and dead son atop the royal portal at Chartres.[29]

This ground-type iconographic convergence of the bereaved mother lamenting in Bethlehem with the bereaved mother lamenting in Golgotha made good medieval Christian sense. For the Crucifixion fulfilled the intent of the Massacre, which was to kill the Messiah.[30] Accordingly, by the logic of prefiguration and fulfillment, the mother mourning her innocent son martyred in Bethlehem anticipated the mother mourning her innocent son martyred in Golgotha. Mary's figural continuity with the Bethlehemite mother was adumbrated as early as the Massacre mosaic of AD 432–440 on the triumphal arch of Santa Maria Maggiore in Rome with its row of mothers holding their sacrificial baby sons in the newly standardized likeness of Mary holding the infant Jesus.[31] The figural continuity was traced in high relief on the mid-eleventh-century wooden door to the church of Sankt Maria im Kapitol in Cologne, where in the Massacre panel a ponderous sorrowful mother holding a son either doomed or dead on her lap (he is too damaged to tell which) is cut in the very mold of the ponderous sorrowful Mary holding Jesus on her lap in the parallel Flight into Egypt panel.[32] Similarly, on a twelfth-century ivory altarpiece in Salerno a compassionate Mary watching the Massacre together with a horrified infant Jesus has a face just like that of the Rachelite Massacre mother

Coppo di Marcovaldo, painted cross, 1260s, detail

(Museo Civico, San Gimignano). (Alinari / Art Resource, NY)

Mosaic, cupola, baptistery, Florence, thirteenth century, detail.

(Alinari / Art Resource, NY)

below her with arms aloft.[33] And to the same effect once removed, the several extant versions of the *Ordo Rachelis,* a liturgical drama of the eleventh and twelfth centuries that was performed on Innocents Day or Epiphany, featured a Rachel fantastically spirited to Bethlehem to mourn the slain Innocents, and it repeatedly termed this Rachel in Bethlehem a sorrowing virgin mother, thereby identifying that sorrowing non-virgin mother in so many words with the sorrowing virgin mother at the cross.[34]

The intriguing confluence of Mary lamenting the dead Christ Byzantine-style in Western art with the second, ground-type model of the mourning mother in Bethlehem was merely extrinsic or formal in one crucial respect. No more than her Byzantine counterparts was Mary in the Western Lamentations self-isolated in her grief over her dead son as was her opposite number in the French Gothic Massacres. On the contrary, she too in every case formed an integral part of a funeral party ritually mourning the Savior in unison while also ritually preparing his body for burial. As against this Mary lamenting in harmony with her son's disciples and

Nicola Pisano, cathedral pulpit, Siena, 1266–1268, detail.

(Alinari / Art Resource, NY)

other relatives, and far more radically than even the ground-type lamenting Massacre mother, the older, lap-type one withdrew into ever deeper spiritual detachment, and the more conspicuously as her numbers multiplied in north central Italy after her powerful, poignant showing in the foreground of a stupendous pulpit that Nicola Pisano sculpted for the Siena cathedral in the 1260s. Later highlights of this increasingly desolate self-enclosure include a striking row of four such mourning mothers in a Massacre painted around 1300 by Giotto's expressionistic coworker Palmerino di Guido in the basilica of Santa Chiara in Assisi,[35] three or four more in what may be Giotto's own Massacre of c. 1305 in the lower basilica of San Francesco in Assisi, two in the front predella of Duccio's majestic *Maestà* of 1308–1311 (plus a ground-type one there too for variety's sake), two dated 1316 carved onto the frontal altar of the Zenone cathedral in Pistoia, another two on a relief panel attributed to Tino di Camaino at the Trinità monastery in Cava dei Tirreni, and two strikingly novel ones on an anonymous fragmentary painting at the Pinacoteca in Bologna[36] and

Duccio di Buoninsegna, *La Maestà*, front predella, 1308–1311, detail
(Cathedral Museum, Siena). (Alinari / Art Resource, NY)

again on a mural in the lower church of the Sacro Speco monastery in
Subiaco.[37] Around 1300 this rash of first-manner Bethlehemite mothers
sorrowing in radical inner retreat from the carnage around them spilled
over into France and the Germanies and even as far afield as Sweden.[38]
But its privileged locus was indubitably Tuscany and Umbria, its grand
masters incontestably Sienese and Perugian. It scaled its highest artistic
heights on Nicola Pisano's son Giovanni's pulpits in bold relief, at once
touching and terrifying, for the Church of Sant'Andrea in Pistoia (1301)
and again for the cathedral in Pisa (c. 1310), each containing fully three
lap-type Bethlehemite Rachels and the latter also a fourth verging on the
ground-type alternative.

Over and beyond the occasional express convergence of the Bethlehemite grieving mother with the grieving mother of God in western Christian art and letters, the two also connected implicitly through juxtapositions of the whole Massacre scene with the whole Crucifixion scene. These
juxtapositions abounded in all artistic media throughout the late Middle
Ages. A mid-thirteenth-century English bible pictured Christ's life in nine
squares arranged three by three, the Massacre proper (complete with a
Rachel symbol and a lap-type lamenting mother) being centered directly
above the Crucifixion (itself complete with a sorrowing Mary).[39] In a frieze

Giovanni Pisano, cathedral pulpit, Pisa, 1302–1311, detail. (Alinari / Art Resource, NY)

English Bible, mid-XIIIth century, MS. Auct. D.3.4, fol. 282v, detail (Bodleian Library, University of Oxford)

Barna da Siena, *Life of Christ*, 1350–1355, detail
(Collegiata, San Gimignano). (Albert Schmidt)

of the same vintage on Notre-Dame at Etampes, the order of the scenes of Christ's infancy drawn from Matthew was reshuffled so that the Massacre and the Passion might appear on adjacent capitals.[40] On Giovanni Pisano's Pistoian pulpit as originally executed, "the corner with the mystical Christ was meant to appear at the upper center, separating the Massacre of the Innocents from the Crucifixion"[41]—or, better, joining the two. The prophet panel to the right of the Massacre on the front predella of Duccio's *Maestà* is inscribed with Matthew's quotation from Jeremiah about Rachel lamenting in Ramah; thus situated, "this prophecy presages the Lamentation over the dead Christ."[42] And an English cope of about 1325 was so embroidered that an Innocent impaled on a spear forms a cross just below the Crucifixion proper at dead center.[43] But this configurative message was most articulate in Barna da Siena's overpowering Crucifixion crowned by a Massacre in his serial depiction of Christ's life painted about 1350 for the Collegiata of San Gimignano. There the Virgin in the Crucifixion swoons diagonally opposite the Rachelite lap-type mourning mother in the Massacre; the Roman centurion (Longinus) piercing Christ's side in the Crucifixion offsets a soldier lancing an Innocent in the Massacre above; a heap of slaughtered Innocents in the upper panel weighs straight down over the dying Savior's head. To achieve this whole richly suggestive vertical alignment, Barna too shifted the Flight into Egypt out of its narrative sequence as given by Matthew "so that the *Massacre of the Innocents* could occupy the lunette above *Christ on the Cross*."[44]

By the time that Western piety conjoined Mary with Rachel figurally in and through that bereaved mother in Bethlehem, such treble composites were no novelty in the Christian repertory. The figure of Mary Magdalen for one had already shaped up in art as "a compound of several of the women mentioned in the different gospel narratives."[45] This many-personed Magdalen acquired a further, figural referent after she threw up her arms in demonstrative grief at Christ's death in Byzantine art. For she thereupon duly followed suit in Italian art,[46] where her gesture served as a further token of Rachel at Christ's bewailing.

I have saved for the last the supreme end product in Western art of that figural tripling from Ramah through Bethlehem to Golgotha: the German Pietà. Its Italian name, preferred even in German from the first to such native variants as *Vesperbild* or *Marienklage*, suggests that the inspiration for it came from Italy. Yet the Pietà itself did not, despite some close approaches to it in and near Giotto's circle.[47] Indeed, for the first century after it emerged in the early 1300s in devotional statues loosely scattered along the Rhine it remained a German product even in Italy, being either imported there from German workshops, produced there locally by itinerant German sculptors, or fashioned there by Italians after German originals.[48] Ever since Drogo's death-ridden "D," a continually

Pietà, early fourteenth century (Veste Coburg). (Foto Marburg / Art Resource, NY)

Workshop of the Master of the Severi Sarcophagus, *Pietà*, c. 1360–1370 (Städtisches Museum, Erfurt). (Foto Marburg / Art Resource, NY)

113

thickening line of reliefs, frescos, and miniatures of the Massacre had featured an inconographical prototype for the Pietà in the lap-type mourning mother.[49] In late pre-Pietà Italian Massacres that lap-type mourning had attained extreme psychological isolation in the very thick of the intense, cruel, and violent action surrounding it. In France meanwhile it reverted closer to its compositional source in Drogo, as when the miniaturist Jean Pucelle, in copying the lap-type twosome from Giovanni Pisano's Pistoian pulpit, distanced it from the Bethlehemite slaughter physically as well as psychologically.[50] Perhaps the lap-type mourning mother's absorption in her grief over her dead son to the exclusion of everything else was why, when the Bethlehemite metamorphosed into the Golgothan twosome on a figural licence, it took the starkly reductive form of freestanding statuary.

This self-contained freestanding German statuary in turn brought the self-enclosed mourning in Golgotha to a still higher level of abstraction from any and every earthly context. It is true that much preaching, drama, and poetry since the early Middle Ages had prepared the way for a last, intimate farewell from Mary to her dead son within the developing story of the Passion and that as of the twelfth century the bittersweet funereal monologues invented for Mary in the Germanies had already separated her spiritually from the other mourners surrounding the dead Christ.[51] But it is equally true, and decisive for its artistic meaning, that the Pietà burst the confines of the Passion itself and therewith removed its subject root and branch from any and every scriptural frame of reference or point of departure.[52] One early authority observed just a bit guardedly: "The Pietà . . . focuses almost exclusively on Mary and Christ alone as an inwardly self-contained group; no more real lamenting, hardly even any more mourning; instead a pained yet controlled absorption, a mute, solitary dialogue between the mother and her dead child."[53] A second early scholar elaborated: "All distracting company has been removed from the mother and son, every tie with the drama unfolding has been severed, and nearly all allusions to the time or place of this lament have been suppressed. All by itself, a mother's timeless, eternal anguish over her son, without bounds, without setting, and without witnesses, touches the devout believer's heart more directly than ever before."[54] And a third early historian of that bleak image insisted succinctly and trenchantly: "The German Pietà is from the first no episode out of the Virgin's laments with all their lively narrative imagery, but a timeless union of the mother with her crucified son—a devotional image divorced from all narrative context."[55] This divorce brought to a head the inner aloneness of the key Massacre mother as in Duccio, Giotto, the Pisanos, and other Tuscan and Umbrian artists active just before the Pietà emerged north of the Alps—the radical unworldliness of that *mater do-*

lorosa oblivious to whatever is not her dead son or her deathless sorrow.

Like an iconographical hyphen connecting the lap-type proto-Pietà derived from Drogo's "D" with the Pietà proper is an early, perhaps the earliest, group of Rhenish Pietàs: those with the dead Christs baby-sized, yet complete with beard and even crown of thorns. The usual understanding of these bizarre halfway specimens relates them, no doubt rightly, to the Virgin and Child as condensing the two ends of Christ's life into a single image.[56] But Erwin Panofsky for one saw them also as the transitional forms they no doubt were, mediating between the proto-Pietà in the Massacre and the Pietà proper.[57]

Whichever Pietàs came first—and this is still a moot question—in them culminated the transcendent triunity of the lamenting mother in Bethlehem with both Rachel before her and Mary after her. Yet at the same time—and this was the paradoxical payoff—the Pietà also cut off the mourning mother of God visually from that same treble continuum. So did the Lamentation in its perfected form lose the deeper, figural dimension of Ramah and Bethlehem behind it even as it contracted forwards into the single plane of the Passion. Nor did that triple composite of Ramah-Bethlehem-Golgotha dissolve all alone, in isolation from the rest of the Christian figural repertory; the whole figural worldview itself disintegrated along with it, marking an apt symbolic end of the Middle Ages.[58] The Massacre did not therewith recede from sight; on the contrary, even as the figural worldview disintegrated, "the fifteenth century honored the Holy Innocents with special veneration"[59]—this, though, no longer for their pivotal figural role, but by reason of their specific fate in its own right, which quintessentialized our all-human fate seen as an execution for no crime. Perhaps it was Fra Angelico who in 1448 last wove a recall of Rachel together with a lap-type and a ground-type mourning mother into a single, prophetic Massacre scene complete with inscriptions drawn from Matthew. Thereafter the fragments of that triunity survived only as occasional stage props in the grandiose dramatic spectacle that the Massacre became for a Raphael or a Poussin once it was relieved of its figural extensions backwards and forwards beyond its own bloody confines—relieved, that is, of all need for the lamenting in Bethlehem to resonate with that in Ramah before it and that in Golgotha after it. A triunitarian disciple of Joachim of Floris, Michael Servetus, in his *Christianismi restitutio* (The Restoration of Christianity) of 1553, could still posit triple figural runs galore including even a new one for lamenting Rachel,[60] but only to be condemned to the flames forthwith first by the Inquisition, then by Calvin's Geneva when he sought refuge there. Remnants of the tattered and faded figural vision with Bethlehem at its midpoint put in a last few fleeting appearances, among them one in that artistic monument of the Counterreformation, Caravaggio's *Entombment,* painted in 1603 for a Chapel of the Pietà, with Mary Magdalen striking the old Rachel pose.[61] Then the entire kaleidoscopic Christian congeries of compound meanings and crisscross allusions came apart definitively even in the face of all the fevered piety suffusing the seventeenth century. And once that figural scheme as a whole lost its organic cohesion, the life went out of its residual components as well. Like the scattered bits of the cut-up Innocents in Basil's seminal fifth-century sermon, those disjointed fragments of a defunct figural complex can now be put back together again only outwardly and at best incompletely.

That lost cohesion was subjective. Where an associative symbolic complex such as Ramah-Bethlehem-Golgotha cohered was within the minds and hearts of the faithful. How that Ramah-Bethlehem-Golgotha complex in particular shaped up, spread, ramified, and ultimately dissolved is therefore a piece of psychohistory. Yet its dynamics were collective, such that my account took little note of the artists, poets, or preachers, let alone the patrons and believers, whose product it was at every stage. It is astonishing, when considered afresh, that a tale such as this one of concepts and images evolving could be told as I did tell it here, impersonally—that it unfolded by an inner developmental logic despite its having been a running result of numberless individual doings over many richly eventful centuries. Such unthinking collaborative unfolding is fraught with special mystery as against group actions induced by particular circumstances or events. Perhaps something of the process involved can be glimpsed from how this minute strand of refined Christian fantasy and illusion conjoining Ramah with Bethlehem first, and then with Golgotha as well, ran its course. But for this purpose the fantasy and illusion must be decrypted.

The Christian figural scheme that in this instance conflated one imaginary lament with a second and then a third by dint of remote equivalences and through multiple, dispersed, allusive signs mimicked the language of the human unconscious. Its figurative devices were the consecrated Freudian ones that shape messages from our psychic depths: condensation, as between Ramah and Bethlehem, Bethlehem and Golgotha, Ramah and Golgotha; displacement, as with Rachel's attribute of the raised arms removed from Ramah to Bethlehem and later to Golgotha; twisted words, such as Rachel's about her children who "were no more"; pictographic ploys, such as Barna's dead innocents literally on Jesus' mind at the Crucifixion; juxtapositions to signify connections, as between the Massacre and the Crucifixion; symbols aplenty, including attributes such as Rachel's raised arms; and the whole smoothed over artistically the way a dream is, only more so. By the same token, in overriding as it did any and every constraint of time, place, or situation, the Christian figural scheme affirmed outright the same wishful deathlessness as governs our mental underworld. The Ramah-Bethlehem-Golgotha continuum specifically stood warrant that all things return even as it put a fable-like spin on cruel death undeserved—on the Massacre symbolizing our mortal lot. This primal sense of the Massacre emerged in all its starkness once that continuum was broken: then, the Black Death aiding, "all the images tending to evoke the horror of death" were assembled in the fourteenth-century churchyard of the Innocents at Paris.[62] But already the alignment of the Massacre mother with Rachel in Ramah on the one side and with Mary in Golgotha on the other was an unconscious denial of death in that the Israelite exiles lamented by Rachel were not really dead[63] any more than Jesus lamented by Mary was really dead. The exiles would return from captivity, and Jesus would rise from the grave, so that the massacred Innocents in between duly survived by association to be named the first martyrs to the Christian faith and thence were privileged to circle the Virgin's head as angels forever.

Pagan elites resisted Christianity for its teachings themselves, to be sure, but just as much for its elevation of an archaic, wishful mode of deconstructing and reconstructing reality to a hieratic device for discerning hidden truths. From the church fathers to the scholastics, Christianity enforced, rationalized, and solemnified a regression to a quasi-magical cast of mind, and this in more than just the figural scheme that I have been illustrating through the figural complex joining Bethlehem to Ramah on the one side and to Golgotha on the other. The regressive thrust of the Christian agenda pokes through those naïve articles of the faith, beginning with miracles, that the Enlightenment had a field day debunking. But my point is a different one: that, doctrinal contents aside, the Christian persuasion represented a step backwards on the rudimentary level of mass consciousness itself. Christian orthodoxy was an offensive waged against straight thinking on behalf of a would-be higher order of meanings and relations actually fetched up out of our species' mental refuse bin. The aura of enchanted superrationality that marked the Christian vision at its loftiest arose out of those subrational depths whence our dearest dreams issue. The Renaissance, the Scientific Revolution, and the Enlightenment—modernity for short—renewed with pagan antiquity in countless more conspicuous ways, but also in the basic way of restoring the reality principle to the privileged place it had won for itself in ancient centers of learning.

Such humanistic, scientific, enlightened restoring was programmatic with the great modernizers and strident with their eager followers. But as can be seen on a small scale from when and how the double figural backdrop to the Lamentation and the Pietà fell away, the battle against the Christian perspective on human existence was won deep down before it was even joined. It was won not by the reality principle militant, moreover, but because that figural mode of thought that was at the very heart of the faith *self-destructed*. The mournful continuity from Ramah to Bethlehem called for a further fulfillment at Golgotha that would transcend Golgotha— for a supreme sorrow that would presage a supreme redemptive joy. But then that further, transcendent fulfillment, by dint of its very transcendence, left Ramah and Bethlehem behind. If this single figural case is indicative, the Christian dream simply dreamed itself out before the Christian scheme was refuted.

CHAPTER SEVEN

Death on a Rampage

The three modes of group process singled out of human history at the start of this inquiry have now been exemplified twice each in some detail. How do or don't the three interact? The present chapter will point out their separate and their conjoint showings in the face of Europe's worst calamity ever, which was also its decisive formative experience: the Black Death of 1348. I say "point out" advisedly: however desirable in itself, a closer study of each mode of group process operant within this lugubrious context would defeat the comparative purpose of this final empirical study of human group process in action.

T he Black Death came to Europe from the Orient by sea.[1] Shipborne from Constantinople to Sicily in October 1347, it invaded the mainland coast at several points from Naples to Catalonia in January 1348, then spread up through France into Bavaria, Burgundy, and southern England by early summer. Zigzagging capriciously, it had overrun most of Europe by 1351, sparing some scattered areas until later.[2] Wherever it struck, it struck without preference as to age, sex, or lifestyle, invading its victims' lungs or else, much more often, covering their bodies with boils, blisters, blotches, and prickly pustules along the lymph tracts out from the neck, the armpits, or the groin. As a rule, sufferers with affected lungs all died within hours, while most with skin sores succumbed within days; occasionally "men and women dropped dead while walking in the streets" after having given no sign of infection.[3] In regions hardest hit, especially cities, putrid corpses commonly lay festering on doorsteps for days; those collected were piled high on planks beside overcrowded graveyards or stacked under thin layers of dirt in open burial pits. The plague recurred locally in its primary, bubonic form about every ten years at first, then less frequently and less intensely over the long run, until the last severe outbreaks in and around Marseilles in 1720, Messina in 1748, and Moscow in 1770–1772. During the first and worst round, the pandemic of 1348 or Black Death proper, fatalities exceeded one European in two.[4]

No prayers and no physics availed for defending against the ghastly pestilence when it first struck. Nor evidently was much gained thereafter from any of the new preventives or remedies that open-minded doctors derived from empirical observation rather than ancient lore. Such pragmatic approaches, which mostly turned on good food and drink, began being tried as early as the second bout of the disease, and the medical innovators claimed and got the credit when the death rate fell. Modern epidemiology was launched. Ironically, it was off to a false start, for what really brought the death rate down emerges in retrospect as immunity both natural and acquired. Most survivors of one bout of the plague who were still around would survive the next one as well: it was as simple as that. On the group level, then, the single effective defense against the infection was physiological.

Effective though it was, that physiological defense was less than foolproof. It came with a complex catch that slowed its workings. Acquired immunity is nontransmissible, and natural immunity is genetically contingent. Hence with each new outbreak of the plague, survivors' children born since the last outbreak were at much higher risk than the survivors themselves. The plague accordingly tended to evolve into a children's disease, with population replacement held back that much more even as the death toll from the plague declined. Nor is that all. Because to have survived any round of the plague was to have either resisted infection or overcome it, the initial round of the plague should have sufficed to turn it into a children's disease outright. The indication is that immunity, natural or acquired, was being lost from one round to the next, though less and less —that the physiological group defense was self-limiting.

Was immunity being suppressed *in order for* the plague to recur? That sounds as sick as the plague itself. In fact it *was* just that sick. Seen as group process, the periodic recurrences of the plague, being so many literal relivings, amounted to a group dysfunction working at cross purposes with the immunological group function. To recap for clarity, once the plague had struck from the outside in 1348 it was endemic across Europe, recurring locally at intervals,[5] and with decreasing intensity by and large, until its last big showing in eastern Europe in the late eighteenth century. In terms of group function and dysfunction, its recurrences describe a maladaptive group process, or traumatic reliving, vying with an adaptive group process of immunization that gradually prevailed. This interplay of resistance and reliving in plagued Europe is a reminder that the pestilence was not simply a pathogen on the loose, but the interaction of a pathogen on the loose with a host now more, now less hospitable.[6] Europe beset with recurrent bouts of the plague may be compared to an individual human organism carrying the germs of the common cold within it but "catching cold" only when its resistance weakens sufficiently.

Traumatic as it was across Europe, the pandemic of 1348 was not exactly a European trauma when it hit for want of a full-fledged prior continental consciousness—of a felt European kinship or shared sense of European identity. Even the most widespread or typical European group reactions to the grim disaster tended to vary regionally. Whatever larger felt identity did preexist in Europe was more Christian than continental:[7] witness the many massacres of Jews touched off by the first flush of the pestilence. But the Black Death itself did initiate a European "synchronicity" that was again manifest not just in its literal recurrences, but also in what the Great Chronicle of Saint-Denis aptly called "the plague of a rebellion": the convulsive social violence that spread as if by contagion across all social divides from the Mediterranean area up through England, the Lowlands, the Empire, and points east, ultimately engulfing the entire continent much like the Black Death before it.[8] To be sure, those fierce and bloody uprisings of the forty-odd years following the Black Death were all grounded in local conditions of life and labor, of property and power. They nonetheless replicated the trauma of the Black Death in some of the standard ways in which a trauma is replicated: in superficial disguise, with active perpetrators replacing passive victims and lending it some semblance of purpose or meaning in the reliving. This traumatic reliving through "the plague of a rebellion" had a posthistory, moreover, unless it was mere coincidence that Europe marked the five-hundredth anniversary of the Black Death in 1848 with an epochal "plague of a rebellion" that likewise broke out in Sicily before it swept the continent.

Groups, like individuals, may go on defending indefinitely against traumatic blows long since received. Thus the posterity of the Black Death is still defending against its traumatic impact through failing efforts to understand its cause. In the late nineteenth century, when another fearful plague ravaged subtropical Asia and circled the globe by sea, researchers pounced on it as the Black Death all over again and exulted at the discovery of the bacillus behind it, named *Yersinia pestis* after its chief discoverer, Alexandre Yersin. They had run the wrong killer to ground. The medieval scourge was incomparably deadlier than *Yersinia pestis;* it was spread person-to-person, not by rat fleas like its later Asian runner-up; it spread much faster, and into greater heat than any rat flea can bear; it mostly covered victims' whole bodies with motley buboes; susceptibility to it varied, and survivors acquired immunity—all in point-for-point contrast with its distant oriental relative.[9] After more than six and a half centuries, Europeans still do not know what hit them in 1348.

One basic shock effect of the Black Death on its survivors appears to have been fairly uniform throughout Europe: it numbed fellow-feeling. Agnolo di Tura observed for Siena: "It seemed to almost everyone that one became stupefied by seeing the pain. . . . There was no one who wept for any death, for all awaited death."[10] The Pope's physician remarked of those stricken: "The father did not visit the son, nor the son the father. Affection was dead."[11] A visitor to papal Avignon concurred: "The sick are treated like dogs by their families" and noted further: "For fear of infection, no doctor will visit the sick."[12] For England the chronicler John of Reading put it tersely: "There was in those days death without sorrow."[13] Trauma need not induce such apathy, but such apathy, whether widespread or particular, tends to be trauma-induced. Paradoxically, at the same time that a shared trauma dissolves affective ties among the individuals affected, as the Black Death did across Europe, it also strengthens the stricken group's psychological cohesion, as the Black Death also did on a continental scale.

Affective numbing aside, reactions to gruesome death on a rampage ran to two opposite extremes that met on the group level. That God was punishing human iniquity with a vengeance was patent to all when the plague first hit Europe. Some, though, chose to repent while there was still time and others to revel and frolic while there was still time.[14] Divergent as were these two reactions at their point of departure, they tended to converge in guilt-ridden debauchery.[15] They did so the more readily since the group reflexes behind them were both adaptive. At the one extreme, penitents scourging themselves morally, then flagellants scourging themselves physically, rehearsed the agonies of the Black Death by way of bracing for it, if sometimes after the fact. As a venerable historian of the pandemic observed: "The pilgrimage of the flagellants from 1348 to 1350 expressed the experience of the plague, as it appeared to the masses, in its full terror and horrible grandeur."[16] At the other extreme, the plague for all its massive grisliness worked as an aphrodisiac. In hard-hit Siena, according to its chronicler Agnolo di Tura, "friars, priests, nuns, lay men and women, all indulged themselves." Once the plague began recurring, some doctors even prescribed pleasure as a preventive—moderately dosed, however, and preferably sweatless.[17] But the revelers exceeded any doctors' prescriptions as they topped their agendas with orgiastic sex, thereby serving, and indeed advertising, the group need to recoup its losses. Such revelry went so far that "in 1394 a papal official threatened with excommunication all those who dared 'to dance . . . or commit unseemly acts' over the graves of the dead."[18]

Orgiastic and sepulchral sex were eccentric effects of an adaptive, restorative group response. More centric an adaptive reaction was the "marrying mania" that raged throughout plagued Europe.[19] In Florence, as a local observer lamented, the common people "married at their will" in the aftermath of the scourge of 1348.[20] A Latin chronicler of the same re-

generative shock effect in Paris noted: "No sooner did the epidemic, pestilence, and mortality come to an end than the surviving men and women
rushed to marry."[21] According to *Piers Plowman,* the marriages contracted
in the wake of the Black Death were loveless.[22] The chronicler John of
Reading concurred: "There was in those days . . . marriage without affection."[23] Even so, marriages proved more fruitful once the plague struck
than they had been before—and especially while it was striking, as more
nurslings died then, with that many more conceptions following. "Everywhere women conceived more readily than ever," observed the Latin
chronicler in Paris.[24] Fertility was straining to replenish numbers. For a
few decades it almost succeeded against all the odds. Florence, exceptional for its rich records, was not so exceptional demographically: although it lost as much as three-quarters of its population in 1348, about
a third in 1363, and nearly a third again in 1374, it had already recouped
a good third of its 1348 losses by 1360 and even its full 1374 losses by
1379;[25] only thereafter, what with children being hit ever harder, did its
restorative thrust appear to flag. Europe as a whole, strain though it
might, could not regain its pre-1348 numbers until the mid-sixteenth
century, nor indeed could Florence specifically until after Italian unification in the latter nineteenth century.[26]

   In the psychological realm, the main adaptive strategem of groups reel-
ing from the Black Death was to inure themselves down through the generations to the experience of sudden, ghastly death on a massive scale. To
this end, even while the dead and dying still littered the streets, churches
across Europe took to displaying grim and grisly relics, mementos, em-
blems, and effigies of death. A collateral preventive or protective purpose
went with the inurement function of such tokens of death: they were pop-
ularly felt to ward off the plague. Johan Huizinga left a celebrated descrip-
tion of the old churchyard of the Innocents in Paris lined with huge heaps
of skulls and bones disinterred to make room for replacements: "In spite of
the incessant burials and exhumations going on there, it was a public
lounge and a rendezvous. Shops were established before the charnel-
houses and prostitutes strolled under the cloisters. . . . Even feasts were
given there. To such an extent had the horrible become familiar."[27] For
good measure, the open ossuary of the Innocents across from Notre Dame
was decorated in 1424–1425 with frescoes and verses depicting the spooky
Dance of the Dead, which was also commonly performed on the
premises.[28] Like the Innocents, the other charnel houses across Europe also
overfilled after 1348 with timely reminders of untimely death.

   The prime reminder of the sort, at least in France and Germany, was the
Dance of the Dead itself, enacted in and beside the courtyard of the Innocents and other graveyards galore beginning a decade or two after 1348,[29]
with figures of all social descriptions, from emperor, king, or pope on down,
being unceremoniously danced away by their skeletal counterparts or else

"Le pape et l' empereur," *La danse macabré des charniers des Saints Innocents à Paris,* ed.
Guyot Marchant, 1485 (Bibliothèque Nationale, Paris).

by a single shrouded mummy. The Dance was, further, depicted in illustrated verses on cemetery, church, chapel, cloister, and charnel walls and
vaults (practically every large town in Europe displayed it in paint[30]) and in
popular prints, chapbooks, and books of hours (it went into at least ninety-
two different French books of hours alone[31]). "Pictures [of the Dance] were
cut into glass, stone, marble, ivory, and gems, and stamped on coins and
medals. Verses and scenes were woven into tapestry, copied on parchment,
cut into wood, and were engraved and painted. They appeared on fireplaces
and even on earthen jugs."[32] Most surviving vernacular versions of the text
are in German, yet French scholars claim priority of authorship for France.
There the poet Jean Le Fèvre, chancellor of Anjou, wrote in his *Respit de la
mort* (Respite from Death) of 1376: *"Je fis de macabré la danse,"* which, whatever or whoever *macabré* was, gave the dance its French name of *danse
macabre.* It is unclear whether Le Fèvre meant that he danced the dance,
that he wrote it up, or even figuratively that he convulsed his way through
the malady itself, yet such is the slim evidentiary basis for his having originated the poem as against strong philological grounds for a German origin
toward 1360.[33] No matter: the single basic French version, however weak its
claim to have been the prototypical first, was imported into Italy, Spain,
England, the Lowlands, and even parts of Germany.[34]

In art as in life, to quote the prodigious medieval art historian Émile Mâle, "death suddenly showed itself in all its horror" with the advent of the Black Death.[35] The Dance of the Dead was only the most popular of four kindred deathly pictorial themes of folk origin that frequently paired off as they swept the mortuary field following the pestilential calamity. The earliest of them, the French or Italian (originally Oriental) fable of the Three Quick and Three Dead, predated the Black Death by nearly a century, but it gained huge new prominence beginning in 1348.[36] It told of three proud dignitaries on horseback coming upon three rotting or rotted corpses in open graves who admonish them: "What you are, we once were. What we are, you will be." (In one variant a nearby hermit does the admonishing.) Here was fair warning, however cheerless, for sinners to relent and repent. Sinners gained no such lead time in the three other, grimmer themes of this overlapping set. The next one to emerge, the Triumph of Death, had already done so in Italian art by 1348, when, however, it acquired new currency in its native Italy and spread abroad. It personified death as a pitiless mass murderer riding roughshod over defenseless victims, as in a gripping fresco of about 1445 painted for the Sclafani Palace

The Triumph of Death, fresco from the Sclafani Palace, c. 1445

(Galleria Nazionale, Palermo). (Alinari / Art Resource, NY)

in Palermo. Typically it mingled with other allegorical themes—originally with the Triumph of Christ as in a small *Allegory of Sin and Redemption* in the Pinacoteca of Siena, then with the Three Quick and Three Dead as in Francesco Traini's powerful mid-fourteenth-century fresco in the Campo Santo of Pisa, or also later with elements of the Dance of the Dead as in Pieter Brueghel's monumentally horrific panel of about 1562 in the Prado.[37] It spilled over into letters in the third of Petrarch's posthumous *Triumphs,* which, though born of the plague, philosophized its brutality away. The third of the four most popular grave themes was the Dance of the Dead, which originated in the immediate aftermath of the Black Death. Finally, Death and the Maiden, a derivative of the Dance of the Dead that lent it scary intimacy, brought up the rear a century or so later to flourish primarily in northern European painting, poetry, and song. In it a lewd and leering figure of death surprises a maiden, or occasionally a matron, luxuriating in her pulchritude. Niklaus Manuel Deutsch gave this simple scenario a bizarre twist on a 1517 panel in Basel with the lush maiden, thickly clad for a change, drawing the ravisher's bony, chilly hand up her ample skirts. The past master of this motif was Hans Baldung Grien, whose grimly grinning figure of death evolved over the 1510s from an insolent killjoy to an impotent lecher.

These four folk themes together served Europe's vital need to adjust to brutal death as a fact of life: they were, in a word, adaptive. But in plagued Europe, as already noted, adaptive and maladaptive group processes were prone to intermix. Coping with the aftereffects of the plague was adaptive, while contriving to reexperience the unassimilated horror of it was maladaptive; even so, survivors might well strike out both ways at once. Thus the Dance of the Dead, which issued from the Black Death as "a pictorial and poetic summation" of it[38] and "one of the motifs that the Christian had before his eyes at all times,"[39] helped inure traumatized Europe to mortality run wild at the same time that through it Europeans relived without relieving the deadening shock of divine and human mercy collapsing together in 1348. That shock has yet to be absorbed.

A model of traumatic reliving, the Dance of the Dead as it first emerged reenacted the impact of the Black Death symbolically in the form of a dramatized and choreographed sermon on death that, like all traumatic re-livings, never once mentioned its traumatic source.[40] In the earliest written version, a couple of dozen sardonic dead would hustle off that many living of diverse worldly conditions, without last rites, to join in a joyless grave-side dance of the damned. So far, so faithful a figurative replay. Indeed, the Black Death called the mortuary tune of the Dance by striking suddenly and swiftly, heedless of status or personal situation, and whisking its victims away with little or no time for them to prepare, especially as priests were no less reluctant than doctors, friends, or relatives to approach the dying in their hour of need. In Sicily, a chronicler related, "even priests

Niklaus Manuel Deutsch, *Death as a Mercenary Embracing a Young Woman,* print, 1517
(Kunstmuseum Basel). (Martin Bühler)

were afraid to visit the sick,"[41] and a letter from papal Avignon confirmed that "priests do not hear the confessions of the sick, or administer the sacraments to them."[42] Hellfire loomed for those who died unconfessed, so it was a tossup whether the rash of deaths or the slew of impending damnations hit survivors harder. The Dance reflected even this tossup through its ambiguity as to whether those being demonically danced away were meant to be just then dying or just then dead.

Faithful as was the dramatic replay of the Black Death in basic respects, it did nonetheless also modify the historic reality in stock ways in which a figurative reliving will commonly rework a traumatic original while working it through. For one thing, in imaginatively reliving the Black Death through the Dance of the Dead, Europeans took control, albeit figuratively and vicariously, of the trauma that had caught them off guard. For another, a trauma routinely escalates in the reliving: the reliving raises the traumatic stakes. Thus the victims in the Dance of the Dead in their monotonous impersonality, and representing as they regularly did a cross-section of society, stood not just for *anyone*, but for *everyone*.[43] Such hyperbole about the drastic mortality from the pandemic was then common coinage, as when Guillaume de Machaut put it that death "killed all and slaughtered all,"[44] or *Piers Plowman* that "death . . . dashed all to dust . . .; he left no man standing."[45] Further, a trauma commonly elicits felt guilt that converts it into a punishment due. Accordingly, God was seen by all in 1348 and its immediate aftermath as a bioterrorist inflicting the Black Death in mass punishment for human wickedness. Pious *Piers Plowman* endorsed the built-in traumatic inconsequence by affirming that "for our guilt he grinds good men to dust."[46] Further, in the early, untempered Dance of the Dead the victims were all pitilessly danced away to damnation as a matter of course, the message being not just that anyone could be damned, but that everyone would be, or indeed already was. Thus the Dance originally went one better, or one worse, than mere bodily destruction: jumping the gun on the divine judgment ahead, it foredoomed the victims of the Black Death one and all as unconfessed sinners. It replayed the trauma of sudden death gigantically as sudden damnation. By refusing even "good men" (in Piers Plowman's wording) the benefit of mitigating circumstances,[47] it reduced to unreason the nominal, sermonic thrust of the Dance as a timely warning to the faithful against the sins of the flesh— sins that the Black Death was in fact perversely fomenting.

On yet another tack, the Dance strove like all traumatic replays to temper the shock effect of the trauma, to dull or deaden the traumatic blow. This it did by fitting the trauma to familiar poetic and artistic imagery as also by affirming its necessity, displaced for the purpose onto the indubitable necessity of death: as a nineteenth-century scholar observed, "the idea of inexorability and ineluctability runs like a red thread through all extant texts from whatever time or place."[48] Yet inherent in every traumatic replay is also, conversely, a straining in vain to guard against that impending traumatic blow, as when unwilling dancers drag their feet. Such indeed was the apotropaic intent of the Dance of the Dead, the superstitious reason why, for all its ugliness and scariness, it was incessantly performed or depicted in sacred public places and peddled in best-selling chapbooks: to hold death at bay by death's own iconic presence. The dance motif in particular had this magical purpose, for dancing was widely held to prevent or cure sickness:[49] thence the sexy choreomania that a Rhenish-Flemish sect of itinerant catalytic dancers, called the *chorisants,* spread across Europe on the trail of the pest beginning in 1374.[50] But not just a magical counteraction of the Black Death was built into the Dance of the Dead; so too was, again true to traumatic form, an implicit denial of the dread affliction in that, with grim grotesquerie, the Dance of the Dead parodied the dance of love, a sexual free-for-all conducted at pagan funerals with pious jollity as if to wipe the loss away.[51] Through the dance motif, then, the Dance of the Dead, while affirming that the sins of the flesh spell death, hinted at their continuance after death. The traumatic illogic cut deep.

Just as the plague itself grew weaker on the whole with successive recurrences, so too the surface text of the Dance of the Dead, in its successive reworkings over the decades, went from stark and chilling to ever more allegorical, from a leveling of ranks to social criticism or even satire, finally from all-damning to merely monitory as the seal on the fates of those danced into death gradually loosened. The old-dead dance partners turned into tutelary dance masters who stood and spoke for death in the abstract, which thereby lost the existential immediacy of sudden mass death that the early versions had imparted. A German historian of the Dance put it wistfully: "The vision from the time of the plague turns into a fantasy on the theme of death, the dance into a mere metaphorical image of dying."[52] The death figures grew weirdly jocular to boot as they cut ever crazier capers, grinning their cheekless, lipless, toothy grins. Hans Holbein the Younger raised the remnants of the Dance to high art in a series of woodcuts of 1523–1526 that took what remained of its ghastly chill away, making death over from a sudden confrontation with sin and damnation into a jarring disruption of earthly joys within a transcendent divine order. Europe's black terror was receding.

The Black Death is commonly said to have undermined old certainties and old authorities, clearing the way for modernity. Actually the prestige of the ancients was due to scale new heights in the Renaissance, as was the authority of the scriptures and church fathers in the Reformation. Even so, the Black Death did push its survivors in Europe along one distinctly progressive path to futurity: it compelled increased attention to this world. I have mentioned medicine. Caught short by the plague in 1348, doctors turned the next times round from applying Hippocrates and Galen to trying new therapies based on direct observation of the dread disease.[53] So also to this same effect did the first recurrence of the plague mark a "decisive break" in testation, at least in central Italy, whereby the dying went from disposing of their worldly goods to investing in memorials to themselves.[54] Again in an increasingly worldly vein, scholasticism yielded to more practical learning in the universities even as the vernacular tongues began replacing Latin in the lower schools.[55] Such new departures, radical though they were, actually fell in with a gradual shift of perspective toward this world that was already under way before the Black Death. This secular trend was conspicuous in art in the form of an increasing humanization of subjects and outlook. Since Giotto at the very latest, art in western Christendom had been drawing closer to worldly visual experience even where it remained suspended in sacred or fabulous realms. How did the Black Death impinge on this slow and, over the long term, steady group process in art?

The likeliest take-off point for an answer is the fact that all across Europe the Black Death gave grim prominence to fleshly death and dying. Integral to the traumatic impact of the pandemic was the everyday experience of putrescent bodies and decomposing corpses of intimates and strangers alike. The death toll of itself is warrant that no survivor can have missed constantly seeing ravaged and rotting victims at close range. "Streets and squares, gardens and vineyards, teemed with the sick and dying":[56] these words on Vienna apply as well to any other town in Europe. The chroniclers all described the patterns of infection in some detail as a familiar spectacle.[57] It was the more conspicuous a spectacle since sufferers with body sores found clothing an irritant; stricken women in particular reportedly ran naked outdoors.[58] Not so much the sick and dying, though, as the dead were egregiously on view. Often they would lie untended on doorsteps—in Padua, according to its chronicler, "the bodies even of noblemen lay unburied"[59]—or else piled high in ditches with little or no cover. "No one could be found to bury the dead for love or money," Agnolo di Tura related for Siena, adding: "I . . . buried my five children with my own hands, and many others did likewise. There were also lots of dead throughout the city who were so sparsely interred that the dogs dragged them out and ate their bodies."[60] The cathedral priory of Rochester recorded similarly for England: "No one could be found to carry the bodies of the dead to burial."[61] And the Great Chronicle of Saint-Denis observed for France: "It was most pitiful to see the bodies of the dead in such great quantities."[62] Johannes Nohl stressed "the general horror inspired by the streets and squares encumbered with corpses. . . . Nowhere were the churchyards sufficient."[63] Outside Vienna, according to the Neuberg chronicle, "five big deep pits were filled to the brim with bodies."[64] The testimonials all concur on the continual, inescapable, unforgettable confrontation with the infected both dying and dead.

It is from this dreadful daily scene that the Dance of the Dead took its cue. The surviving images of the Dance suggest that in its earliest performances the old dead were enacted as rotting corpses. Bodily rot was at home in Europe's literature even before the Black Death. It figured prominently in the poems of the Three Quick and Three Dead, themselves richly precedented.[65] The grisly French verses for the Dance of the Dead were in keeping with this "all-out creaturely realism" of late medieval letters.[66] The first graveyard figure in the illustrated French text of the Dance displayed in the cemetery of the Innocents set the sepulchral tone by inviting spectators to "look at us / dead, rotten, stinking, naked."[67] This earthy idiom was on a par with that of Eustache Deschamps apostrophizing a human carcass toward 1400 as "carrion for worms, turd putrid and vile, . . . garnished with lice, louse-eggs, and filth, piss, spittle"[68] and with that of the rustic German poet of the same vintage who made out the fair female form to be "a dung keg, a putrid dish, a smelly sink, a foul tub, a rotten carcass, a mouldy casket, a bottomless sack, a tattered pocket" as seen from the vantage point of death.[69] François Villon, haunted by mortality as he frequented the Innocents a generation later, described the dying body in that same stark vein: "The gall bursts on the heart / Then sweats God knows what sweat."[70] Not to be outdone, his contemporary Pierre de Nasson poetized with mortuary flourish: "Oh man, stinking rot!"[71] All in all, the various German verses for the Dance were one whit less graphic, more traditionally biblical-ascetical, than the single French script. A tack-on to the oldest text for the Dance, the Latin-German version of about 1360, sounded what promptly became the monotonous refrain of all German rewrites: a solemn reminder that we are all mere flesh due to fester as fodder for worms.[72]

Strange to relate, in contrast to this aggressive verbal earthiness suffusing the Dance of the Dead as inscribed or recited inside or outside graveyards throughout Europe for streams of visitors all sadly familiar with the stark sight of death and putrefaction, the corpses illustrating it pictorially there and elsewhere were strictly fanciful. This disconnection between text and image was profoundly Christian, the Word being sacred and likenesses being prohibited by the terms of Christian Holy Writ.[73] The old dead in the Dance all derived from emblematic ancient models, including notably a gutted and mummified corpse, and again a fiddler who sets fresh corpses dancing.[74] Those fresh corpses for their part, in all known depictions of the Dance, kept their mortal flesh and dress, with no trace of the pest about them, as if death had just rudely cut in on their daily occupations for no earthly reason. True, realistic depiction was no more appropriate to ambulatory newcomers to death than to gamboling mummies or skeletons,[75] which is why artists kept the figures in the Dance at an allegorical remove from earthly reality. But neither did material likenesses of dead bodies—such as filled the streets, graveside garrets, and open burial pits in plague times for all to see—come into illustrations of any of the other themes that the Black Death spawned or boosted. There too the dead, whether in a Dürer print or a comic strip–like chapbook, were stylized male bone men or else stereotypical male mummies—the latter usually eviscerated, and with worms crawling where their genitals had been.[76] The devout poet John Gower illuminated this last iconographical nicety when he railed righteously: "Who used to think the vice of lechery so sweet! A serpent now sucks his private parts."[77]

Very much as a whole, and for all their brooding obsession with fleshly decay, artists did not face the putrescent reality squarely. Where Traini's Pisan fresco depicts the Three Quick and Three Dead, we might—pushing it—construe the middle one of the three corpses (one fresh, one rotting, and one skeletal) as a gesture of the first hour toward charnel realism: arguably its hands and face show faint signs of discoloration (the rest of the corpse is covered).[78] Was it, then, painted under the immediate shock effect of the Black Death? This was long taken for granted because of the sudden topicality of its theme in 1348; the stronger indications are, though, that it was produced earlier.[79] In any case, no painter in Italy or elsewhere followed Traini's timid lead after 1348 even in depicting the Three Quick and Three Dead, which alone of the four overlapping macabre themes required at least one decomposing corpse.[80] Not until the late fifteenth century did the resistance to human putrefaction in art sacred or profane lift sufficiently for the dead Christ to begin turning lurid, and for a couple more centuries even this immortal forerunner drew no mortal corpses in his cadaverous train.[81] The constant symbolic reminders of death after 1348 did serve to inure Europeans to the worst of the plague that had caught them traumatically short; with the one tardy, divine exception just noted, however, the accurate image of death did not gain entry into the visual arts before the late baroque. In the allegorical repertory, fantastic figures of death did duty for both adaptive self-inuring and, as regards the Dance of the Dead specifically, traumatic reliving, while outside of allegory as well the trend toward this-worldliness in art remained likewise impervious to the deathly fallout from the plague.[82]

If, unlike the literature, the visual art inspired by the Black Death could not deal realistically with the death that was its subject, neither could it handle the disease itself any better than the doctors could. Not only were the new dead asymptomatic in the iconography of the Dance of the Dead; in no Triumph of Death that I know, from the writhing hecatomb in the Sclafani Palace to the visionary intensity of Pieter Brueghel's panorama of death run amok, did the Black Death mark the victims distinctively. The Black Death looms behind, but only behind, the miniatures on death and burial done shortly after 1400 in the circle of Jean de Berry.[83] Even the rare direct depictions of the pandemic raging, including illustrations in chronicles that themselves describe it graphically, long concealed its bodily signs. A stylized depiction of a mass burial in the annals of Gilles li Muisis, abbot of Saint-Martin in Tournai, dating from the first plague years, shows only closed coffins.[84] The dead bodies strewn together in an allegory of the Black Death in a Lucca chronicle of about 1400 give no hint of infection.[85] Black Death buboes were symbolized from the start as arrows or lances shown raining down on victims, striking them by preference in the neck or groin, shot by God the Father or even by Christ more often than by a subservient, evil figure of death.[86] Buboes were first pictured in their own right only a century or so after 1348, and only seldom and sketchily for starters, in naïve and awkward woodcuts of barbers lancing them, or again in a crude fresco on a chapel wall in Savoy that shows a surgeon lopping one off a woman's neck while other sufferers wait their turn beneath a demon aiming a spear at them and an angel lamely interceding.[87] Full-fledged, honest-to-goodness skin sores at least suggestive of pestilence debuted in art with chromatic extravagance on a web-footed gnome in the Athanasius segment of Matthias Grünewald's Isenheim altarpiece of 1511–1516 between two patron saints of the plague-stricken, Anthony and Sebastian, on the panel wings.[88] Meanwhile around 1480 Domenico Ghirlandaio had painted, tenderly yet unsparingly, an old man's face deformed by elephantiasis: nascent realistic art was, then, somewhat less shy of body sores per se than of buboes specifically. In one holy case, though, that restraint perforce lifted at least symbolically: Saint Rock, who survived the Black Death in 1348 to become the protector of Europe's plague-stricken, was shown after the early fifteenth century pointing to a single, bulging and even, before the century ended, suppurating bubo misplaced onto his knee or thigh.[89]

Back to artists long shunning rotting corpses like the plague: as with Saint Rock's bubonic attribute, an exception again points up the rule, this one a small but glaring exception at the dead center of the secular art of the era. A tiny strain of grimly decomposing bodies haunted mortuary sculpture for a couple of centuries after the pandemic of 1348. If, as Émile Mâle noted, "nothing in earlier art pointed ahead to these frightful images," nothing in the art of their own time pointed sidewise to them either.[90] At intervals a small breed of Europeans of means had their tombs adorned with sculptured portraits of themselves as loathsome cadavers—emaciated, shriveled, mouldy, as a rule worm-eaten, sometimes already skeletal. These so-called *transis* were frequently topped by old-style *gisants*, or second, fine likenesses of themselves in all their earthly splendor.[91] The *transi* tomb, though apparently a byproduct of the Black Death, did not evoke it directly, nor did any known specimen shelter a plague victim. The earliest known *transi* tomb, built by 1370 for a nobleman from the region of Lausanne, François de La Sarra, represented his face and genitalia being eaten by toads and the rest of him by worms.[92] The *transi* mini-vogue peaked around 1450, just when King René of Anjou commissioned for himself a topsy-turvy take-off on the two-tier tomb, with his two bodies

Transi of Cardinal Jean de Lagrange, 1390s
(Musée du Petit Palais, Avignon). (A. Guerrand)

(the one incorruptibly regal, the other corruptibly creatural) conflated into a robed *transi* sitting upright, crown in hand, on the higher level and for good measure his regal body lying in state below.[93] As in the Dance of the Dead, so in the body language of the *transis,* worldly eminence went the way of all flesh. The proud flesh itself followed suit in all its nakedness: in a spinoff of the *transis,* at least three hideous decomposing women were sculpted in chapels across France in the mid-sixteenth century with inscriptions reading: "My once fair body is now rotten."[94] The *transis* influenced a few miniatures on death done for Jean de Berry soon after 1400,[95] while the two-tier tomb came into a sprinkling of drawings, engravings, and illuminations as a *vanitas* or memento mori.[96] This whole eccentric mortuary fashion came to both glory and grief when Germain Pilon designed a spectacular double-decker for Valentine Balbiani in 1572–1584, one of the last of its kind as well as one of the few done for a woman alone: it turned the original monitory *transi* message around through a couple of cute baby angels affirming survival on high despite the body's corruption below. Jacques de Gheyn paid last respects to the outgoing *transi* tomb when in 1599 he engraved one with a contrasting king and peasant standing above their indistinguishable rotted corpses.[97] In its very singularity, the *transi* tomb gives the full measure of how far the rest of art then still was from the faithful lifelikeness and deathlikeness toward which it was slowly and haltingly advancing.[98]

Let me back up a little before lunging farther forward. Europeans collectively suffered the shock effect of the Black Death for decades and even centuries after the event. It permeated their culture from top to bottom, or more usually from bottom to top. Art bore its impress above all in allegories of death, the most notable being the Dance of the Dead, which reenacted it in symbolic form. At the same time, art was retreating ever farther from the Mosaic injunction against making likenesses and was reflecting human reality with ever-increasing precision while progressively humanizing religious and mythological subjects. Graveside portraiture led the realist way: around the turn of the thirteenth to the fourteenth century "the art of the funerary portrait fast attained the sharpest verity,"[99] though with its subjects shown only at their living best, as they hoped to appear when resurrected. By the mid-fifteenth century, art as a whole had achieved luminous fidelity in depicting persons: there can be no improving on a Jan Van Eyck or an Andrea Mantegna for acute this-worldly rendition of human subjects. Even in portraiture, though, and pronouncedly outside of it, the truth of artistic rendition at the time was not the whole truth. It kept the dirt of life at a distance. It did not so much idealize (the usual term) as sanitize and refine. It eschewed rough textures, crude surfaces, the everyday, above all anything coarse or sordid. Plague sufferers and casualties accordingly fell outside its purview except that a single, minor strand of mortuary sculpture, the *transi* tomb, took the gruesome reality of fleshly rot—the traumatic cold core of the Black Death—to its extreme limit and even beyond. In the rest of art, the entombed Christ alone got a grisly touch of death toward 1500, not least because his holy flesh was proof against corruption.[100] The eventual transition to convincing, if still not decomposing, human corpses in painting can be seen working itself out in plague scenes once these were free of attendant saints and angels, from Poussin's of 1630–1631 to those of Bertholet Flémal and Michiel Sweerts modeled on Poussin's, then those of Micco Spadaro and Carlo Coppola some three decades after Poussin's.[101] Decomposition finally registered in all its obscene ugliness with Valdés Leal's *Hieroglyphs of Our Last Days* of 1672 (probably inspired by the Three Quick and Three Dead[102]) and, in sculpture, with Fischer von Erlach's 1692 *transi*-like personification of the plague defeated.[103] In fine, the Black Death had put body rot on the artistic agenda thematically several centuries before artists either could or would render it realistically apart from a smattering of ghastly *transis* inside death's own precincts.

An even bigger issue than body rot in plague-shocked Europe was "the horrors of sudden death."[104] In Italy, which inclined to privilege beauty even in portraiture, Ghirlandaio's old man with elephantiasis was an oddity. There in reaction to the Black Death the celebration of comely flesh passed more easily into both high art and low life than did any shuddering at corpses. Even in the lugubrious north the joyous Italian alternative to penitential brooding might peep naughtily through the pictorial strictures on demonized female flesh, as in a Lucas Cranach or a Hans Baldung Grien. In Spain, though, the Italian carnal antidepressant never caught on in any which way. On the contrary, Spanish artists excelled at dramatizing death: Valdés Leal, the baroque master of the macabre, was one of a breed that culminated in Francisco Goya and his nightmarish etchings of 1810–1814, *The Disasters of War*. French Romanticism took up the funereal torch next, beginning with Géricault's lurid studies of severed heads in the late 1810s.[105] (Both Goya and Géricault also painted plague victims feelingly if none too graphically.[106]) Not, though, until the Realist era of the mid-nineteenth century did death again top the French and hence the European artistic agenda, and then to the undramatic and untouching programmatic effect of being stripped of all meaning beyond what met the eye, of being reduced to a mere "visual fact."[107] Only then could the dead at long last draw the keen, placid, dispassionate look appropriate to a still life, as in Arnold Böcklin's *Dead Girl's Head* of 1879.   *

At this Realist end point of a thousand-year pictorial development, artists finally achieved full documentary objectivity to their own satisfaction—just in time for the camera to do the job for them. They thereupon moved away from reflecting visual experience to deconstructing and reconstructing it. But even while realism in art was still working its slow way toward the bare factuality achieved in the mid-nineteenth century, the fantastic in art was expanding its visionary range. There even more than in realism, death celebrated its new artistic triumph in breadth and depth. For no sooner did the Black Death stop recurring biologically in Europe in the early 1770s than, right on the nose, the artistic agenda thrown up by it revived. And it revived as pure fantasy play, detached from all historic reference, relieved of all stylistic restraint, drained of all traumatic affect as far as met the eye. The Dance of the Dead, recrudescent beginning punctually in the early 1770s, dominated this traumatic throwback. It "appeared most frequently in the graphic arts, but it emerged in almost every conceivable popular medium as well: posters; cheap novels; trinkets and objets d'art; journalism and keepsake books; travel journals and articles promoting the preservation of medieval sculpture and art; works directed at bibliophiles, for whom the dance of death incanabula became (and remain) fashionable for collections; and historical scholarship directed at a broad audience, along with philological scholarship for a more limited readership."[108] Period depictions of those medieval deadlings' antics were reproduced; new ones were fashioned; together the two sorts overran the market. So did folk songs and ballads both old and new to the beat of the graveyard Dance. High culture and low reveled equally in that spectral two-step. Gottfried August Bürger's high-camp "Lenore" of 1773 kicked off the vogue in verse with a macabre Dance of the Dead at the grim finale as a dead soldier home from the wars bears his bride to the altar. Old Goethe and young Flaubert followed Bürger's lyrical lead. So did Heine in Germany; Quinet, Gautier, and Baudelaire in France; Scott, Beddoes, Browning, and Hardy in England; and even European-minded Poe in America.[109] "There has been much talk of late about the Dance of the Dead," began a French treatise of 1852 on its history that concluded with an original forty-four-page oratorio, *Danses des morts*, orchestrated for all the instruments shown in medieval illustrations.[110] Liszt's "Totentanz," Saint-Saëns's "Danse macabre," Mussorgsky's "Songs and Dances of Death," and Glazunov's "From the Middle Ages" struck more enduring, if less authentic, notes. At the height of its comeback, the modish motif served as the offstage motive for a drama of a couple's ritualized, self-destructive behavior, Strindberg's *Dance of Death*.[111] In art, letters, and music alike, the social hierarchy and biblical resonances of the medieval conception had fallen away. In return, its erotic thrust had surfaced, intimating a bacchanal;[112] already in Bürger's ballad the Dance was styled a "nuptial round."[113] The tone was by turns playful, festive, ironic. By the fin de siècle, reanimating the historic scene, the morgue was back in fashion with Parisian strollers as in the very heyday of the Innocents, only without its period grimness.

Over and beyond the Dance of the Dead, the morbid grew sexy within the resurgent Black Death complex as a whole, from Matthias Claudius's beguiling new lyrics of 1775 for "Death and the Maiden," with Death bidding the Maiden "sleep snugly in my arms,"[114] through Antoine Wiertz's resplendent *La belle Rosine* of 1847, with its elegantly undraped statuesque beauty serenely facing down a standing skeleton, to Edvard Munch's *Death and the Maiden* of 1894, with its fleshy maiden crushing her boneman in a bear hug. Baudelaire set the outré standard with his poem "La charogne" of 1856 celebrating a putrid carrion spreading its legs like a woman in heat.[115] Three years later "La danse macabre" by Baudelaire saluted "the charm of madly titivated emptiness" in a waggish female figure of death.[116] That same year Baudelaire hailed as likewise *"full of emptiness"* a sculpture by Émile Hébert of a *transi* rising from the grave to receive a fair maiden into death.[117] Hébert's macabre twosome descended from the Dance of the Dead by way of Death and the Maiden, with the erotism implicit in its medieval referents now at dead center in a tender embrace. Erotism apart, Hébert's *transi* is as authentically deathlike as any produced in the aftermath of the Black Death, and horrifically gorgeous besides.[118]

In the prolonged aftermath of 1348, the *transis* proper had been by contrast only a creepy sideshow, arresting beyond their small numbers. For the rest, art after the Black Death had stuck to its earlier sluggish pace in coming to face the earthly reality of human rot in the raw. Did the *transis*,

138

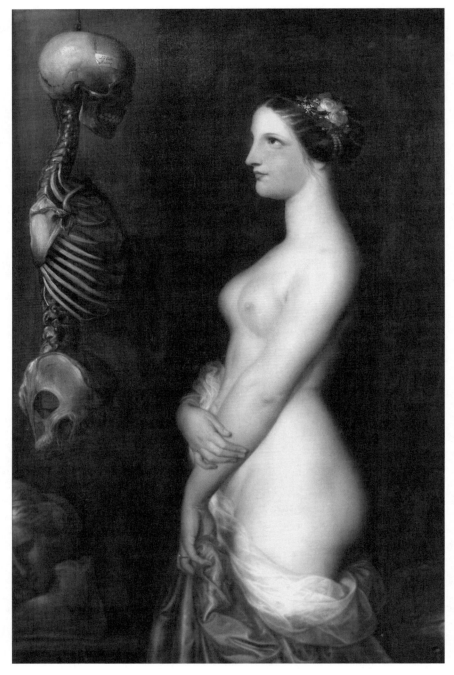

Antoine Wiertz, *La belle Rosine*, 1847 (Musée Wiertz, Brussels)

Émile Hébert, *Et toujours! Et jamais!* 1859
(private collection, Boston). (Dana Salvo)

then, few as they were, drain the full shock effect on style in art of the haunting European spectacle of agonizing or putrifying bodies heaped high and scattered wide? Nowhere else in art at all odds, and least of all in the themes of sudden death that proliferated in the wake of the plague, did the manner of rendering such bodies bear any trace of that traumatic shock. Running its own course on its own schedule, the increasing worldliness of Europe's artistic vision simply passed the traumatic Black Death by. At the same time the deathly trauma, on its flip side a "great source of artistic inspiration . . . imprinted on our collective unconscious" (I am quoting, of all people, a microbiologist),[119] could come to full artistic fruition only after it ceased recurring outright. The symbolic had the last word against the real.

Open Questions

It is high time to synthesize.

Animal populations curtail their fertility whenever overpopulation threatens. Europeans curtailed their fertility in the late nineteenth century when overpopulation threatened. Animal fertility increases with available food or space. When the Black Death freed up available food and space, European fertility increased despite the macabre circumstances. The indication is that the human animal engages in adaptive behavior on the group level just like other animals—that on the whole the individuals composing a group do what its welfare calls for, such as reproduce more or less, though they do not do so with that welfare in mind. Clear as is this indication, it comes with a conceptual catch. We cannot, or cannot yet, locate the springs of unsuspecting cooperative action anywhere in the individual organisms of any species, let alone outside of those organisms. Because of this conceptual catch, historians commonly ignore the evident fact of purposive behavior in concert by human groups. I have preferred to ignore the elusive springs of such behavior and instead study how it works.

It works adaptively for the most part, as in fertility adjustment. No other form of human group process so clearly shows its evolutionary source as does the adaptive kind, and even it departs its animal original in that the existential needs it serves are not always material needs like food and space. What overrode natural fertility in marriage in late-eighteenth-century America and France was ideology, although a century later by contrast a material adaptive imperative, the threat of overpopulation, overcame a deeply embedded moral resistance to marital birth control throughout Europe. Nor does adaptive pressure necessarily confront a human group from the outside the way it does other animal societies. The pressure to adapt was generated within the group itself in both historic cases just cited—by a gender tug-of-war in revolutionary America and France, then by a tumbling death rate in Europe as a whole.

The Black Death, however, did strike Europe's population from the outside. When it struck, it created Europe psychologically through the identical, indiscriminate misery it sowed on all sides. Once it struck from the outside, though, Europe internalized it in order to cope with it: it became endemic. This adaptive coping is hard to sort out from the maladaptive reliving of the devastating blow throughout Europe over the centuries that followed. The adaptive process turned on survivors' immunity, the maladaptive process on survivors' loss of immunity. Adaptation won out in the long haul as the pestilence recurred with irregularly diminishing range, frequency, and mortality. This physiological blend of recurrence and resistance proved bracing. Whereas the same plague depressed the Middle East enduringly, Europe throve on surmounting it, from Petrarch's *Triumphs* and Boccaccio's *Decameron* on. By the late eighteenth century, all Europe was immune.

Where adaptive defenses prove inadequate, as they did in Europe when the Black Death first struck, maladaptive, or traumatic, reliving constitutes a second distinct form of group process prominent in human history. Does the French cavalry case presented in the introduction hold up as a model for traumatic reliving? Europe relived the Black Death in kind, which is how the French relived their suicidal cavalry charge at Courtrai. The Germans also relived in kind their 1918 trauma of defeat, as—to recur to the introduction again—the Belgians did their 1914 trauma of invasion. The Belgians and Germans relived their traumas straight, moreover, with simplistic literalness. This is how Europeans kept reliving the Black Death in their bodies until immunity prevailed, and how the French kept up their headlong horseplay until their tactical turnabout behind the Maginot Line. But while plagued Europe relived its trauma in kind, physically, it also relived that same trauma figuratively, as in the Dance of the Dead. Romantic Europe likewise relived both in fact and in fancy, on the barricades and in creative works, its trauma of the dream of reason bearing monsters. Yet straight reliving in kind is the rule with human groups as far as my meager source base discloses, with reversed reliving and figurative reliving only bringing up the rear.

My summation has so far left out of account a factor essential for understanding reliving by groups, in particular reversed reliving and figurative reliving. In the course of evolution the individual human organism developed a deviant, devious mind of its own, and individual traumatic reliving arose with a greater variety of twists and turns than the group kind ever developed. Individual traumatic reliving may have been the original form or may have derived from, and fed back into, the group form. In either case, reversing a trauma in reliving it, being more frequent with individuals, appears to have originated with individuals. Similarly, as the individual trauma is typically a mental blow, it looks like the germ of the mental group trauma, such as the dream turned nightmare of 1789–1794 that bedeviled Romantic Europe. Only in individuals, moreover, do mental and physical trauma ever fuse as far as our historic sample goes. Hitler's trauma of his mother's death was mental, his interlinked gas trauma physical: he relived the hybrid in kind, physically by proxy, through the Final Solution. Comparably, Leopold III, who drove his queen to her death at the wheel of his roadster with no physical harm to himself, relived his devastating mental blow physically by proxy, through the military destruction of Belgium. More to our purposes, individual and group trauma can interact. Hitler and his Germans, like Leopold and his Belgians, relived separate traumas symbiotically: leader and led enabled each other's reliving. Apparently a group will relive through a leader a trauma that featured a leader. The figure of Ludendorff in Germany's 1918 trauma of defeat is discernible behind Hitler leading its reliving. So too is the figure of Albert I in Belgium's 1914 trauma of invasion discernible behind Leopold III leading its reliving. On the other hand, no single armored horseman personified for the French their traumatic cavalry charge at Courtrai, and not even Robespierre quite personified the traumatic Reign of Terror for Romantic Europe, so that neither event needed a leader to be relived.

What with individual and group reliving impinging on each other, my frame of reference for group reliving cries out to encompass some of my earlier published findings on traumatic reliving by individuals and groups alike.[1] Two of the emotional casualties that I shall now add to my little stock may be unfamiliar: brilliant, bewitching young Lou Salomé was traumatized when Friedrich Nietzsche, who had taken her on as his disciple in the making, cast her off as an adventuress on the make, and middle-aged Luigi Pirandello traumatically had his wife committed when she found cause to accuse him of incest with their daughter.

Trauma may be self-inflicted, as was the case with the death of God: "*We killed him*—you and I," cries the mad fellow in Nietzsche's apt parable. Freud fantasized relivings of self-inflicted group traumas in prehistory and history: totemism as the ritual reenactment of the ancestral gang-murder of a tribal father, then Jahweh as the comeback of a gang-murdered Moses, himself a reedition of that tribal father.[2] Fantasized relivings always raise the traumatic stakes in the way that Freud's tribal father graduated stagewise through lordly Moses to the Lord himself. So do successive real-life relivings escalate if they can, though adaptive maneuvers may counter the escalation. I say "if they can" because it would be hard to hoist the death of God any higher; instead it has been relived, among other ways, through the lapsed Christian creed reviving piecemeal in godless guises only to lapse each time anew.[3] Serial reliving, over and over, is standard except where, as in Hitler's bunker, the escalation is terminal. Like piecemeal reliving, escalation helps to disguise the trauma being relived and so to keep the fact of reliving under wraps. Individual reliving comes with thicker wraps than group reliving. Reversals, which also disguise reliving, are routine with individuals, as with a Hitler hell-bent on "poisoning the poisoner," or with young Rilke's mistress and schoolmistress Lou Salomé doing unto him just what her own master and schoolmaster Nietzsche had traumatically done unto her. Because the group military replays considered above were so blatantly literal except only the Maginot Line reversal, military trauma has a prototypical look to it.

A trauma may strike only gradually or hit home only slowly. The death of God was first being registered long after the fact when Nietzsche asked in his inspired parable: "Does not night and more night keep coming?"[4] Autobiographic accounts of deconversion nonetheless tended to compress and even to objectify it, thereby fitting it to the basic traumatic mold of a bolt out of the blue.[5] Comparably, Lou Salomé's and Luigi Pirandello's big traumas, though both mental and relived mentally, were physicalized in fantasy: Lou, cast off by Nietzsche, saw herself as pushed downstairs,[6] and Pirandello reconfigured his wife's charge of incest as a scream of horror.[7] Besides thus reliving trauma through fiction, writers since antiquity have dealt in fictional traumatic reliving. Fictional traumatic reliving is physical as a rule. It is mostly individual too, though in Pirandello's *Six Characters in Search of an Author* the six parties to an unresolved incest drama (actually Pirandello's own offstage) must keep replaying it together forever. Through that group of six at loose ends seeking its fugitive author to bring it closure, Pirandello also invoked the group trauma of the death of God.[8]

Relived traumas are all relived in actuality even if some—the Black Death, or the revolution of 1789 run amok—are also relived in fantasy first and last. An apparent exception is the death of God, which has been relived in fantasy only because it occurred in fantasy only. Groups that relive enlist the parties to the original where they can or else the closest available surrogates. Individuals take greater liberties, as when Leopold relived a traumatic automobile accident, and Hitler two traumatic poisonings, in politics.[9]

Not every trauma, however elemental, entails reliving, nor is all reliving traumatic. A trauma may instead be unthinkingly defended against after the fact—an adaptive reaction—or it may be recalled obsessively along with its attendant affect. One prerequisite for reliving may be for those traumatized to put the affect behind them until they relive, as did the survivors of the Black Death, or more typically to block it at the very source, like the untroubled deicides in Nietzsche's parable or like Lou Salomé shrugging off Nietzsche's rejection of her. A reliving can be identified on structural grounds, but whether its cause was traumatic cannot. The Dance of the Dead was visibly the Black Death remembered as in a bad dream; we cannot see, though, but only feel, that the Black Death behind it was traumatic. Conversely, a child will commonly relive a parent's life for no traumatic reason. At an outré extreme all its own was the doubleheader I once studied of a crown prince who relived in kind a royal cousin's mysterious death, whereupon his successor, another cousin, relived the crown prince's mysterious death in turn.[10]

Beneath all its accrued complexities, the generic formula remains: groups or individuals alike may relive staggering blows repeatedly. The fact of reliving is never conscious with them, nor is the original traumatic affect recognized when it revives. Unconsciously meanwhile, to relive a trauma is to be right back in the traumatic original. Only on a poetic license do Pirandello's Six Characters reenact their trauma deliberately and with insistent literalness, the way a trauma is relived unconsciously. One of them tells the Stage Manager, who commonsensically thinks it is all behind them: "No, it's happening now, it's happening forever."[11] At the same time, relivings are of the relivers' own devising on the surface. For this reason, to control or master the original may look like the relivers' purpose, as if their reliving were an attempt to absorb the traumatic blow, or to inure themselves to it, or to bind the enduring affect, as Freud's concept of a repetition compulsion implies. But there is no absorbing or inuring or binding where the traumatic outcome is each time confirmed and indeed exceeded. Nor deep down do relivers even hope to avert the impending blow. Ostensibly they guard against it, yet they make it come, and feel it coming, as surely in actual as in fantasy reliving. An individual reliver's frequent reversal of roles from victim to victimizer may look like "getting even" but never feels like it. In sum, the foregone conclusion of traumatic reliving points away from control to uncontrol. So above all does the tendency of reliving to degenerate into a mere sterile routine. Today the Belgian or German reliving of World War I through World War II may appear to have been conclusive, but wait: the French cavalry wound did not heal in over half a millennium's latency. Trauma dies hard if ever.[12]

A trauma, or psychic gash, will not be denied. The attendant affect, if it is repressed, will buck the repression in disguise through phobias, nightmares, or—most dramatically—reliving. Such reliving is of itself self-punitive. As if to drive the point home, relivers tend in addition to culpabilize and punish themselves *within* a trauma as relived, though groups less so than individuals. True, the blanket damnation in the Dance of the Dead came with the trauma being relived (the Black Death seen as God's punishment for human sin), as did the criminality in the German reliving of World War I (the 1918 defeat bore the stigma of imputed war guilt), but both relivings also scaled the blame and the penalty higher. At the deepest level, those who relive a trauma already feel that they had it coming, that it served them right, that they brought it on themselves. I say at the deepest level without meaning to suggest, on the contrary, that this gut feeling never shows outright. It was outspoken in plagued Europe and demonstrative in the foolhardy French cavalry charge even if it was vociferously denied by Germany defeated in 1918 and by Belgium invaded in 1940. It surfaced after the traumatically failed Revolution of 1789 in the Romantics' tragic view of humankind as unworthy of its own highest ideals; conversely, a seer was needed to apprise ex-Christians not of God's death, which was no news, nor even of their inner loss, which was poignant enough, but of their guilt (*"We killed him*—you and I"). It is this sense that the trauma was somehow deserved that gets magnified in the reliving. And just because "it's happening now, it's happening always," it is always due, always coming, hence relived ad infinitum and rightly called a fate.

Dysfunctional it is, but traumatic reliving is also creative. Fantasy relivings fill our libraries and museums. Factual relivings, maniacally impelled, pervade our histories. Trauma-driven group process is the blood and guts of large-scale, titanic events full of sound and fury. Adaptive group process is dull by contrast. Territories break up or merge, cities grow or decline, households expand or contract, nations centralize or decentralize, as real or felt group needs change. Such adaptive group process, though it suffuses all of history, is little chronicled in its time as compared with the disruptive episodes of traumatic failure to adapt. Historians often reconstruct its workings with great verve and even excitingly, but that is something else.

Alongside adaptive and maladaptive group process come, finally, long-range patterned developments in the ways of approaching, reflecting, or adorning human life. These ways encode the basic sense of self and world prevalent within a culture. They are accordingly peculiar to human consciousness even if a rudimentary cultural group process may be found in communal display by lower animals. Individual works of culture will bear a personal stamp and convey a personal message. Yet they all partake of patterned developments with a direction and meaning unknown to the thinkers or artists behind them. Walter Abell was right that the medievals' shrinking monsters reflected their perception of shrinking existential perils. For comparative purposes, however, it were better to put a finer point on it and say instead that the monsters shrank as the world ceased *looking* scary—that the change was first and last subjective. So too did realism advance in art in step with a secular and this-worldly outlook—with the earth seen less and less as a way station between nonexistence and life eternal, and more and more as our native habitat. Likewise, the figural outlook self-destructed even as magical yielded to rational thinking. Ex-Christendom's highest values went from Being to Doing to Having in keeping with a progressive human self-impoverishment or self-estrangement. Such basic shared outlooks vary from one culture to another even within roughly equivalent material circumstances.[13]

Humans enter into multiple groups. Thus the French were reliving their cavalry trauma even while they were caught up in Europe's Black Death trauma and later in the French, then also the European, demographic transition. Adaptive group process operates only in preexisting groups: thence the temptation to see the Europe-wide demographic transition of the 1870s and after as so many national adaptations (Europe's nations being more coherent on average than Europe as a whole) despite the demonstrable continental unity beneath it. Similarly, a cultural group process can occur only within a common culture. Does group trauma too strike only preexisting groups? It might appear so from the examples of France's noble horse cavalry and of Germany's 1918 trauma of defeat, with group consciousness especially acute in an embattled army or nation. Europeans of the cosmopolitan Enlightenment would be no exception where their shared ideology was on trial in revolutionary France 1789–1794. The traumatic Black Death, however, first gave Europe the basic psychological unity manifest in its adaptive and maladaptive reactions alike since 1348.

I have said that the fact of reliving a trauma is never conscious. I would call it unconscious if I were dealing with individuals alone. As it is, the implication that groups have unconscious mental systems like individuals stays my hand despite their parallel ways of reliving. A group unconscious would complete a rough equivalence with Freud's model for the individual psyche, since the adaptive function in groups corresponds to the conscious self-preservative function in the individual, while the cultural process argues a group faculty akin to the individual superego. But that facile analogy only makes the group unconscious suspect. On my scant evidentiary basis, all inferences from group process to its generative source would be premature.

How far, then, have we come in our inquiry? Nowhere close to a science of group process, but a few steps beyond establishing the need for one. Group process has been seen as regulating population, informing culture, and shaping values. It has also been seen inducing mass pathology and spreading death and destruction. Perhaps its workings can be more instructively subdivided than into my three main forms, which may even leave crucial modes of group action out of account. Further, the interrelation of individual and group purposes demands attention outside of traumatic reliving and closer scrutiny even there. Above all, the issue of the physical locus of group purposes cannot be left aside indefinitely. Yet whatever the heuristic inadequacy of my approach, I hope to have scored at least two points with it. First, individual drives and motives are not alone in fueling human history. Take warfare: it is almost universally chalked up to human aggression conceived individually, whereas in point of fact it submerges individual in collective determinants, as has been shown for Hitler's Germany and beyond.[14] And second, those large-scale activities and developments that we call historic—the agricultural revolution, the mass migrations, the rise and fall of states and empires, the growth or decline of populations—are collective human doings with as strong a claim as individual human doings to be seen as motivated on their own level. But grant just these two points and already our broad-gauged histories all need rewriting. For while they do generally deal in coherent, active entities the likes of peoples or cultures, they do not deal with them in the psychohistorical terms in which such entities cohere and act. It is time to call a misdeal.

And what of history on the live end of it: the present? To understand the ongoing play of human history requires knowing which groups are playing and how they play. Adaptively, the stakes are perilously high on the global level, what with ozone depletion, energy exhaustion, and increasing poverty amid increasing plenty. This is known individually and even governmentally the world over. Yet we adapt in group formation, primarily as nations, and hence competitively. Europe alone has (since the Black Death) acted adaptively as a continent in some measure, and it is now institutionalizing its group identity by national consent. But what is emerging is as much exclusive as inclusive—a Fortress Europe consolidated in defense of its shared economic advantages against the disinherited of Africa and Asia. Not even in Europe, where the Enlightenment taught human oneness the whole eighteenth century long, has that oneness gelled. For it to gel worldwide might take a global trauma. Heightened global warming could, like its polar opposite, the Ice Age, traumatize the human breed en bloc. Meanwhile, the Twin Towers trauma was felt well outside its target area, but America's self-absorbed, frenetic, enraged traumatic recall—a losing defense against reliving—soon spoiled that broad solidarity. In any case, trauma unites only at the price, beyond the pain it inflicts, of the aggression it breeds. Witness bellicose Israel with the Holocaust trauma as its legitimation. Worse, witness Bush's America with the Twin Towers trauma as its sanction, fomenting the very terrorism it is fighting. And all the while, ever more lethal weaponry—atomic, chemical, biological—is posing an escalating peril to all concerned or unconcerned whether it is manned by trauma-driven governments or only piecemeal by group process in person, the suicide bomber.

All is not darkness. As against the human divisiveness of adaptive and maladaptive group process, culturally the human breed is inching together. Historians are learning global history. The Global Village is as much a cultural as a technological fact. A common humanity of sorts even sounds through mounting pop violence when terrorists dance to the same tunes and lyrics as their victims. Still in all, human survival is a bad bet on balance except that no one could collect on its loss. The first thing needful to redress the balance is to see the down side of the balance straight. Groups are selfish adaptively, ruthless maladaptively, and disconnected culturally from their adaptive and maladaptive moments. But before all else, such group moments elude individual self-awareness—and here my inquiry can only end where it began.

Notes

Preface

1. The germs of this book can be found in my "Group Process," *Clio's Psyche* 7 (2000): 102, 141–44, 154–55; "Fiction as Social Fantasy," *Journal of Social History* 27 (1994): 679–700; "Marianne au foyer," *Population* 55 (2000): 81–103, 395–96; "Hitler Looks East," *History of Childhood Quarterly* 3 (1975): 85–102; "Notes on Romanticism," *Journal of Psychohistory* 10 (1983): 43–64; "Being, Doing, Having," ibid., 22 (1994): 223–33; "Three Mourning Mothers," ibid., 25 (1998): 449–77; and "Europe's Culture of Death," in *The Psychology of Death in Fantasy and History,* ed. Jerry S. Piven (Westport, Conn.: Praeger, 2004), 119–35. All needed permissions have been granted.

Introduction—Group Process

1. Group process as defined here is thus distinct from the workings of transient groups such as crowds or mobs, the deliberate operations of stable groups, and the individual psychology of group membership, all of which Freud treated in his *Group Psychology and the Analysis of the Ego* (1921) as if to set the agenda for the psychoanalytic study of group behavior.

2. Wynne-Edwards, *Animal Dispersion*. Wynne-Edwards here extended to the whole animal kingdom the homeostatic principle developed by Carr-Saunders in *Population Problem* (1922) of self-regulating human population density tending to maximize well-being rather than numbers.

3. For the history of the issue in biology, see Wilson, "The Group Selection Controversy"; Dugatin, *Cooperation Among Animals*, especially 3–13; Wilson and Sober, "Reintroducing Group Selection," and Sober and Wilson, *Unto Others.*

4. Some new theoretical departures in biology are nonetheless suggestive for group process in human history. One is the modeling of colony-level behavior, such as patterns of foraging in Camazine and Sneyd, "Honey Bees." Another is complexity theory and especially the Gaia hypothesis, nicely reconciled with superorganisms in Turner, *The Extended Organism*, especially 179–212.

5. Franks, "Army Ants," 139.

6. T. S. Eliot [London] to his father, 23 XII 1917, quoted in Eliot, *The Waste Land,* xiii.

7. Sean Wilder to me, 10 III 2001.

8. Campbell and Jacobs, "Arbitrary tradition." (The delusion—about how far a fixed point moves—dwindled away in four or five generations.)

9. For the periodic fatal surges of lemmings, see Wynne-Edwards, *Animal Dispersion,* 479–80.

10. Counting only 25 years per generation at an intrinsic growth rate under 2.5 percent: see further p. 27.

11. See Coale and Watkins, *Decline,* 39 (fig. 2.3) and 293–313.

12. The danger was not primarily a biochemically signaled spatial overcrowding as argued by Hall, *The Hidden Dimension,* 15–28 and 184–86, since fertility declined no more and no sooner in urban than in rural areas.

13. Markowitz, *The Psychodynamic Evolution of Groups,* 115–70.

14. Ibid., 140.

15. Ibid., 147.

16. Ibid., 116–17.

17. Ibid., 135.

18. Binion, "Repeat Performance," 15–61; *Introduction à la psychohistoire,* 29–33; "Ketzerisches zur Kriegsfrage," 123–24; *Freud über Aggression und Krieg,* 33–34; "Traumatic Reliving in History," 240–47.

19. Abell, *The Collective Dream in Art,* 119–46, 163–65, 170–227.

20. Ibid., 133.

21. Ibid., 138.

22. Ibid., 194.

23. Ibid., 198.

24. Ibid., 131.

25. Ibid., 132.

26. Ibid., 137.

27. Ibid., 139.

28. Ibid., 171.

29. Ibid., 172.

30. Ibid., 175.

31. Ibid., 182.

32. Ibid., 201.

33. Ibid., 224.

34. Ibid., 226.

1—The Guilty Family

1. Gide, *Les nourritures terrestres,* 74.

2. Ibsen, *Samlede verker,* vol. 5, 42 ("Vildanden").

3. Ibid., 46.

4. Quoted in Ibsen, *Hedda Gabler,* 135.

5. Ibsen, *Samlede verker,* vol. 4, 201 ("Et Dukkehejm").

6. Ibid., 199.

7. Ibid., 205.

8. Ibid.

9. Quoted in Ibsen, *The Wild Duck,* 83, from Ibsen's notes.

10. Strindberg, *Kammarspel,* 191 ("Spöksonaten").

11. Strindberg, *Kammarspel,* 279 ("Pelikanen").

12. Ibid., 266.

13. Vallès, *L'enfant,* 301. Salleron, 78, calls this novel from the social depths "one of the most vehement protests ever launched against the family."

14. Turgenev, *Sobranie sochinenii,* vol. 3, 139 ("Otsi i deti").

15. Shaw, *Collected Plays,* vol. 4, 187 ("Misalliance").

16. Ibid., 246.

17. Wilde, *Oscar Wilde,* 459.

18. Butler, *The Way Of All Flesh,* 325.

19. Reuter, *Aus guter Familie,* 45.

20. Ibid., 40.

21. Ibsen, *Samlede verker,* vol. 6, 252 ("John Gabriel Borkman").

22. Ebner-Eschenbach, *Aus Spätherbsttagen*, vol. 1, 126 ("Der Vorzugsschüler").

23. Ibsen, *Samlede verker*, vol. 5, 25 ("Vildanden").

24. Strindberg, *Dödsdansen*, 227.

25. Schnitzler, *Gesammelte Werke*, vol. 2:3, 298 ("Der Ruf des Lebens").

26. Synge, *Plays, Poems, and Prose*, 125 ("The Playboy of the Western World").

27. Ibid.

28. Ibid., 127.

29. Ibid., 139.

30. Ibid., 165.

31. Ibsen, *Samlede verker*, vol. 5, 411 ("Hedda Gabler"): "slikt noe *gjør* man da ikke!" The usual English translation—"People don't do such things!"—blunts Ibsen's point.

32. Ibid., vol. 4, 260 ("Gengangere").

33. Ibid., 245.

34. Ibid., 279.

35. Hauptmann, *Sämtliche Werke*, vol. 1, 121 ("Das Friedensfest").

36. Shaw, *Collected Plays*, 113.

37. Ibid., 182.

38. Butler, *The Way of All Flesh*, 131.

39. Strindberg, *Kammarspel* ("Spöksonaten"), 175.

40. Ibid., 183.

41. Ibid., 209.

42. Zola, *La terre*, 498.

43. Ibsen, *Samlede verker*, vol. 4, 157 ("Et Dukkehejm").

44. Ibid., 165.

45. Granville-Barker, *The Voysey Inheritance*, 59. Further: ibid., 100, on familial evils, and ibid., 106, on families shrinking.

46. A broader survey of just the parent-child conflict in European fiction is Wais, *Das Vater-Sohn Motiv in der Dichtung bis 1880* and *Das Vater-Sohn Motiv in der Dichtung 1880–1930* (both Berlin: Gruyter, 1931), and in German fiction alone Eichbaum, "Jugendprobleme."

47. Fine, "Enfant et normes familiales," 458.

48. Thus the heroine of Colette's *La vagabonde* (1910) fled domestication in the very footsteps of Ibsen's Nora. More to the point, while the leading authors of the period were mostly male, their public was not; for a woman's deeply felt kinship with Ibsen's female characters in their time, see Andreas-Salomé, *Henrik Ibsens Frauen-Gestalten*.

49. Madaule, "La famille dans la littérature française," finds a single significant clearcut affirmation of the family in French fiction for this period: Charles Péguy's sacred poem *Ève*.

50. Not counting a holograph note on his *Queen Mab*: Rogers, *Shelley*, 266, 301ff.

51. See, e.g., [Drysdale], *Elements*. In France even radical feminism did not target the family: Offen, "Depopulation, Nationalism, and Feminism," 648–76; Hause, *Women's Suffrage*.

52. Naquet, *Religion, propriété, famille*, 228–310, and *Le divorce*, 108–9, 184–85, and passim. Naquet's divorce law passed the French parliament in 1884 on the ground of family interest: Desforges, "La loi Naquet," 107. In *Vers l'union libre* Naquet recurred to free love for the communist future. Like Naquet pushing divorce, Léon Blum in *Du mariage* called for premarital free love for the sake of improving marriage.

53. Le Play, *L'organisation de la famille*, 9 and passim.

54. See, e.g., the authoritative Morel, *Traité de dégénérescences*, 47–63, 561–72; Möbius, *Über Entartung*, passim.

55. Hareven, "Crossroads," xviii; Burnett, *Destiny Obscure*, 261, also 53. Further: Mitterauer and Sieder, *Vom Patriarchat zur Partnerschaft*; Barbagli, *Sotto lo stesso tetto*.

56. "Increased births following upon increased deaths seems to be a fairly common demographic phenomenon, almost as if the population automatically sought to maintain its numerical equilibrium in the face of sudden losses": Herlihy, *Pistoia*, 95.

57. A good summary is Livi Bacci, "Forerunners." The evidence is compelling for French dukes and peers beginning in the late seventeenth century and strong as well for the Genevan bourgeoisie from before 1600, the Genoese patriciate from 1600, Rouen's bourgeoisie from 1630, and the Milanese patriciate after 1750. In the tricky Milanese case, interpregnancy intervals lengthened, which would suggest longer lactation replacing wet-nursing except that protogenesic intervals lengthened as well: Zanetti, *La demografia del patriziato milanese*, 87, 134–74, 200. Herlihy, *Pistoia*, 86, infers a possibility of customary marital birth control from a 1424 smallish post-plague bumper crop of Pistoian babies more likely due to "younger marriages" (and, I would add, to half of Pistoian nurslings dying in the plague, so that their mothers resumed ovulation that much earlier). Still less plausibly, Herlihy and Klapisch-Zuber, *Les Toscans*, 439–42, suggests possible marital birth control in poorer Tuscan households because in 1427 they counted fewer living children than did richer households; for marriages at all odds those data hardly substantiate Bernardino's Tuscan preachments of 1427 invoking the cries of babies "thrown into your Arno and your privies or . . . killed in their mothers' bellies": Cohn, *Death and Property in Siena*, 31. E. A. Wrigley argued birth control in tiny Colyton (Devon) 1647–1719 from the wives' relatively long last birth intervals (after a plague, with marriage ages soaring), but later he conceded that his results were open to question: Wrigley, "Family Limitation in Pre-Industrial England," reprinted in Wrigley, *People, Cities and Wealth;* and Wrigley, "Marital Fertility," 423, for his concession and for "how sensitive a very small sample can be to minor data changes . . . because of the very small numbers involved." Further: Morrow, "Family Limitation in Pre-Industrial England"; Coale and Watkins, *Decline*, 411n.

58. Hecht, "Le Siècle des Lumières."

59. Van de Walle, "Motivations and Technology"; Watkins, "Conclusions"; Seccombe, "Starting to Stop," 151–52.

60. Robert Graves, born in 1895, experienced *a contrario,* as one of ten siblings, "a diminution of parental affection": Graves, *Goodbye To All That,* 12.

61. Spicq, *Agapè,* vol. I, 70–71, 73–74, 266–67; vol. II, 209; vol. III, 130–31, 135, 151–52.

62. I take this term and concept from Kern, "Explosive Intimacy."

63. Ibsen, *Samlede verker,* vol. 4, 260 ("Gengangere").

64. Knodel, *Decline,* 69–70; Keyfitz and Flieger, *Population,* 56; Gaukey, *Demography,* 194; Festy, *La fécondité,* 88–106.

65. This effect of birth control was first described by Demos, "Oedipus and America," 29–30.

66. Tolstoy, *Kreutzerova Sonata,* 73.

67. Strindberg, *Kammarspel* ("Spöksonaten"), 209.

68. James, *What Maisie Knew,* 55.

69. The proof that this was no mere literary convenience is Frank Wedekind's *Spring Awakening* (1891) with its ten finely individualized children. Fittingly, only one of those children is known to have a sibling, while the little heroine takes charity to "working-class families with too many children."

70. Further, Ibsen and Wedekind each had five siblings, Tolstoy four, Butler three, Shaw and Hauptmann two each, and Maupassant one; Hauptmann had two marriages and Tolstoy, Zola, Ibsen, and Wedekind one each; Strindberg had four children from his first marriage and two from his third, Hauptmann three from a first marriage and two from a second, Wedekind two and Ibsen one from a single marriage each.

71. For that pagan premise: Rawson, "The Roman Family," 9–12. For the Christian sequel: Klapisch-Zuber, "La famille médiévale," 479–89.

72. Hélène Bergues, ed., *La prévention des naissances,* 203–5, 247–51, and passim.

73. For some emphatic Tuscan exceptions in the fifteenth century see Herlihy and Klapisch-Zuber, *Les Toscans,* 440–42.

74. Hélène Bergues, ed., *La prévention des naissances,* passim.

75. Tolstoy, *Kreutzerova Sonata,* 108.

2— Ideology in the Bedroom

1. As measured by the Princeton Ig index, which totalizes age-specific marital fertility rates adjusted to a standard age-distribution of married women.

2. Fernand Braudel, *L'identité de la France,* 172–73, 181.

3. As measured by the Princeton Ig index; Weir, "Family Reconstitution," 150–52, 158, and passim.

4. Ganiage, *Trois villages,* 85–86; Chamoux and Dauphin, "La contraception avant la Révolution française," fig. 6; Lachiver, *La population de Meulan,* 151, 210; Dupâquier and Lachiver, "Sur les débuts," 1395, 1398–1402; Henry, "Quart sud-ouest," 995–98; Henry and Houdaille, "Quart nord-ouest," 916; Houdaille, "Quart nord-est," 377–78; Keyfitz, *Applied Mathematical Demography,* 329–30; Henry, "Quart sud-est," 878–80; John Knodel, "Espacement des naissances," 473–88, 493–94; Dupâquier and Lachiver, "Du contresens"; Flinn, *The European Demographic System,* 104–7, 109–11, 117, 128–29; Mroz and Weir, "Structural Change," 77 (spacing "changed little in the south, but contributed importantly to the overall decline of fertility in the north"); Weir, "Estimation," 350; Weir, "Family Reconstitution," 156–58.

5. On the English experience, the documentation in Seccombe, "Starting to Stop," is conclusive.

6. To misquote Pascal, "le *corps* a ses raisons que la raison ne connaît pas." Cf. Henry, "Natural Fertility," 90–91; Wrigley, "Fertility Strategy," 148; Bideau, "Les mécanismes autorégulateurs," 1047–48; Coale, "Decline of Fertility," 9–10; Santow, "*Coitus interruptus,*" 42–43.

7. Gautier and Henry, *Crulai,* 116; Valmary, *Familles paysannes,* 140; Giachetti and Tyvaert, "Argenteuil (1740–1790)," 45–46; Bardet et al., "Les paysages humains," 832; Henry, "Quart sud-ouest," 1001; Henry and Houdaille, "Quart nord-ouest," 911, 920–21; Weir, "Family Reconstitution," 156–57. On birth spacing versus birth stopping in the Old Regime, see Knodel, "Espacement des naissances"; Dupâquier and Lachiver, "Du contresens"; Bardet, *Rouen,* vol. 1, 272–75, 281–83, 303. And on conceptions varying seasonally from one locale to another: Zinc, *Azereix,* 80–83.

8. Goubert, *L'ancien régime,* 196.

9. Sauvy, "Essai d'une vue d'ensemble," 389–90; Goubert, "Reinterpretation," 45. Against explanations based on modernization in general: Vinovskis, "Socioeconomic determinants," 396, and "A Multivariate Regression Analysis," 256.

10. Wrigley, *People, Cities and Wealth,* 287–91; Chesnais, *La transition démographique,* 89–90, and "La transition démographique," 1061–62; cf. Weir, "New Estimates," 322.

11. Spagnoli, "Unique Decline," 425, 438, and passim.

12. Goubert, "Legitimate Fertility," 321–30; Le Bras, "Coït interrompu"; Blum, Houdaille, and Tugault, "Baisse de la fécondité"; Blum, "L'évolution de la fécondité"; Wrigley, *People, Cities and Wealth,* 292–321.

13. Sauvy, "Essai d'une vue d'ensemble," 379—and in the same volume Bergues, "Sources et documentation," 24: "France had taken a hundred-year lead over the rest of the world."

14. Sauvy, *La prévention des naissances,* 13.

15. Goubert, "Historical Demography," 46 (similarly 44: "No other country in the known world experienced so early and so rapid a decline"), and *L'ancien régime,* 196.

16. Braudel, *L'identité de la France,* 173, 181.

17. Chaunu, "Postface," 557.

18. Dupâquier et al., *Histoire de la population française,* jacket and 1.

19. Van de Walle, "Motivations and Technology," 138.

20. Van de Walle, "Alone in Europe."

21. Leasure, "La baisse de la fécondité aux États-Unis de 1800 à 1860." Three researchers stated in the selfsame journal five years later that "in France . . . birth control . . . appeared very much earlier than elsewhere": Blum, Houdaille, and Tugault, "Baisse de la fécondité," 503.

22. Bardet and Dupâquier, "Contraception," 3.

23. Whereas in the eighteenth century before the transition the total fertility rate seems to have remained under six children per woman in France, the weighted average of results from the main local studies for America (white population) is over seven. These studies yield, in decreasing order of magnitude, over eight for Plymouth and Sturbridge; between seven and eight for Deerfield, Hampton, Hingham, and the patricians of Philadelphia; between six and seven for Nantucket, the Quakers, and a sampling of New England as a whole; below five for Andover, and below three for Germantown: see respectively Demos, "Plymouth Colony," 270, and Osterud and Fulton, "Family Limitation," 488, 492; Temkin-Greener and Swedlund, "Fertility Transition," 31, Kilbourne, "Fertility Transition," 212, Daniel Scott Smith, "Population, Family and Society," 320–21, 336, and Louise Kantrow, "Philadelphia Gentry," 31; Cole, "Family, Settlement, and Migration," 184; Byers, "Fertility Transition," 21–22, Wells, "Family Size," 75, and Higgs and Stettler, "Colonial New England Demography," 290; Greven, *Four Generations,* 183, and Wolf, *Urban Village,* 264. This approximate average of seven matches one derived from genealogical registries in 1916–1917—cited by Wells, *Revolutions in Americans' Lives,* 92—and accords mutatis mutandis with the later census returns as analyzed in Coale and Zelnik, *New Estimates,* fig. 10, and Smith, "'Early' Fertility Decline in America," 73, and "The Peculiarities of the Yankees," 2.

24. Respectively: Withey, "Household Structure"; Kilbourne, "Fertility Transition"; Greven, *Four Generations;* Smith, *Population, Family and Society;* Osterud and Fulton, "Family Limitation"; Temkin-Greener and Swedlund, "Fertility Transition"; Byers, "Fertility Transition"; Wells, "Family Size," "Family History," and *Revolutions.* No dating is possible either for Germantown in Pennsylvania as per Wolf, *Urban Village,* for want of sufficient data or for the region of Sandwich in Massachusetts as per Cole, "Family, Settlement, and Migration," because of continual migration in and out.

25. Higgs and Stettler, "Colonial New England Demography," 282–94.

26. Wells, "Family Size," 79–81; Smith, *Population, Family and Society,* 330–34; Temkin-Greener and Swedlund, "Fertility Transition," 37; Kantrow, "Philadelphia Gentry," 28; Byers, "Fertility Transition," 30–34. Cf. above, n. 7.

27. Bloch, "Pour une histoire comparée," 47, 30, 28, 30, 44, 49; similarly, Braudel and Spooner, "Prices," 437.

28. Goubert, "Historical Demography," 45. Further: Rose, "Feminism," 182.

29. Butler, *Awash;* Smith, "The peculiarities of the Yankees," 14.

30. Smith, "Population, Family and Society," 73–74 (the birth rate began to decline some eight decades before the death rate). Comparably, age at marriage was falling throughout America (Sturbridge alone appears as an exception) even while it was rising in France.

31. Sauvy, "Essai d'une vue d'ensemble," 385; Kantrow, "Philadelphia Gentry," 21–30.

32. Flandrin, *Familles,* 214–17, 229–30; Chaunu, "Postface," 558–59.

33. Henry, "Quart sud-ouest"; Henry and Houdaille, "Quart nord-ouest"; Houdaille, "Quart nord-est"; Henry, "Quart sud-est."

34. Weir, "Family Reconstitution," 155.

35. Chaunu, "Postface," 562, 559.

36. Gautier and Henry, *Crulai,* 122, 119.

37. Ganiage, *Trois villages,* 86.

38. Dupâquier and Lachiver, "Sur les débuts," 1402.

39. See, e.g., Dupâquier, "La constitution de la famille," 31 ("the French Revolution . . . brought about changes in the constitution of the family: the later age at marriage was now supplemented by a generalized limitation of births"), and "Révolution et population," 75 ("it was rather through its long-term consequences and by the population shuffles it produced that the Revolution appears to have generalized and accelerated the process of deliberate limitation of births already underway in a few sectors").

40. Blum, "L'évolution de la fécondité," 157.

41. Landry, *La révolution démographique,* 40. Reinhard, "La Révolution," 426, could still affirm that in France the political revolution and the demographic revolution proceeded "from the same profound transformation of ideas."

42. The survey of the French transition conducted by the Institut National d'Études Démographiques (n. 33 above) hardly lends itself to regional comparisons as to politics and demography, as the four quarters of the country were each politically heterogeneous and each represented by demographically heterogeneous villages, with no significant trends distinguishing any quarter. (Henry and Houdaille, "Quart nord-ouest," 920 and 922, claimed that births before the transition were more widely spaced in the southwest than in the northwest quarter, but the opposite held for women aged 20–24, the most fertile category; see also Blum, "L'évolution de la fécondité," 158, and Weir, "Family Reconstitution," 157–58.) Moreover, such regional comparison is out of the question for America, where the loyalists mostly fled abroad after the victory of the rebels.

43. Smith, "Family Limitation." Smith pointedly distinguished "domestic feminism" from feminism proper.

44. Smith, "Family Limitation," 231; cf. Smith, *Population, Family, and Society,* 352–55, 361–67.

45. Ibid., 352–55, 363–65. Wells, *Revolutions in Americans' Lives,* 96, opts instead for breastfeeding and coitus interruptus; Wells, "Family History," 13, adds prostitution.

46. Stengers, "Les pratiques anticonceptionnelles," passim, including 420–22 on the "sin of Onan" as a clerical euphemism for withdrawal.

47. Norton, *Liberty's Daughters,* xv; cf. xv–xvii, 232–35. Of subsequent studies, the most germane is Klepp, "Revolutionary Bodies," 910–45. The thesis of "domestic feminism" competes in America above all with approaches that turn on religious, ethnic, or regional factors (and are subject mutatis mutandis to the same objections as in France): see, e.g., Leasure, "La baisse," and Smith, "The Peculiarities of the Yankees."

48. Degler, *At Odds,* 189; cf. 181–95, 207, and passim; see also Davidson, *Revolution and the Word,* 116–17. Leasure, "La baisse," 669, and "A Hypothesis," 106–10, argued the influence of the Revolution in this same sense on both sexes without distinction.

49. Drinker, *Not So Long Ago,* 55, 59.

50. McLaren, "Abortion in France," 485; see also Traer, *Marriage and the Family,* 16, 138–39, and passim, and Klepp, "Revolutionary Bodies," 916.

51. Archives Parlementaires, *Recueil complet,* 50.

52. Cerati, *Le Club,* 173.

53. Perrot, "Avant et ailleurs," 17; cf. Hunt, "Révolution française," 51.

54. Ariès, "Sur les origines," 471.

55. Bergues, "Sources et documentation," 37.

56. Hunt, "Révolution française," 42.

57. Bergues, *La prévention des naissances,* 149–61, 221–32, 253–307, and passim; Van de Walle, "Alone in Europe," 267–69, and "Motivations and Technology," 140–41, 145–48, 152, 163–64, and passim; Flandrin, *Familles,* 208–12; Théré, "Limitation des

naissances," 432–34; Darnton, *Best-Sellers,* 112, 408–9; Van de Walle and Muhsam, "Fatal Secrets," 262–63, 275–76, and passim.

58. Bergues, "Sources et documentation," 227.

59. See, e.g., Jean-Marie Gouesse, "En Basse-Normandie."

60. Ibid., 248.

61. Proctor, *Women, Equality, and the French Revolution,* 57–61.

62. Coale, "Decline of Fertility," 21; Knodel and Van de Walle, "Lessons from the Past," 393, 409, 410; Watkins, "Conclusions," 431–32. Princeton dated the start of a transition accordingly from the passage of the threshold of -10% even though it necessarily began earlier. By a curious coincidence, I myself once postulated an identical critical threshold of -10% and automatic process for the decline of illiteracy: Binion, "Considérations sur la disparition de l'analphabétisme," 121–28.

63. See Houdaille, "Quart nord-est," fig. 8, and Henry and Houdaille, "Quart nord-ouest" fig. 10. The corresponding studies of the southwest and southeast quarters of the country provide no comparable data: see Henry, "Quart sud-ouest," 977–1023, and "Quart sud-est," 855–82.

64. Weir, "Estimation," 350; see also Ganiage, "Trois villages," 85–86.

65. In France the Church's teachings on the marital obligation to multiply actually varied over time: see Gouesse, "En Basse-Normandie," 236–37, 257–58.

66. The Enlightenment gave maternal breastfeeding high marks: it meant fewer confinements, more children surviving, and healthier and more attractive mothers, all by eminently natural means. See Duncan, "Happy Mothers and Other New Ideas in French Art," 570–83; Hecht, "Le Siècle des Lumières et la conservation des petits enfants," 1589–1620. Enlightened approval of reduced fertility helped to prepare the moral basis for the contraceptive revolution.

67. Van de Walle and Muhsam, "Fatal Secrets," 261–79; Gouesse, "En Basse-Normandie," 231–61.

68. Goubert, *L'ancien régime,* 196.

69. For this danger, see above, pp. 6–7, 27.

70. Demos, "Shame and Guilt in Early New England," 70.

71. Ibid., 75–76.

72. Ibid., 69 (phrase borrowed from Ruth Benedict).

73. Duncan, "Happy Mothers and Other New Ideas in French Art," 570–83; Sylvana Tomaselli, "Moral Philosophy and Population Questions in Eighteenth-Century Europe," 7–29; Klepp, "Revolutionary Bodies," 926. Van de Walle, "Motivations and Technology," 164: Pierre Bayle attributed childbearing itself to the false shame attached to barrenness. But the criteria for shame over infertility varied across Europe: see Santow, *"Coitus interruptus,"* 26, 28.

74. In France the collapse of the Church under the Revolution facilitated this process of interiorization: see John T. Noonan, Jr., "Intellectual and Demographic History," 390. In European moral philosophy, it was above all Kant who linked the one moral regime to the other by converting Rousseau's "general will," in which the moral judgment of others was sovereign, into a subjective categorical imperative, which, though supposedly derived from pure reason, bore the traces of its origin in communal censure.

75. Bloch, *Apologie pour l'histoire ou métier d'historien,* 101.

76. On "gender depolarization" in the nineteenth and twentieth centuries: Kern, *The Culture of Love,* 199–217.

3—A Community of Fate

1. Hitler to Stahlhelm leaders, 11 May 1929: Tyrell, *Führer befiehl...,* 319–20 ("the natural inner will of the people . . . the people's will proper . . . the real inner will of the people").

2. Hitler, *Mein Kampf,* 144 ff.

3. Bundesarchiv Koblenz NS26/51/208-9; Jäckel and Kuhn, *Hitler,* 427.

4. Maser, *Hitlers Briefe und Notizen,* 276; Jäckel and Kuhn, *Hitler,* 423.

5. Phelps, "Hitler als Parteiredner im Jahr 1920," 327; Jäckel and Kuhn, *Hitler,* 259. In all likelihood "to the east" ("nach Osten") is a mistake for "to the outside" (*"nach aussen"*), as the somewhat fuller report in the *Völkischer Beobachter* of 25 November 1920 on the same Party meeting contains no such indication: see Bundesarchiv Koblenz NS26/51/18-20; Jäckel and Kuhn, *Hitler,* 262–63.

6. Zechlin, "Ludendorff im Jahr 1915," 352.

7. Hahlweg, *Der Friede von Brest-Litowsk,* 118. Hitler first met Ludendorff in April or May 1921.

8. Maser, *Hitlers Briefe und Notizen,* 268; Jäckel and Kuhn, *Hitler,* 422.

9. Eduard August Scharrer to Wilhelm Cuno, 30 December 1922: Bundesarchiv Koblenz R431/2681/88; Jäckel and Kuhn, *Hitler,* 773.

10. Jäckel and Kuhn, *Hitler,* 870.

11. Viereck, "Hitler the German Explosive," 236; Jäckel and Kuhn, *Hitler,* 1023.

12. Jäckel and Kuhn, *Hitler,* 1115; Horn, "Ein unbekannter Aufsatz Hitlers aus dem Frühjahr 1924," 280–94; Jäckel and Kuhn, *Hitler,* 1217; Kuhn, *Hitlers außenpolitisches Programm,* 99–104.

13. Hitler, *Mein Kampf,* 741–42.

14. Ibid., 519, 523–24, 524. What Hitler added applied as well to his speech on "the true causes of the World War," which he delivered on 31 May 1921 like the one on Brest-Litovsk cited above, n. 3.

15. Ibid., 525–26, 527.

16. Binion, *Hitler Among the Germans,* 1–35 and passim; and pp. 54–56 of this work.

17. Jäckel and Kuhn, *Hitler,* 89 (letter to Adolf Gemlich, 16 September 1919: "racial tuberculosis of the peoples").

18. For the power-political implications of Hitler's anti-Semitism, see Binion, "'Der Jude ist weg,'" 347–72 and 396–401.

19. Bayerisches Hauptstaatsarchiv, Allgemeines Staatsarchiv, Sonderabgabe I1478/76, and Jäckel and Kuhn, *Hitler,* 120 (speech of 6 April 1920); cf. Phelps,"Hitler als Parteiredner im Jahr 1920," 302 (speech of 11 May 1920), and Jäckel and Kuhn, *Hitler,* 132: "The evil must be grasped by the root."

20. Koerber, *Adolf Hitler,* 29; Jäckel and Kuhn, *Hitler,* 620.

21. Tyrell, *Führer befiehl...,* 49–50; Jäckel and Kuhn, *Hitler,* 703.

22. Scharrer to Cuno, fol. 88; Jäckel and Kuhn, *Hitler,* 773.

23. Jäckel, *Hitlers Weltanschauung.*

24. Weinberg, *Hitlers zweites Buch,* 225.

25. Jacobsen and Jochmann, *Ausgewählte Dokumente zur Geschichte des Nationalsozialismus 1933–1945* (unpaginated).

26. Sauer, "Die Mobilmachung der Gewalt," 749–50; cf. O'Neill, *The German Army and the Nazi Party 1933/39,* 40–41.

27. Jacobsen and Jochmann, *Ausgewählte Dokumente zur Geschichte des Nationalsozialismus 1933–1945* (unpaginated). Further: Henrikson, "Das Nürnberger Dokument 386-PS (das "Hossbach-Protokoll")," 175.

28. Jacobsen and Jochmann, *Ausgewählte Dokumente zur Geschichte des Nationalsozialismus 1933–1945* (unpaginated).

29. Hitler, *Mein Kampf,* 750–52.

30. Weinberg, *Hitlers zweites Buch,* 128.

31. Treue, "Hitlers Denkschrift zum Vierjahresplan 1936," 204, 206.

32. Jacobsen, *Nationalsozialistische Aussenpolitik 1933–1938,* 427: Laqueur, *Russia and Germany,* 170, 176–95, 196–98; Henke, *England in Hitlers politischem Kalkül 1935–1939,* 95–96; Kuhn, *Hitlers aussenpolitisches Programm,* 196–98.

33. Sommer, *Deutschland und Japan zwischen den Mächten 1935–1940*, 31, 34 (9 June and 22 July 1936).

34. Buchheit, *Hitler, der Feldherr*, 167.

35. Hillgruber, *Hitlers Strategie*, 145, and *Deutschlands Rolle in der Vorgeschichte der beiden Weltkriege*, 105.

36. Halder, *Kriegstagebuch*, 336–37.

37. Krausnick, "Judenverfolgung," 365.

38. Jacobsen, *Aussenpolitik*, 459, n. 21.

39. Binion, *Hitler Among the Germans*, 3–14 and passim.

40. Binion,"Hitler's Concept of 'Lebensraum,'" 187–215, and *Hitler Among the Germans*, 53–58.

41. Preiss, *Adolf Hitler in Franken*, 40.

42. Bayerisches Hauptstaatsarchiv, Allgemeines Staatsarchiv, Sonderabgabe I 1478/104; Jäckel and Kuhn, *Hitler*, 134 (speech of 4 March 1920).

43. Phelps, "Hitler als Parteiredner im Jahr 1920," 316; Jäckel and Kuhn, *Hitler*, 222 (speech of 5 September 1920).

44. Phelps, "Hitler als Parteiredner im Jahr 1920," 318; Jäckel and Kuhn, *Hitler*, 222 (speech of 20 September 1920).

45. Bayerisches Hauptstaatsarchiv, Allgemeines Staatsarchiv, Sonderabgabe I 1478/248; Jäckel and Kuhn, *Hitler*, 257–58 (speech of 5 November 1920).

46. Kursell, *Adolf Hitlers Reden*, 67; Jäckel and Kuhn, *Hitler*, 909 (speech of 20 April 1923).

47. Koerber, *Adolf Hitler*, 73; Jäckel and Kuhn, *Hitler*, 960n (speech of 1 August 1923).

48. Koerber, *Adolf Hitler*, 84; Jäckel and Kuhn, *Hitler*, 989 (speech of 21 August 1923).

49. Kursell, *Adolf Hitlers Reden*, 157 ("Aussprüche Adolf Hitlers").

50. Preiss, *Adolf Hitler in Franken*, 30 (speech of 2 March 1925).

51. Bundesarchiv Koblenz NS26/54/145 (speech of 26 March 1927).

52. Bundesarchiv Koblenz NS26/55/3 (speech of 30 September 1928: newspaper résumé).

53. For additional examples, see Binion, "Hitler Looks East," 105–8.

54. *Völkischer Beobachter*, 27 January 1921: Bundesarchiv Koblenz NS26/51/34-35.

55. A few examples out of hundreds: *Völkischer Beobachter*, 28 April 1921; Bundesarchiv Koblenz NS26/51/114; Jochmann, *Im Kampf um die Macht*, 70–78 (speech of 28 February 1926); Bundesarchiv Koblenz NS26/55/123-34 (speech of 9 November 1928); Preiss, *Adolf Hitler in Franken*, 90–91, 100 (speech of 8 December 1928), and 160–61 (speech of 13 November 1930); Bundesarchiv Koblenz NS26/52/76 (speech of 7 November 1930) and 90–92 (speech of 8 November 1930).

56. On the problematics of Hitler's racism in terms of his expansionism, see Binion, "'Der Jude ist weg,'" 347–72, 396–401. (If Jews were parasites that debilitated their host nations, then on Hitler's own terms Germany's expansionist interest was to promote Jewish emigration to prospective enemy nations as against persecuting and then exterminating Jews at home and abroad.)

57. Bundesarchiv Koblenz NS26/55/140 (speech of 9 November 1928). Hitler drew the cover term *freedom* from his earlier, revisionist vocabulary: "For freedom we need in the first instance solidarity in our own land," he typically declared on 1 August 1923 (Preiss, *Adolf Hitler in Franken*, 11). A rich early source for the use of cover terms is Hitler's speech of 28 February 1926 to Hamburg's "National Club": Jochmann, *Im Kampf um die Macht*.

58. Bundesarchiv Koblenz NS26/52/76, 79, 82. In Hitler's vocabulary, "foreign markets" and "foreign supplies" fronted for "land and soil." Compare the wording in the speech of 27 January 1932 (below): "if we want to develop a new domestic market or to solve the problem of [living] space."

59. Ibid., 103.

60. Preiss, *Adolf Hitler in Franken*, 177.

61. Domarus, *Hitler*, 84–88. "Ferment of decomposition" was a familiar epithet for the Jews (attributed to Theodor Mommsen); by pluralizing it ("ferments"), Hitler ostensibly broadened the reference. While he stressed Marxism and the class struggle to exemplify the Jews' work of decomposition, he might also cite other divisions wrought by Jews among Germans, including "the division into parties promoted by Jewish influence and pushed to a drastic extreme" (*Völkischer Beobachter*, 27 January 1921: Bundesarchiv Koblenz NS26/51/36).

62. Preiss, *Adolf Hitler in Franken*, 186 (speech of 30 July 1932).

63. Vogelsang, "Hitlers Brief an Reichenau vom 4. Dezember 1932," 437.

64. Vogelsang, "Neue Dokumente zur Geschichte der Reichswehr 1930–1933," 434–35.

65. This holds even if Hitler did conclude that, once "political power" were regained, expansionism would be pursued either economically or ("and probably better") militarily: ibid. Cf. above, n. 58.

4—The Sublime and the Grotesque

1. Thorslev, "Incest as Romantic Symbol," 50.

2. *Don Juan*, X:53.

3. *Prometheus Unbound*, IV:471.

4. 13 July 1831.

5. Chateaubriand, *Oeuvres romanesques et voyages*, 139 *("criminelle passion")*.

6. Alfred de Vigny, *Éloa ou la soeur des anges*, Chant Troisième.

7. Grillparzer, *Die Ahnfrau*, V, 2:3011–12 (1817).

8. Maigron, *Le romantisme et les moeurs*, 312–50 and passim. For third-tier Romantic suicides, see ibid., 315, n. 1.

9. Alfred de Vigny, *Moïse*.

10. "Midnight Musing," lines 2–5.

11. See Koch, *Heinrich von Kleist*, 303–7 and passim.

12. Schenk, *The Mind of the European Romantics*, 64.

13. Durkheim, *Le suicide*, 315.

14. *Hallin's Lovelife*.

15. *Nachtwachen von Bonaventura*, Achte Nachtwache.

16. Diary entry, 12 September 1839: Kaplan, *Mother Death*, 90.

17. *Childe Harold*, III:72.

18. Ibid., III:90.

19. "The Infinite."

20. Kaplan, *Mother Death*, 188; entry of 20 November 1847.

21. Chateaubriand, *Oeuvres romanesques et voyages*, 144.

22. Letter 1. (Frankenstein's own fate parallels the narrator's.)

23. "Bitte," Lieder. ("*Will einer merken lassen / Dass er es mit Gott hält, / So muss er keck erfassen / Die arge, böse Welt.*")

24. *Childe Harold*, III:113.

25. *Adolphe*, ch. X.

26. Balzac, *Le père Goriot*, 309.

27. Alfred de Vigny, *Moïse*.

28. Edgar Allan Poe, "Eleonora," first paragraph.

29. Letter to Thomas Butts, 11 September 1801.

30. Letter 84.

31. Preface to *Mary Tudor* (1833).

32. *William Shakespeare*.

33. "À celle qui est voilée," *Les contemplations*. (*"Je suis le proscrit qui se voile, / Qui songe et chante loin du bruit, / Avec la chouette et l'étoile, / La sombre chanson de la nuit."*)

34. "Rêverie de Charles VI" (*"Il semble que Dieu dise à mon âme souffrante: / Quitte ce monde impur, la foule indifférente"*).

35. Furst, "Novalis' *Hymnen an die Nacht* and Nerval's *Aurélia*."

36. Christian Grabbe, *Hannibal*, V:iv.

37. *Don Juan*, II:204.

38. Thorslev, "Incest as Romantic Symbol," 41.

39. *Ode to a Nightingale*, III.

40. *Heinrich von Ofterdingen*, II.

41. *Ode to a Nightingale*, VIII.

42. "Intimations of Immortality from Recollections of Early Childhood," V.

43. Percy Bysshe Shelley, "Mont Blanc," III.

44. III:113–14.

45. Georg Büchner, *Dantons Tod*, I:v.

46. Poe, "Eleonora," first paragraph.

47. Abrams, "English Romanticism," 31.

48. *Lectures on the Philosophy of World History*.

49. Books Tenth, Eleventh.

50. "Nachtrag zu dem Raisonnement des Herrn Professor Kant über das Verhältnis zwischen Theorie und Praxis."

51. "Signatur des Zeitalters" (1820), quoted by Schenk, *The Mind of the European Romantics*, 12.

52. "An die Deutschen."

53. "Donnernd bebt die Erd' in Felsenklüften."

54. "Religious Musings."

55. Letter to George Coleridge, early April 1798.

56. "Der Zeitgeist." (*"Du in der dunklen Wolke . . . / Zu wild, bang ists ringsum, und es / Trümmert und wankt ja, wohin ich blicke."*)

57. Untitled poem sent to Friedrich Schlegel.

58. *Europe and the Revolution* (1821).

59. *Elements of Politics*.

60. "Last Song" (1809/1810).

61. *The Spirit of the Age* (1825).

62. Shelley to Byron, 8 September 1816, in Byron, *Correspondence*, 25; preface to *The Revolt of Islam* (1817).

63. *Childe Harold*, IV:97; cf. Byron, *Correspondence*, 148.

64. Honour, *Romanticism*, 19.

65. Honour, *Neo-Classicism*, 186. I elided the words "and the betrayal of its principles under the Empire" because the belief at issue was already overturned by the Terror, as Honour's own examples show, whereas Napoleon had his enthusiasts among the Romantics.

66. Examples from Bousquet, *Les thèmes du rêve*, 227–29.

67. Shelley, *Frankenstein*, 57, 74, 188, 173, 186.

68. *Don Juan*, IV:30–36.

69. Büchner, II:v.

70. "Fuyons, mon âme...," *Recueillements poétiques*.

71. Balzac, *Le père Goriot*, scene of Vautrin's arrest.

72. Büchner, I:i.

73. For the scholarly linkage of Romanticism with the Revolution, see especially Abrams, "English Romanticism," passim.

5—Being, Doing, Having

1. Jean-Paul Sartre devoted the last fourth of his *Being and Nothingness* to the concepts of Being, Doing, and Having in the abstract, calling them "the cardinal categories of human reality" and again "the three great categories of concrete human existence." The terms have been used elsewhere in a variety of special philosophical or psychological ways—especially Being, as when Erich Fromm in *To Have Or To Be?* championed it as an antithesis of object-dependence.

2. *Galateo* (1550–1555).

3. Erasmus, *The Education of a Christian Prince*, 151–52.

4. That Castiglione spoke for his times in his advocacy of Being is confirmed by the contrast between *The Book of the Courtier* and its rival for celebrity in High Renaissance letters, *The Prince* by Machiavelli. For Machiavelli, the test of a prince's personal worth lay in his effective action, which often turned on trickery. True, Machiavelli advised the Prince that in the last resort "those methods alone are good, are certain, are lasting, that depend on yourself and your own ingenuity" (Ch. XXIV), which might seem to shift the stress back to Being; the political workability of those self-devised "methods" remained no less the supreme test of their worth for Machiavelli. But Machiavelli shocked his times precisely because he judged political qualities solely by their efficacy.

5. Raffael, *Castiglione*, Musée du Louvre.

6. Perhaps its closest rival is Jacopo Pontormo's majestic *Portrait of a Lady in a Red Dress* of 1532–1533: Städelsches Kunstinstitut, Frankfurt/Main.

7. Rosenberg, Slive, and Kuile, *Dutch Art and Architecture*, 102; Haak, *Rembrandt*, 162–63. Rembrandt's *Self-Portrait* of 1640 and Titian's *Man with the Blue Sleeve*, National Gallery, London.

8. Gracián, *Obras completas*, ed. Arturo del Hoyo, 154 ("Oráculo manual y arte de prudencia," 1647): "5. Hombre en su punto. No se hace hecho; vase de cada día perficionando en la persona, en el empleo, hasta llegar al punto del consumado ser."

9. Gracián, *Obras completas*, 254 ("El heroe," 1637): "los empeños plausibles."

10. Ibid., 245.

11. Ibid., 264–66.

12. Correas, 256a.

13. Montaigne, *Essais* ("De la praesumption," 1580), 745.

14. Edmund Spenser, *The Faerie Queen* (1589), 6.9.3, quoted by Greenblatt, *Renaissance Self-Fashioning*, 2.

15. Pascal, *Oeuvres complètes*, 1123 ("Pensées," 1662).

16. Mascarille (the fake marquis) in Molière, *Les précieuses ridicules*, Scene IX.

17. Carlyle, *Carlyle's Complete Works*, 154 ("The English" in "Past and Present"). Cf. Emerson, *Complete Essays*, 150 ("Self-Reliance"): "But do your work, and I shall know you."

18. Aging Diderot had turned this corner already. Blum, *Diderot*, 125, quotes Diderot in 1773: "we can only give the name good to one who does good" and comments that "the verb of activity . . . had replaced the verb of essence."

19. Stendhal, *Le rouge et le noir*, Book I, ch. 12: "Between himself and the most heroic deeds, the young peasant [Julien] saw nothing but a lack of opportunity."

20. Smiles, *Self-Help*, 383.

21. *The Concert*, National Museum of Women in the Arts, Washington, D.C.; *Self-Portrait*, National Gallery of Art, Washington, D.C.

22. Museo del Prado, Madrid; Kunsthistorisches Museum, Vienna. Except occasionally where they posed as Saint Luke painting the Virgin, the rare painters who depicted themselves full-face and nominally on the job in the age of Being gave the merest

token hint of that job itself while highlighting themselves overdressed in their Sunday best: see the self-portraits by Catharina van Hemessen, Öffentliche Kunstsammlungen, Basel (1548); Isaac van Swanenburgh, Stedelijk Museum, Leiden (1568); Abraham de Vries, Rijksmuseum, Amsterdam (1621); David Teniers II, Gemäldegalerie der Akademie der Künste, Vienna (c. 1650); etc. It may be relevant that the self-portrait of an artist at work, being perforce done through a mirror, is perforce inauthentic insofar as the mirror image must be reversed as to left-and-right and the artist's eyes redirected to the work in progress.

23. William Hogarth, *David Garrick as Richard III,* Walker Art Gallery, Liverpool; François-André Vincent, *Mademoiselle Duplant,* Museu Calouste Gulbenkian, Lisbon.

24. Maurice Quentin de La Tour, *Madame de Pompadour,* Musée du Louvre, Paris.

25. Alfred Lord Tennyson, "The Charge of the Light Brigade" (1855).

26. Benjamin Price, quoted by Briggs, *Victorian People,* epigraph to ch. 6.

27. Nightingale, *Cassandra,* 36.

28. Henry James, *The Portrait of a Lady,* Chapter XX.

29. Earlier partial exceptions tended to stress the picturesque: thus Antoine Raspal's lovely *Sewing Studio* (toward 1760), Musée Réattu, Arles. Most nearly precursive of *Work* is William Hogarth's print cycle *The Industrious and Idle Apprentice* (1747).

30. 1849 (destroyed), 1857 (Musée du Louvre), 1852–1865 (Manchester City Art Gallery).

31. Bulwer-Lytton, *England and the English,* 57.

32. Fichte, *Sämtliche Werke,* 249; quoted by Robertson, 153.

33. Hess, *Ausgewählte Schriften,* 131 ("Philosophie der Tat," 1843).

34. *Zur Genealogie der Moral,* I:13.

35. Ibid., III:8.

36. *John Gabriel Borkman* (1896), Act III.

37. Ibid., Act IV.

38. Thomas Mann, *Tod in Venedig* (1912).

39. Henry James, *The Portrait of a Lady,* Chapter XIX.

40. William James, *The Principles of Psychology,* 291.

41. Simmel, *Philosophie des Geldes,* 355–56 and passim. Leopold II of Belgium concurred: he had the Antwerp railroad station, which he inaugurated in 1905, adorned "with the heraldic motif of the beehive standing not, as one might at first think, for . . . industrious labor as a social good, but symbolizing the principle of capital accumulation": Sebald, *Austerlitz,* 12.

42. Wells, *Tono-Bungay,* 249.

43. Lowenthal, *Literature,* 110–18.

44. Ortega y Gasset, *La rebelión de las masas,* 92.

45. Packard, *The Hidden Persuaders,* 23.

46. Packard, *The Waste Makers.*

47. Galbraith, *The Affluent Society,* xxii. Here and immediately below I quote from Galbraith's résumé of his 1958 work in his new preface to it dated 1984.

48. Ibid., xii.

49. Ibid., xxxii.

50. Ibid., xvii.

51. Ibid., xii. Galbraith himself accorded consumption great social value when, over a quarter century later, he expressed the huge success of *The Affluent Society* in terms of its "sales of some millions of copies": ibid., xi. No wonder he could then report no headway made against those dominant values in America: ibid., xi–xxxvii ("*The Affluent Society* Revisited") .

52. Perec, *Les choses,* 18.

53. Ibid., 25.

54. Ibid., 38.

55. Ibid., 86.
56. Ibid., 141.
57. Fourastié, *Le grand espoir*, 382.
58. Baudrillard, *Le système des objets*, 241.
59. Ibid., 282. Further: ibid., 283: "The disappointed demand for totality at the heart of the project is the source of the systematic and indefinite process of consumption."
60. Closets, *Le bonheur en plus*, 261.
61. Ibid.
62. Ibid., 263.
63. Ibid., 260.
64. Stoetzel, *Les valeurs*, 210–14.
65. Baudrillard, *La société de consommation*, notes this desire on the consumer's part for ever new needs, arguing that it is no mere artifact of advertising but (somehow) "a product of the mode of production" (103).
66. On such paradigmatic consumers: Baudrillard, *La société de consommation*, 53.
67. Noble *"scheinen"* vs. bourgeois *"leisten und schaffen"*: quoted by Auerbach, *Mimesis*, 396, from *Wilhelm Meisters Lehrjahre*, Book 5, Chapter 3.
68. Ortega y Gasset, *La rebelión de las masas*, chapters 1, 7, and passim.

6—Three Mourning Mothers

1. On the Christian origins and uses of the concept: Auerbach, "Figura," 11–76. On its Jewish roots and uses: Funkenstein, *Perceptions of Jewish History*, 13–14, 98–121. On its centrality to the medieval outlook: Auerbach, "Figura," 61ff. and passim. For "figure" and "figural" (or "typological") in my usage below: ibid., 28–49.
2. Matthew 2:18 (Jeremiah 31:15: "are not"). In Jeremiah's Hebrew and Matthew's Greek (as also in the Latin of the later Vulgate), this phrase could mean equally *were dead* or *were absent*, about like the English *were gone* (cf. Genesis 5:2). Though the Lord promptly cleared up the ambiguity for Rachel (Jeremiah 31:16: "they shall come back"), Matthew exploited it to establish a figural continuity from Ramah to Bethlehem.
3. Matthew 2:17.
4. Swarzenski, "Quellen zum deutschen Andachtsbild," 142; Reiners-Ernst, *Das freudevolle Vesperbild*, 75; Küppers, "Marienklage," 279; Belting, *The Image and its Public*, 32.
5. Swarzenski, "Quellen zum deutschen Andachtsbild," 142; Reiners-Ernst, *Das freudevolle Vesperbild*, 31–32; Meiss, "Sleep in Venice," 360–61; Tselos, "The Pietà," 63.
6. Lafontaine-Dosogne, *Histoire*, 168. Further: Brandt, "Michelangelo's 'Pietà,'" 91.
7. For Joachim as against much of his artistic discipleship, the second recurrence was still to come. (Joachim drew largely on Augustine: Auerbach, "Figura," 41.)
8. Kötzsche-Breitenbruch, "Zur Ikonographie," 104–15.
9. On this Oriental gesture: Maguire, "The Depiction of Sorrow," 158–60. Ramah was no more Oriental than Bethlehem, but European depictions tended to Europeanize the Massacre apart from that gesture.
10. On Rachel in eastern Christian art: Lafontaine-Dosogne, "Iconography," 230–34.
11. Bibliothèque Nationale, Paris, lat. 9428, fol. 31a. On Drogo and his sacramentary: Pfister, "Drogon," 101–45; Koehler, *Die karolingischen Miniaturen*, 101–5; Simon,"Studies on the Drogo Sacramentary"; Calkins, "Drogo Sacramentary," 17–23.
12. Koehler, *Die karolingischen Miniaturen*, 101; Simon, "Studies," vii, xiii.
13. Körte, "Deutsche Vesperbilder in Italien," 16–17, published one such ninth-century–B.C. statuette as a chance prefiguration of the Pietà. Musée des Beaux-Arts, Lyon, *Bronzes antiques de Sardaigne*, catalogues three (Nos. 15, 25, 33) and reproduces

one different from Körte's that Ariès, *L'enfant,* 54 and n. 3, calls "a sort of pietà." Less clear-cut, but older, is a damaged wooden statue in the Egyptian Museum in Cairo of a woman with what looks like a tiny dead man lying on her lap and three tinier girls standing there.

14. Louvre, Paris, signed "Douris," 490–480 B.C.; cited by Janson, *History of Art,* 98, as "strongly prophetic of the Christian Pietà." Cf. Vermeule, *Aspects of Death,* ch. V, figs. 3, 21, 28.

15. Cf. Körte, "Deutsche Vesperbilder in Italien," 17. Partial exceptions in classical sculpture include Menelaus holding the limp body of Patroclus on the battlefield (copy in the Loggia dei Lanzi, Florence) and a Gaul between killing his wife and killing himself (Museo delle Terme, Rome).

16. Maguire, *Art and Eloquence,* 27, and "The Classical Tradition," 96. (Euripides' Agave had done just this in a passage of *The Bacchae* applied to Mary and the dead Christ in the Byzantine compilation *Christus patiens.*)

17. Maguire, *Art and Eloquence,* 27, and "Classical Tradition," 96.

18. A finer but severely mutilated version survives in the monastery of Santo Domingo de Silos (Burgos), and a more sophisticated, classicistic one adorns the tomb of Doña Blanca, Abbey of Santa Maria la Real, Logroño (Navarre).

19. On the lesser lap-type variant with the son still alive, cf. below, n. 31.

20. Three on the nave of Sant'Angelo in Formis, Capua; five in the Gospel Book of Otto III, Clm. 4453, Cim. 58, f. 30v, Staatsbibliothek, Munich—otherwise virtually identical with Codex Egberti, f. 15v, in Trier, and with Henry III's Pericope, b. 21, f. 13r, in the Staatsbibliothek, Bremen.

21. Gr. 74, 510, Bibliothèque Nationale, Paris; Golden Gospel Book of Echternach 156412, Germanisches Nationalmuseum, Nuremberg; Gr. 1156, f. 280v, Vatican Library, Rome; Add. 39627, f. 11r, British Museum, London; etc.

22. For this received view: Grabar, "L'asymétrie," 9–24.

23. Heimann, "Capital Frieze," 80; Demus, *Romanesque Mural Painting,* pl. 153; Sauerländer, *Gothic Sculpture in France,* 386, 388–91, 394; Crown, "The Winchester Psalter," 81, fig. 9 (possibly an interpolation by Viollet-le-Duc—and in that case visibly after the Chartres window). For a vertical departure from the lap-type, see Lapeyre, *Les façades,* fig. 62, on Le Mans; Cahn, "The 'Tympanum' of Saint-Pierre," 119–26; and below, n. 50.

24. They may include the Alsatian church window shown in Bruck, *Die elsässische Glasmalerei,* plate 17, now destroyed, but this was more likely the nineteenth-century restorer's handiwork after a period original: cf. nn. 413, 440.

25. "Childhood of Christ" Window, Saint Pierre-Saint Paul Cathedral, Troyes; Ingeborg Psalter 1695, f. 18v, Musée Condé, Chantilly (evidently modeled on the Chartres window: cf. Panofsky, "Zur künstlerischen Abkunft," 127); Bible Moralisée, Lat. 11560, f. 86, Bibliothèque Nationale, Paris; Psalter and Hours, Lat. 1073A, f. 7v, Bibliothèque Nationale, Paris; Codex Vindobonensis 2554, f. 16r, Österreichische Nationalbibliothek, Vienna; Lewis 185, f. 6v, Philadelphia Free Library. (Cf. n. 406 for the Christian and pagan sources of this dismemberment.) A non-kneeling Massacre mother with arms aloft might likewise have a decapitated infant at her feet as in the Saint-Trophime cloister, Arles, c. 1190. The west portal of Le Mans Cathedral, c. 1158, shows a mother bent over her dead (?) son but raising him upright.

26. Millet, *Recherches,* 489–90; Tselos, "The Pietà," 59–60.

27. Millet, *Recherches,* 495; Kartsonis, *Anastasis,* 167, 169, 185, 229; Tselos, "The Pietà," 56–57.

28. Schiller, *Ikonographie,* 187–88; Millet, *Recherches,* passim; Tselos, "The Pietà," 63–67.

29. On the Byzantine impress: Lafontaine-Dosogne, *Histoire,* 153–88. On the relevant compositional factors of the evolving Lamentation (Jesus grounded, head left; Mary kneeling, left arm around his chest): Millet, *Recherches,* 489–516; Tselos, "The Pietà," 57–67.

30. On the Crucifixion as fulfillment in Matthew's gospel itself, see Binion, *Sounding the Classics*, 21–31.

31. Hofstätter, "Bethlehemitischer Kindermord," 341, 343. Later the lap-type Massacre subgroup-of-two with the son still alive was normally modeled after Mary holding the infant Jesus: see, e.g., Cotton Caligula, A VII, f. 7 r, British Museum; Smith-Lesouëf 20, f. 11v, Bibliothèque Nationale; plate 12 of the Golden Gospel Book of Echternach 156412, Germanisches Nationalmuseum, 1053–56; the mid-twelfth-century painted arch of the Saint-Aubin abbey in Angers; or the early-thirteenth-century miniature from the Waldkirch Psalter, Codex Breviary 125, f. 45v, in Württembergische Landesbibliothek.

32. On this pronounced resemblance: Hamann, *Die Holztür*, 14; Wesenberg, *Frühe mittelalterliche Bildwerke*, text to plates 55–58. For a later, Byzantine equivalence, cf. Millet, *Monuments byzantins de Mistra*, 93.3 (church of the Brontochion, Mistra). How closely the two like figures in Cologne were meant to neighbor is uncertain, as the door panels are no longer in their original order: Schäfke, *St. Maria im Kapitol*, 22.

33. Cathedral museum, Salerno.

34. Young, *Ordo Rachelis*, 18, 30, 33, 35, 47, and *Drama*, 112, 116. (Cf. nn. 406 and 415 for a parallel Byzantine identification of the dead Christ with a mutilated innocent.)

35. Boskovits, "Un pittore 'espressionista' del trecento umbro," 115–30 and fig. 3; Todini, *La pittura umbra*, 138–39; Lunghi, "La decorazione pittorica," 204–30. A fifth mother at the back of the row holds no child.

36. Variously attributed hit-and-miss to Simone da Bologna, Jacopo de' Bavasi, and Andrea de' Bartoli.

37. School of Meo da Siena (?), on the Santa Scala. For a Perugian miniature in this series see Previtali, *Giotto e la sua bottega*, fig. 169a. For a Tuscan one see Palazzo Pubblico, Siena, *Il gotico a Siena*, 51, and Soldano, *Miniature*, Table XXV,1.

38. Hours of Jeanne d'Évreux, 1325–1328; south portal, Worms cathedral, c. 1300; two wooden sculptures from a shrine (Västergötland), late 13th century. Jean Pucelle, painter of the Hours of Jeanne d'Évreux, derived this mourning mother specifically from Giovanni Pisano's Pistoian pulpit a quarter century later (see just below): Ferber, "Jean Pucelle and Giovanni Pisano," 69. Comparing Giovanni's figures with Pucelle's derivative, Ferber aptly notes: "In both cases . . . the mothers' grief has them oblivious to the grisly deeds taking place behind and above them."

39. Auct. D.3.4, f. 282v, Bodleian Library, Oxford. (Square four of the nine already shows Herod ordering the Massacre.)

40. Nolan, "Narrative," 173–74, 178—but cf. n. 44 below. Comparably, the Massacre appears just below and after the Passion on late-thirteenth-century panels of a window in the Saint-Martin church in Louze, but this may not be the original sequence.

41. Mellini, *Giovanni Pisano*, 65. (Giovanni's sequence was rearranged in the early nineteenth century.)

42. Wilkins-Sullivan, "Some Old Testament Themes," 606.

43. Christie, *English Medieval Embroidery*, 159–61 and Plate CXII.

44. Borsook, *Mural Painters*, 2nd ed., 45; cf. n. 40 above. Duccio may have been Barna's source for this shift (reminiscent of the one in Notre-Dame at Étampes): Borsook, *Mural Painters*, 1st ed., 138; White, *Duccio*, 121; Wilkins-Sullivan, "Some Old Testament Themes on the Front Predella of Duccio's Maestà," 607–8, and Ragusa and Wilkins-Sullivan, Letters, 646–49. On this same shift, cf. Bucher, *The Pamplona Bibles*, 23.

45. Dillenberger, *Style and Content*, 80.

46. *Lamentation*, Perugia, mid-thirteenth century [Swarzenski, "Italienische Quellen," 129]; *Lamentation* (Italian), Yale University, mid-thirteenth century; *Lamentation*, Baptistery, Florence, late thirteenth century; *Entombment* (Guido da Siena

workshop), Pinacoteca, Siena, late thirteenth century; *Crucifixion* (Cimabue), upper church of San Francesco, Assisi, c. 1290. The Rachel gesture is displaced onto another mourner behind Mary Magdalen at Christ's feet in both Bartolo di Fredi's and Andrea di Bartolo's Lamentations of about 1388.

47. Swarzenski, "Italienische Quellen," 130–31; Körte, "Deutsche Vesperbilder in Italien," 9–11. Most intriguing is the Pietà-like fresco in the Basilica di Santa Chaira, Naples, though precious little of the original remains.

48. Körte, "Deutsche Vesperbilder in Italien," passim.

49. Swarzenski, "Quellen zum deutschen Andachtsbild," 142; Panofsky, "Reintegration," 490–91 and n. 42, and *Early Netherlandish Painting*, vol. 1, 44 and n. 2; Wilkins-Sullivan, "Some Old Testament Themes," 605 (one of the grieving mothers in Duccio's Massacre "holds her dead son in her lap in a pose anticipating the *Pietà*").

50. Ferber, "Jean Pucelle and Giovanni Pisano," 69; cf. above, n. 38. Comparably, a Romanesque portal in Nuaillé-sur-Boutonne depicted the Massacre through a mother and child alone on their arch-stone: Dahl, "Nuaillé-sur-Boutonne," 301; Crozet, *L'art roman en Saintonge,* 137. Their vertical embrace anticipates one on the cathedral in Le Mans with the mother kneeling, which may have derived from the royal portal in Chartres. The space around the lap-type mourning was already self-contained in Worms and Stockholm too: cf. above, n. 38.

51. Pinder, "Die dichterische Wurzel der Pietà," 145–63, and *Die Pietà,* 3–4; Reiners-Ernst, *Das freudevolle Vesperbild,* 8–37; Dobrzeniecki, "Medieval Sources of the Pietà," passim.

52. Around 1325 a church in Westhofen (Alsace) may have included a Pietà in a stained-glass sequence of scenes from the life of Christ: Bruck, *Die elsässische Glasmalerei,* 53 and plate 16. However, Schauenbourg, "Mémoire du Baron de Schauenbourg," 261–63, does not mention this image among the fragments of the church before it was restored, no doubt after post-1325 models (cf. above, n. 25). The Pietà pose crept into Lamentations abroad later in the fourteenth century, but that was something again: Swarzenski, "Italienische Quellen der deutschen Pietà," 130.

53. Passarge, "Das deutsche Vesperbild im Mittelalter," 3.

54. Körte, "Deutsche Vesperbilder in Italien," 8–9.

55. Reiners-Ernst, *Das freudevolle Vesperbild,* 36–37.

56. Compare nn. 4–6 above.

57. Panofsky, "Reintegration," 491, and *Early Netherlandish Painting*, vol. 1, 44 n.2—perhaps picking up on Lill, "Die früheste deutsche Vespergruppe," 660–62, and Swarzenski, "Quellen zum deutschen Andachtsbild," 142 n. 7.

58. On this disintegration see also Auerbach, "Figura," 61 and 236 n. 43, and Huizinga, *Waning,* 194 and passim.

59. Huizinga, *Waning,* 148.

60. Servetus, *Christianismi restitutio,* 457 *("ploratus Rachel, quasi tertio repetitus")* and passim. The third figural term of Rachel's lamenting in Servetus is not Mary's lamenting, but a chorus of the sons of God, the church, and the angels in heaven.

61. Cf. n. 46 above. On the problematical subject matter of this painting: Graeve, "Stone of Unction," 223–38; Tselos, "The Pietà," 55–56, 68, and passim.

62. Huizinga, *Waning,* 148.

63. Jeremiah 31:16.

7—Death on a Rampage

1. My account of the Black Death relies throughout on Cohn, *The Black Death Transformed,* and personal communications from the author in addition to the other sources cited below.

2. It spared much of Flanders and Poland as well as Nuremberg until the second big wave, Milan until the third, Iceland and sparsely populated stretches of Finland indefinitely.

3. Chronicler of Meaux Abbey, London, quoted in Horrox, *The Black Death*, 69. The chronicler for Padua attributed the sudden deaths to "blood poisoning": ibid., 35. Some commentators add a secondary septicemic to the secondary pneumonic plague.

4. Benedictow, *The Black Death 1346-1353*, 245-384.

5. Whenever it recurred, it might nonetheless spread into areas it had originally missed.

6. Cohn, *The Black Death Transformed*, 250-51.

7. See Hay, *Europe*.

8. Mollat and Wolff, *Ongles bleus: "synchronisme"* 143, 271; quotation 180, from the Great Chronicle of Saint-Denis. Further: ibid., 109, 139, 143, 185, 271-72. The expression "plague of a rebellion" was not unprecedented: TeBrake, *A Plague of Insurrection*, 1, quotes the *Chronicon comitum Flandrensium* calling the Flemish rebellion of 1325-1328 "this plague of people rebelling against their superiors"; cf. Pirenne, *Histoire de Belgique*, 305.

9. Cohn, *The Black Death Transformed*, with its exacting, exhaustive comparison of the two plagues, lays the false equivalence to rest. See also Cohn, "The Black Death," 703-38.

10. Horrox, *The Black Death*, 246.

11. Guy de Chauliac, quoted by Bulst, "Der schwarze Tod," 57. Ibid., 57-58: "When pest accounts composed independently of one another are read comparatively, it is especially striking how many of them use almost the same words at times to depict the social breakup brought about by the plague."

12. Horrox, *The Black Death*, 44, 43.

13. Ibid., 74. Further: Aberth, *Apocalypse*, 154.

14. Nohl, *The Black Death*, 207-26, 263; Ziegler, *The Black Death*, 271-72; Deaux, *The Black Death 1347*, 145; Aberth, *Apocalypse*, 151-55. The *locus classicus* for this account of the bipolar reaction to the Black Death is Giovanni Boccaccio's introduction to *The Decameron* of 1348-1353.

15. Nohl, *The Black Death*, 207-8, 263-64; Ziegler, *The Black Death*, 87; Tuchman, *A Distant Mirror*, 114.

16. Nohl, *The Black Death*, 327. Further: Graus, *Pest—Geissler—Judenmorde*, 38-59; Aberth, *Apocalypse*, 155-58. Nominally they were reenacting Christ's torture.

17. Cohn, *The Black Death Transformed*, 242-43.

18. Herlihy, *Black Death*, 64.

19. Nohl, *The Black Death*, 212.

20. Matteo Villani, quoted by Meiss, *Florence and Siena*, 67.

21. Jean de Venette, quoted by Mollat and Wolff, *Ongles bleus*, 109; cf. Horrox, *The Black Death*, 57.

22. Wenzel, "Pestilence," 132.

23. Horrox, *The Black Death*, 74.

24. Ibid., 57. Further: Aberth, *Apocalypse*, 134-35.

25. Rodolico, *La democrazia fiorentina*, 35; Cohn, *Women in the Streets*, 22, and *The Black Death Transformed*, 192-93. Recovery data for 1360-1374 are unavailable.

26. Other Tuscan towns such as San Gimignano have yet to regain their pre-1348 numbers.

27. Huizinga, *Waning*, 13; cf. Dimier, *Les danses macabres*, 21-22.

28. Chaney, *La danse macabré*, 4-5, 9-10. For consistency I write "Dance of the Dead" throughout even though it gradually became a "Dance of Death" with a single dance master representing or personifying death: see Stegemeier, *Dance of Death*, 6, 9-10.

29. On the Dance of the Dead as originally performative: Kastner, *Les danses des morts*, viii and 135-310; Dimier, *Les danses macabres*, 14, 27-29; Williams, "The Dance of Death," 229; Carco, *La danse des morts*, 22-24 and passim; Chaney, *La danse macabré*, 3; Mâle, *L'art religieux*, 361-63; Clark, *Dance of Death*, 93; Brion-Guerry, *Le*

thème, 59 n. 3; Saugnieux, *Les danses macabres*, 30–32; Tuchman, *A Distant Mirror*, 505–7; Collins, *Dance of Death*, 14, 24; Wirth, *La jeune fille et la mort*, 21–22; Aberth, *Apocalypse*, 205–7. Possibly a first remote allusion occurs in a Netherlandish poem of about 1350, *Maugis d'Aigremont*, that mentions a dance in a circle "as if by dead men [*als van doden*]": Huet, "La danse Macabré," 161–63; Siciliano, *François Villon*, 245 n.2. The Dance of the Dead continued to be performed in sermonic masques and dramas well into the sixteenth century. A far-fetched supposed precedent for it is cited by Clark, *Dance of Death*, 93–94: at the nuptials of Alexander III of Scotland in 1285 a military dance came to an eerie halt after a spectral figure glided among the dancers.

30. Nohl, *The Black Death*, 37. It was still being depicted in Breton ossuaries as late as 1635 and 1639–1640: Croix, *La Bretagne*, 1185 n. 175.

31. Mollaret and Brossollet, *La peste*, 73; cf. Stegemeier, *Dance of Death*, 63.

32. Stegemeier, *Dance of Death*, 6.

33. Rosenfeld, *Der mittelalterliche Totentanz*, convincingly attributes a Latin original to a Dominican writing in or near Würzburg toward 1360. Further: Rosenfeld, "Der Totentanz," 74–82; Hammerstein, *Tanz und Musik des Todes*, 29. "*Faire la danse de macabré*" may have meant to have the plague: Stegemeier, *Dance of Death*, 50–52, 62–64.

34. Saugnieux, *Les danses macabres*, 46–53, however, argues that the Spanish *Dança general* came out of an independent Aragonese tradition.

35. Mâle, *L'art religieux*, 347.

36. It was French for Glixelli, *Les cinq poèmes*, and Rotzler, *Die Begegnung*, Italian for Brion-Guerry, *Le thème*, Rosenfeld, *Der mittelalterliche Totentanz*, Tenenti, *La vie et la mort*, and *Il senso*, and Pavel Chihaia, *Immortalité*. For Aberth, *Apocalypse*, 196–99, it came to Italy pictorially in the eleventh century but was first poetized in late-thirteenth-century France.

37. Brion-Guerry, *Le thème*, passim; Tenenti, *La vie et la mort*, 19–23.

38. Aberth, *Apocalypse*, 206.

39. Mâle, *L'art religieux*, 365.

40. See especially Rosenfeld, *Der mittelalterliche Totentanz*, 58–61, 182, and passim, and "Der Totentanz," 81–82. A free adaptation of the Innocents text into English by the Benedectine monk John Lydgate toward 1346 did twice mention the plague: Aberth, *Apocalypse*, 210–11. The object lesson in traumatic reliving provided by the Dance of the Dead suffices to refute the tack taken by (among others) Binsky, *Medieval Death*, 133, that the Dance was "an internal development of medieval visual culture itself" and only chanced to originate after the Black Death.

41. Horrox, *The Black Death*, 40.

42. Ibid., 44.

43. Rosenfeld, *Der mittelalterliche Totentanz*, 297 ("All mankind is reflected in the representatives of the several estates"); Wirth, *La jeune fille et la mort*, 55 ("humanity in its entirety"); Kaiser, *Der tanzende Tod*, 36 ("Death fetches all"); Goodwin, *Kitsch and Culture*, 51.

44. Guillaume de Machaut, *Le jugement dou Roy de Navarre*, l. 364 (*"tout tuoit et tout acouroit"*).

45. Quoted by Wenzel, "Pestilence," 133.

46. Ibid. (The ill-chosen image of grinding to dust had evidently lost its literal meaning for the Plowman.)

47. According to a papal bull of 1336, largely ignored outside the Dance of the Dead, one was already saved or damned at the moment of death: Hammerstein, *Tanz und Musik des Todes*, 24, 29. In even the earliest versions of the Dance a preacher or a death figure speaks of heaven *or* hell, but the option is foreclosed for those present because they have died unprepared.

48. Hammerstein, *Tanz und Musik des Todes*, 43.

49. Rosenfeld, *Der mittelalterliche Totentanz,* 293–300 and passim; Graus, *Pest— Geissler—Judenmorde,* 50; Horrox, *The Black Death,* 58.

50. Nohl, *The Black Death,* 250–59; Schumacher, *Die Krankheitsdarstellungen,* 72–75, 77–78, 89–90; Stegemeier, *Dance of Death,* 25; Graus, *Pest—Geissler—Judenmorde,* 49–52. Ibid., 51: "The unorganized, ecstatic impulse that so clearly and unmistakably broke through the 'dancing,' as it does through all spontaneous mass movements, contrasted sharply with the regulated ritual, with the downright 'standardized' procedures, of the flagellants."

51. Olds, "Love and Death," 5. Further: Stegemeier, *Dance of Death,* 17; Deaux, *The Black Death 1347,* 208; Kaiser, *Der tanzende Tod,* 66–67.

52. Rosenfeld, *Der mittelalterliche Totentanz,* 284; "Der Totentanz," 57, 82–83.

53. Cohn, "The Black Death," 707–10.

54. Cohn, *Cult of Remembrance,* 282 and passim; Cohn, "Group Process," 147.

55. Herlihy, *Black Death,* 70–73.

56. Nohl, *The Black Death,* 34. Further: ibid., 35, on "villages and boroughs."

57. Horrox, *The Black Death,* 4–5.

58. Nohl, *The Black Death,* 14; Deaux, *The Black Death 1347,* 151.

59. Horrox, *The Black Death,* 34.

60. Lisini and Iacometti, eds., *Cronache sinesi,* 55.

61. Horrox, *The Black Death,* 70.

62. Ibid., 58.

63. Nohl, *The Black Death,* 22.

64. Horrox, *The Black Death,* 61.

65. Glixelli, *Les cinq poèmes,* 28; Chihaia, *Immortalité,* 49–53.

66. Auerbach, *Mimesis,* 236 (*"hüllenlose kreatürliche Realistik"*) and passim.

67. Chaney, *La danse macabré,* 15: *"regardes nous / Mors, pourris, puans, descouvers."*

68. *"Comment nostre povre charongne est orde et vile, viande a vers"* ("Wherein our poor carcass is foul and filthy meat for worms"): Deschamps, *Oeuvres complètes,* 121 (*"Charoingne a vers, fiens pourris et ors, . . . / Garnis de poulz, de lentes et d'ordure, / Pissat, crachat").*

69. Burdach, *Vom Mittelalter zur Reformation,* 55 (*"ein kotfass, ein unreine speise, ein stankhaus, ein unlustiger spulzuber, ein faules as, ein schimelkaste, ein bodenloser sack, ein locherete tasche"),* 312–13.

70. François Villon, *Testament,* 316–17: *"Son fiel se creve sur son cuer, / Puis sue, Dieu scet quelle sueur!"*

71. Quoted by Dubruck, *Theme of Death,* 84 (*"Hé homme, puante pourriture!").*

72. Rosenfeld, *Der mittelalterliche Totentanz,* 37–38, 319–20, 319 n. 1.

73. John 1:1; Exodus 20:4.

74. Helm, *Skelett- und Todesdarstellungen,* 1–49; Stegemeier, *Dance of Death,* 8–16; Rosenfeld, *Der mittelalterliche Totentanz,* 18–23, 25–29; Wirth, *La jeune fille et la mort,* 38–43; Collins, *Dance of Death,* 15–17; Aberth, *Apocalypse,* 188–90.

75. For the skeletons: Helm, *Skelett- und Todesdarstellungen,* 70–76. Standing mummies crawling with vermin came closest to naturalism on their own symbolic terms in memento mori unrelated to the Black Death, such as engagement or marriage portraits with companion pieces showing the couple after death: see, e.g., Buchner, *Das deutsche Bildnis,* 171–75.

76. Two singular exceptions are a skeletal mummy holding a lantern beneath an intact penis in Pieter Brueghel's *The Triumph of Death* and Hans Baldung Grien's early drawing of *Death with an Inverted Banner* (1505?) based on his still earlier drawing of a live *Banner Carrier* (1504).

77. Horrox, *The Black Death,* 351. Lecherous necrophagous vermin went back in Christian art at least to serpents and toads feasting on Eve's breasts and her genitalia respectively atop the early-twelfth-century Moissac cathedral portal.

78. Traini apparently illustrated a derivative fourteenth-century south-Italian poem with the three corpses unequally decomposed: cf. Glixelli, *Les cinq poèmes,* 33–34, 39, 43, and Chihaia, *Immortalité,* 189–204. Chihaia, *Immortalité,* 203, following Baltrušaitis, *Le moyen âge fantastique,* 239–40, sees in Traini's corpses the three stages of bodily decomposition from "tumefaction" through "greenish viscosity" to "ivory-colored skeleton."

79. Polzer, "Aspects," 107–19. Bellosi, *Buffalmacco,* attributes it to Buonamico Buffalmacco rather than Traini and dates it c. 1336; cf. Baschet, "Image et événement," 28, 33.

80. Tenenti, *La vie et la mort,* 24 and passim: after Traini, Italian art in particular kept death symbolic and abstract.

81. Binion, *Love Beyond Death,* 85–86.

82. Cf. Wenzel, "Pestilence," 148–52: "the medieval plague experience left a surprisingly small and unremarkable imprint on the artistic consciousness and imagination in England," with art and letters not so much abstracting it away as avoiding the whole subject.

83. Meiss, *French Painting,* figs. 151–59, 163–66; Polzer, "Aspects," 116. Jean de Berry also had the fable of the Three Quick and Three Dead carved onto the portal of the church of the Innocents in Paris in 1408, though how realistically is unknown.

84. Polzer, "Aspects," 111, 114.

85. Ibid., 115.

86. Mollaret and Brossollet, *La peste,* 61–66; cf. Meiss, *Florence and Siena,* 77; Dinzelbacher, "Die tötende Gottheit," 5–138, and "La divinità mortifera," 147–50 and passim. The symbolism was age-old: *Iliad* I:46 likens a plague to burning arrows shot at mankind by Apollo.

87. Biraben, *Les hommes et la peste.* Further: Schumacher, *Die Kranksheitsdarstellungen,* 90: "Interestingly, not the period of the 'Black Death' itself, but only the later plague years after 1470, witnessed their depiction."

88. These sores suggest ailments besides the plague, especially ergotism: see Hayum, *The Isenheim Altarpiece,* 17–22; Matossian, *Poisons of the Past,* 12 and passim; Monick, *Evil,* 89–102. The next big step toward plague realism was Tintoretto's in his works of the mid-1500s in the Scuola di San Rocco, Venice.

89. Mollaret and Brossollet, *La peste,* 84–90. On the "countless" images of Saint Rock and those "almost as numerous" of Saint Sebastian later: Schumacher, *Die Kranksheitsdarstellungen,* 46, 47. From first to last the iconography of plague saints was comically coy and stylized compared with the graphic accounts of their afflictions in the Saints' Lives. My chief sources for images of the plague were in London: the Wellcome Trust and especially the Warburg Institute (picture files of plague saints Rock, Sebastian, and Christopher as well as of plague victims).

90. Mâle, *L'art religieux,* 350. Connections drawn by Chihaia, *Immortalité,* 127–48, 218, and passim, to late-thirteenth-century south-German allegorical figures of the Prince or the Lady of the World crawling with vermin behind their fine fronts, and 209–54, to the Traini fresco following Morganstern, "The La Grange Tomb," 63–65, are tenuous at best.

91. On these grisly *gisants* see Panofsky, *Tomb Sculpture,* 63–66; Cohen, *Metamorphosis;* Chihaia, *Immortalité,* 209–54; Aberth, *Apocalypse,* 229–57.

92. Panofsky, *Tomb Sculpture,* 64; Cohen, *Metamorphosis,* 3 n. 5 and figs. 31–32; Chihaia, *Immortalité,* 7, 209–26, and passim.

93. Wescher, *Jean Fouquet,* 59–60 and fig. 11; Panofsky, *Tomb Sculpture,* 65–66 and fig. 11; Cohen, *Metamorphosis of a Death Symbol,* figs. 33–35.

94. Mâle, *L'art religieux,* 350–52.

95. Meiss, *French Painting,* figs. 156–59, 162–63, and 165–66.

96. Panofsky, *Tomb Sculpture,* figs. 266 a/b, 268; Cohen, *Metamorphosis,* figs. 10, 115.

97. Tapié, *Les vanités*, 49.

98. Mâle, *L'art religieux*, 350, rightly qualifies all such generalizations with the reminder that many images of death from the aftermath of the Black Death have been lost; thus a church in Avignon once held a panel painting of "a woman's decomposed corpse," and the illuminator Jean Bourdichon reportedly painted "a cadaver devoured by worms."

99. Duby, *Fondements*, 144.

100. The closest approach I have seen from before the baroque to a faithful depiction of dead bodies besides Christ's is a weird 1518 engraving by Agostino Veneziano after a drawing by Rosso Fiorentino of the resurrection of the flesh.

101. Nicolas Poussin, *Plague of Ashdod*, c. 1630–1631, Musée du Louvre, Paris; Bertholet Flémal, *The Plague of the Philistines*, [date?], Musée de l'Art Wallon, Liège; Michiel Sweerts, *Plague in an Ancient City*, c. 1652, Los Angeles County Museum of Art; Micco Spadaro (Domenico Gargiullo), *Piazza del Mercatello*, 1656–1660, Museo Nazionale di San Martino, Naples; Carlo Coppola, *The Pestilence of 1656 in Naples*, after 1656, Princeton University Art Museum. See further: Mattia Preti, two *bozzetti* on the plague of 1656, 1656–1659, Museo Nazionale di Capodimonte, Naples.

102. Hospital de la Santa Caridad, Seville: Trapier, *Valdés Leal*, 57.

103. *Pestsäule*, Im Graben, Vienna.

104. Stegemeier, *Dance of Death*, 6.

105. Théodore Géricault, *Heads of Executed Prisoners*, 1818, Nationalmuseum, Stockholm; *Study of the Head of a Corpse*, c. 1819, Art Institute, Chicago; various preparatory sketches for *The Raft of the Medusa*.

106. Francisco Goya, *A Plague Hospital*, c. 1808–1812, Marquesa de la Romana collection, Madrid; Théodore Géricault, *Plague Scene*, c. 1822–1823, private collection, Paris. Both were history paintings if properly titled.

107. Nochlin, *Realism*, 64. Further: Musée d'Orsay, Paris, *Le dernier portrait*.

108. Goodwin, *Kitsch and Culture*, 13. Further: Collins, *Dance of Death*, 45–49.

109. For further examples, see Goodwin, *Kitsch and Culture*, passim.

110. Kastner, *Les danses des morts*, vii, appendix.

111. Goodwin, *Kitsch and Culture*, 4–12.

112. Ibid., 45–46.

113. On the Dance of the Dead as a "round": Stegemeier, *Dance of Death*, 21–22; Hammerstein, *Tanz und Musik des Todes*, 49–51.

114. Stegemeier, *Dance of Death*, 195. In the old folk song that Claudius redid (ibid., 190–93), Death "shows himself to be quite heartless and cruel" (ibid., 194).

115. Baudelaire, *Oeuvres complètes*, 105.

116. Ibid., 160–70 (*Les fleurs du mal*, XCVII).

117. Ibid., 829 (Baudelaire's stress).

118. On the Wiertz painting and Hébert sculpture, see further: Binion, "Europe's Culture of Death," 128–31.

119. Quotations from microbiologist Henri Mollaret in *Le Monde* (Paris), 16 October 2001, 20.

Epilogue—Open Questions

1. See also Binion, "Traumatic Reliving in History." Other researchers have, like Joel Markowitz, instanced traumatic reliving in history, albeit in different conceptual terms, but only Markowitz's treatment of the Courtrai syndrome provides the information necessary for even a summary comparative analysis like this one.

2. Sigmund Freud, *Totem and Taboo* and *Moses and Monotheism*. Freud's traumatic replay climaxes with the Crucifixion.

3. See Binion, *After Christianity* and *Love Beyond Death*.

4. Friedrich Nietzsche, *Die fröhliche Wissenschaft,* III:125.

5. Locus classicus: Andreas-Salomé, "Die Stunde ohne Gott."

6. In her "Geschwister": Binion, *Frau Lou,* 416–38.

7. In his *Six Characters in Search of an Author:* Binion, *Soundings,* 130.

8. On traumatic reliving in fiction, see further: Binion, *Sounding the Classics,* 7–44; *Soundings,* 4; "Traumatic Reliving in History," 244–45.

9. Trauma-savvy Pirandello nonetheless had the psychiatrist in his *Henry IV* use the same original parties to an individual trauma in restaging it around the victim except only a daughter as stand-in for her mother.

10. Binion, "From Mayerling to Sarajevo," where I considered the two relivings as quasi-traumatic.

11. Pirandello, *Maschere nude,* 97; Binion, *Soundings,* 130–31.

12. On this uncertainty as to Germany, see Binion "Germany: New and Old," 379–86.

13. Cf. Trigger, *Early Civilizations,* 110: "I have documented significant variation from one early civilization to another only in terms of art styles and cultural values."

14. See further: Binion, "Ketzerisches zur Kriegsfrage," 117–24.

Sources

Archival Sources

For the chapter "A Community of Fate" I utilized the Bundesarchiv in Koblenz and the Bayerisches Hauptstaatsarchiv in Munich in addition to published sources as cited. Full archival references are in the notes.

Visual Sources

For the chapters "Death on a Rampage" and "Three Mourning Mothers" I used the photographic collections of the Wellcome Institute and especially the Warburg Institute, both in London, besides viewing monuments and art collections across Europe and America. My principal pre-Pietà visual sources for "Three Mourning Mothers" were these:

Mothers bringing children to Massacre:

Mosaic, triumphal arch, Santa Maria Maggiore, Rome, 432–440.

Rachel-type Massacre mothers:

Ivory carving, Staatliche Museen, Berlin, c. 430.
Ivory book cover (North Italian), Codex Lat. 10077, Bayerische Staatsbibliothek, Munich, 5th century.
Ivory book cover, Cathedral, Milan, 5th century.
Ivory book cover (Metz), Douce Manuscript 176, Bodleian Library, Oxford, c. 800.
Ivory plaque, Bibliothèque Nationale, Paris, 9th century.
Pericope, Codex Egberti 24, f. 15v, Stadtbibliothek, Trier, 977–993.
Fresco, nave, Urbano alla Caffarella, Rome, early 11th century.
Pericope of Henry III, b. 21, f. 13r, Staatsbibliothek, Bremen, 11th century.
Ivory altar front, Cathedral Museum, Salerno, 12th century.
Enamel plaque, No. 17.190.444, Metropolitan Museum of Art, New York, 12th century.
Stone tympanum (from St. Pierre Cathedral, Etampes), Museum, Etampes, 12th century.
Mosaic, crossing, Cathedral, Monreale, late 12th century.
Manuscript, Theol. Lat. 2, 487, f. 24v, Staatsbibliothek, Berlin, 1251–1275.
Column decoration, St. Julien Church, Poncé-sur-le-Loir (Sarthe), 13th century.
Fresco (Italian), choir, Basilica of St. Martin, Aimé (Savoie), mid-13th century.
Psalter, Pal. Lat. 26, f. 8v, Vatican Library, Rome, mid-13th century.
Psalter of Robert de Lisle (Madonna Master), f. 124v, British Library, London, c. 1310.
Enamel statuette base, Musée du Louvre, Paris, early 14th century.
Fresco, St. Gallus Chapel, Oberstammheim, early 14th century.

Baptistery vault decoration, Basilica of San Marco, Venice, 14th century.
Fresco, Zeno Church, Lüen, Switzerland, late 14th century.

Massacre mothers with dead child or children on lap:

Drogo Sacramentary (Metz), Lat. 9428, tableau 82a, f. 31a. Bibliothèque Nationale, Paris, c. 850.
Wooden door, Sankt Maria im Kapitol, Cologne, 1050.
Ivory panel, lower Rhine, Victoria and Albert Museum, London, 379–1871, late 11th century.
Fresco, Saint-Jacques-des-Guérets (Loir-et-Cher), early 12th century.
Bronze door, Cathedral, Benevento, 12th century.
Manuscript, Cotton Caligula, A VII, f. 7r, British Museum, London, late 12th century.
Sculpture, archivolt, west front, Santo Domingo Cathedral, Soria, late 12th century.
Sculpture, Tomb of Doña Blanca, Abbey of Santa Maria la Real, Logroño (Navarre), late 12th century.
Sculpture, archivolt, Santo Domingo Monastery, Silos (Burgos), 12th–13th century.
Sculpture, external arch, St. Pierre Church, Nuaillé-sur-Boutonne, 13th century.
Fresco (Palmerino di Guido), Basilica of Santa Chiara, Assisi, c. 1300.
Fresco (Theoskepastos of Trebizond), Kariye Camii, Istanbul, 1310–1320.
Hours of Jeanne d'Évreux (Jean Pucelle), 54.1.2, f. 69r, Cloisters, Metropolitan Museum of Art, New York, c. 1325–1328.
Panel painting (Simone da Bologna or Jacopo de' Bavasi or Andrea de Bartoli), Pinacoteca, Bologna, early 14th century.
Panel painting (Tuscan), Museum, Fiesole, 14th century.
Fresco, nave, Monastery Church, Pomposa, 14th century.
Wooden polyptych, right wing, Marienberg Church, Helmstedt, 14th century.
Panel (Matteo di Giovanni), National Gallery, Naples, 1488.
Panel (Master of Schloss Lichtenstein), Alte Pinakothek, Munich, early 16th century.

Massacre mothers with live children on lap:

Gospel Book of Otto III, Clm. 4453, Cim. 58, f. 30v, Bayerische Staatsbibliothek, Munich, 10th–11th century.
Manuscript, Golden Gospel Book of Echternach 156412, f. 19v, Germanisches Nationalmuseum, Nuremberg: 1053–1056.
Manuscript, Lectionary 9428, f. 13r, Bibliothèque Royale, Brussels, early 11th century.
Mural, arcade, Saint-Aubin Abbey, Angers, 1150.
Fresco, choir, east wall, Saint-Aignan Church, Brinay-sur-Cher, mid-12th century.
Gumpertsbibel, f. 322v, University Library, Erlangen, by 1195.
Psalter (Waldkirch), Codex Breviary 125, f. 45v, Württembergische Landesbibliothek, Stuttgart, 1201–1215.
Bible (English), Auct. D.3.4., f. 282 v, Bodleian Library, Oxford, early 13th century.
Wooden sculpture (Västergötland), Inventory No. 5669:3-4, Nationalmuseet, Stockholm, late 13th century.
Triptych, Kunsthalle, Hamburg, late 14th century.
Panel, Germanisches Nationalmuseum, Nuremberg, late 14th to early 15th century.

Massacre mothers cradling severed infant head:

Fresco, Church of Saint-Jacques-des-Guérets (Loir-et-Cher), early 12th century.
Bronze door, Sophia Cathedral, Novgorod, mid-12th century.
Ingeborgpsalter, Manuscript 1695, f. 18v, Musée Condé, Chantilly, c. 1200.

Bible Moralisée, Codex Vindobonensis 2554, f. 16r, Österreichische Nationalbiblio-
thek, Vienna, early 13th century.
Bible Moralisée, Lat. 11560, f. 86r, Bibliothèque Nationale, Paris, early 13th century.
Stained glass, Childhood of Christ Window, St. Pierre St. Paul Cathedral, Troyes,
1240–1250.
Psalter and Hours, Lat. 1073 A, f. 7v, Bibliothèque Nationale, Paris, c. 1260.
Psalter (French), Lewis 185, f.6v, Free Library, Philadelphia, c. 1260.

Lap- and Rachel-type Massacre mothers:

Manuscript, Gr. 74, f. 510, Bibliothèque Nationale, Paris, 11th century.
Manuscript, 1156, f. 280v, Vangelo del Vaticano, Rome, 11th century.
Ivory plaque (Cologne?), Victoria and Albert Museum, London, late 11th century.
Fresco (School of Montecassino), nave, Sant'Angelo in Formis, Capua, 11th–12th century.
Stone sculpture, east archivolt, St. Trophime Cloister, Arles, c. 1190.
Stone sculpture, south portal, Cathedral, Worms, c. 1300.
Fresco (Barna da Siena), Collegiata of San Gimignano, 1350–1355.
Gospel Book, Add. 39627, f. 11r, British Museum, London, 1356.

Ground-type Massacre mothers:

Stained glass, Chapel of the Virgin, "Childhood of Christ" window, Cathedral, St. De-
nis, c. 1145.
Stone sculpture, embrasures, Portail Royal, Cathedral, Chartres, 1145–1155.
Stained glass, central window, west façade, Cathedral, Chartres, c. 1145–1155.
Stained glass, Church, Westhofen (Alsace), c. 1325.
Antiphonary, I, f. 113v, Biblioteca Capitolare, Padua, 14th century.
Breviary for Charles V, Lat. 1052, f. 308r, Bibliothèque Nationale, Paris, late 14th century.

Lap- and Lamentation-type Massacre mothers:

Manuscript, Smith-Lesouëf 20, f. 11v, Bibliothèque Nationale, Paris, 13th century.
Fresco (Giovanni Pietro and Giuliano da Rimini), Santa Maria in Posto Fuori, Ravenna,
late 15th century.

Betwixt and Betweens:

Manuscript (Sedulius), Carmen Paschale, M.17.4, f. 16r, Plantin-Morelus Museum,
Antwerp, 10th century.
Fresco, nave, Church of St. Martin, Zillis, 12th century.
Manuscript 500, f. 21r, Bibliothèque Communale, 12th century.
Sculpture, external arch, west side, Cathedral, Le Mans, mid-12th century.
Marble pulpit (Nicola Pisano), Cathedral, Siena, 1266–1268.
Antiphonary (Sienese), Corale 33–35, C. 168, Cathedral Museum, Siena, c. 1290.
Manuscript (Tuscan), Supplicationes Variae, Plut. 25, 3, f. 368v, Laurentian Library,
Florence, 1293–1300.
Marble pulpit (Giovanni Pisano), Church of Sant'Andrea, Pistoia, 1301.
Marble pulpit (Giovanni Pisano), Cathedral, Pisa, 1302–1311.
Panel painting in tempera (Duccio di Buoninsegna), Maestà, front predella, Cathedral
Museum, Siena, 1308–1311.
Metal altar front, Zenone Cathedral, Pistoia, 1316.
Manuscript (Maestro dei Cavali), Antiphonary F, Initial C, Manuscript 9, f. 100r,
Biblioteca Capitolare di S. Lorenzo, Perugia, 1320–1330.

Fresco (Pietro Lorenzetti), Santa Maria dei Servi, Siena, 1330.
Fresco (Giotto and school), Lower Church of San Francesco, Assisi, early 14th century.
Sculpture (Tino di Camaino), Trinità Monastery, Cava dei Tirreni, early 14th century.
Cope (English), Museo Civico, Bologna, 14th century.
Fresco, Markov Monastery, Serbia, after 1371.
Fresco (Giusto dei Menabuoi), Baptistery, Padua, 1376.
Stone sculpture, west portal, St. Lorenz Church, Nuremberg, 14th century.
Fresco, Basilica of San Nicola, Tolentino, 14th century.
Decoration (School of Meo da Siena?), Santa Scala, Sacro Speco Monastery, Subiaco, 14th century.
Hours of Gian Galeazzo, Landau Finaly 22, f. 29r, Biblioteca Nazionale Centrale, Florence, late 14th century.
Panel painting (Niccolò di Tommaso), Uffizi Gallery, Florence, late 14th century.
Panel painting (Bartolo di Fredi or Andrea di Bartolo), Walters Art Gallery, Baltimore, late 14th century.
Manuscript, Landau Finaly, Biblioteca Nazionale Centrale, Florence, late 14th century.
Fresco (Andrea da Lecce), Cathedral, Atri (Abruzzo), mid-15th century.
Panel painting (Fra Angelico), San Marco Museum, Florence, mid-15th century.
Fresco (Theophanes), Lavra Monastery, Mont Athos, 1535.

Pre-Pietà Lamentations:

Wall painting, Panteleiman Church, Nerezi (Macedonia), c. 1164.
Tempera on parchment attached to wood (Master of the San Matteo Crucifix), Museo Nazionale, Pisa, early 13th century.
Painted cross (Coppo di Marcovaldo), Museo Civico, San Gimignano, 1260s.
Mosaic, cupola, Baptistry, Florence, 13th century.
Painted cross (Salerno di Coppo), sacristy, Cathedral, Pistoia, 13th century.
Georgian miniature (Millet, *Monuments byzantins de Mistra. Matériaux pour l'étude de l'architecture et de la peinture en Grèce aux XIVe et Xve siècles,* 495), late 13th century.
Fresco (Giotto), Arena Chapel, Padua, 1305–1308.
Tempera on parchment attached to wood (Pacino di Bonaguida), Pierpont Morgan Library, New York, c. 1303–1320.
Rohan Hours (Rohan Master), Lat. 9471, Bibliothèque Nationale, Paris, 1414–1418.
Painting (Rogier van der Weyden), Capilla Real (Granada), 1435–1438.
Painting (Caravaggio, *Entombment*), Vatican Museum, Rome, 1603.

Printed Sources

The works listed here are only those referenced in the notes. They do not include familiar literary classics cited by chapter or verse.

Abell, Walter. *The Collective Dream in Art: A Psycho-Historical Theory of Culture Based on Relations between the Arts, Psychology, and the Social Sciences.* Cambridge, Mass.: Harvard University Press, 1957.
Aberth, John. *From the Brink of the Apocalypse.* New York: Routledge, 2001.
Abrams, M. H. "English Romanticism." In *Romanticism Reconsidered*, ed. Northrop Frye, 26–72. New York: Columbia University Press, 1963.
Andreas-Salomé, Lou. *Henrik Ibsens Frauen-Gestalten.* Jena: Diedrichs, 1891.
———. "Die Stunde ohne Gott." In *Die Stunde ohne Gott und andere Kindergeschichten.* Jena: Diedrichs, 1921.
Archives parlementaires de 1787 à 1860. *Recueil complet des débats législatifs et politiques des Chambres françaises* 1re série (1787–1799), vol. 78. Paris: Paul Dupont, 1911.

Ariès, Philippe. "Sur les origines de la contraception en France." *Population* 8 (1953): 465–72.

Auerbach, Erich. "Figura." In *Scenes from the Drama of European Literature*, 11–76. New York: Meridian, 1959.

———. *Mimesis. Dargestellte Wirklichkeit in der abendländischen Literatur*. Bern: Francke, 1945.

Baltrušaitis, Jurgis. *Le moyen âge fantastique. Antiquités et exotismes dans l'art gothique*. Paris: Armand Colin, 1955.

Balzac, Honoré de. *Le père Goriot*. Paris: Garnier, 1963.

Barbagli, Marzio. *Sotto lo stesso tetto. Mutamenti della famiglia in Italia dal XV al XX secolo*. Bologna: Il Mulino, 1984.

Bardet, Jean-Pierre, *Rouen aux XVIIe et XVIIIe siècles. Les mutations d'un espace social*, 2 vols. Paris: Sedes, 1983.

Bardet, Jean-Pierre, Pierre Chaunu, Jean-Marie Gouesse, Pierre Gouhier, Anne and Jean-Marie Valez. "Les paysages humains, XVIe-XVIIIe siècles." In *Histoire de la Normandie*, ed. Michel de Boüard, 319–46. Toulouse: Privat, 1970.

Bardet, Jean-Pierre, and Jacques Dupâquier, "Contraception: les Français les premiers, mais pourquoi?" *Communications* 44 (1986): 3–33.

Baschet, Jérôme. "Image et événement: l'art sans la peste (c. 1348–1400)?" In *La peste nera: dati di una realtà ed elementi di una interpretazione. Atti del XXX Convegno storico internazionale. Todi, 10–13 ottobre 1993*, 25–48. Spoleto: Centro Italiano di Studi sull'Alto Medioevo, 1994.

Baudrillard, Jean. *La société de consommation: ses mythes, ses structures*. Paris: Denoël, 1970.

———. *Le système des objets*. Paris: Gallimard, 1968.

Beck, Herbert, and Horst Bredekamp. "Kompilation der Form in der Skulptur um 1400." In *Städel-Jahrbuch*, Neue Folge 6, 129–57. Munich: Prestel, 1977.

Bellosi, Luciano. *Buffalmacco e il Trionfo della Morte*. Turin: Einaudi, 1974.

Belting, Hans. *The Image and Its Public in the Middle Ages*. New Rochelle, N.Y.: Caratzas, 1981.

Benedictow, Ole J. *The Black Death 1346–1353. The Complete History*. Woodbridge: Boydell, 2004.

Bergues, Hélène. "Sources et documentation." In *La prévention des naissances dans la famille. Ses origines dans les temps modernes*, ed. Hélène Bergues, 19–50. Paris: Presses Universitaires de France, 1960.

Bideau, Alain. "Les mécanismes autorégulateurs des populations traditionnelles." *Annales: Économies, Sociétés, Civilisations* 38 (1983): 1040–57.

Binion, Rudolph. "Considérations sur la disparition de l'analphabétisme." *Population* 7 (1953): 121–28.

———."Europe's Culture of Death." In *The Psychology of Death in Fantasy and History*, ed. Jerry S. Piven, 119–35. Westport, Conn.: Prager, 2004.

———. *Freud über Aggression und Krieg: Einerlei oder zweierlei?* Vienna: Picus, 1995.

———. "From Mayerling to Sarajevo." In *Journal of Modern History* 47 (1975): 280–316.

———. "Germany Old and New." *Journal of Psychohistory* 19 (1992): 379–86.

———. *Hitler Among the Germans*. New York: Elsevier, 1976.

———. "Hitler's Concept of 'Lebensraum': The Psychological Basis." *History of Childhood Quarterly* 1 (1973): 187–215.

———. *Introduction à la psychohistoire*. Paris: Collège de France and Presses Universitaires de France, 1982.

———. "'Der Jude ist weg.' Machtpolitische Auswirkungen des Hitlerschen Rassengedankens." In *Die deutsche Frage im 19. und 20. Jahrhundert*, ed. Josef Becker and Andreas Hillgruber, 347–72, 396–401. Munich: Ernst Vögel, 1983.

———. "Ketzerisches zur Kriegsfrage." In *"so ist der Mensch...". 80 Jahre Erster Weltkrieg*, 117–24. Vienna: Historisches Museum der Stadt Wien, 1994.

———. *Love Beyond Death. The Anatomy of a Myth in the Arts.* New York: New York University Press, 1993.

———. "Repeat Performance. Leopold III and Belgian Neutrality." Chapter in *Soundings Psychohistorical and Psycholiterary.* New York: Psychohistory Press, 1981.

———. *Soundings Psychohistorical and Psycholiterary.* New York: Psychohistory Press, 1981.

———. *Sounding the Classics. From Sophocles to Thomas Mann.* Westport, Conn.: Greenwood, 1997.

———. "Traumatic Reliving in History." *Annual of Psychoanalysis* 31 (2003): 237–50.

Binsky, Paul. *Medieval Death. Ritual and Representation.* Ithaca: Cornell University Press, 1996.

Biraben, Jean-Noël. *Les hommes et la peste en France et dans les pays européens et méditerranéens,* vol. 2. Paris: Mouton, 1976.

Blake, Judith, and Prithwis Das Gupta. "Reproductive Motivation versus Contraceptive Technology: Is Recent American Experience an Exception?" *Population and Development Review* 1 (1975): 229–49.

Blayo, Yves. "Mouvement naturel de la population française de 1740 à 1829." *Population* 30 (1975): 15–64.

———. "La population de la France de 1740 à 1860." *Population* 30 (1975): 71–122.

Bloch, Marc. *Apologie pour l'histoire ou métier d'historien.* Paris: Armand Colin, 1949.

———. "Pour une histoire comparée des sociétés européennes." *Revue de synthèse historique* 46 (1928): 15–50.

Bloch, Peter. "Die Pietà Schnütgen." In *Museion; Studien aus Kunst und Geschichte für Otto H. Förster,* ed. Heinz Ladendorf, 211–14. Cologne: Schauberg, 1960.

Blum, Alain. "L'évolution de la fécondité en France aux XVIIIe et XIXe siècles. Analyse régionale." *Annales de démographie historique 1988:* 157–77.

Blum, Alain, Jacques Houdaille, and Yves Tugault. "Baisse de la fécondité dans la valée de la Garonne." *Population* 42 (1987): 503–26.

Blum, Carol. *Diderot: The Virtue of a Philosopher.* New York: Viking, 1974.

Blum, Léon. *Du mariage.* Paris: Ollendorf, 1907.

Bois, Paul. *Paysans de l'ouest. Des structures économiques et sociales aux options politiques depuis l'époque révolutionnaire dans la Sarthe.* Le Mans: Vilaire, 1960.

Borsook, Eve. *The Mural Painters of Tuscany from Cimabue to Andrea del Sarto.* Garden City, N.J.: Phaidon, 1960; second edition, Oxford: Clarendon Press, 1980.

Boskovits, Miklós. "Un pittore 'espressionista' del trecento umbro." In *Storia e arte in Umbria nell'età comunale,* ed. Francesco Ugolini, vol. 1, 115–30 and figure 3. Perugia: Centro di Studi Umbri, 1971.

Bousquet, Jacques. *Les thèmes du rêve dans la littérature romantique.* Paris: Didier, 1964.

Brandt, Kathleen Weil-Garris. "Michelangelo's 'Pietà' for the Capella del Re di Francia." In *"Il se rendit en Italie": Études offertes à André Chastel,* 77–119. Rome: Edizioni dell'Elefante, 1987.

Braudel, Fernand. *L'identité de la France. Les hommes et les choses.* Paris: Arthaud-Flammarion, 1986.

Braudel, Fernand, and Frank C. Spooner. "Prices in Europe from 1450 to 1750." In *The Cambridge Economic History of Europe,* vol. 4, *The Economy of Expanding Europe in the Sixteenth and Seventeenth Centuries,* ed. Edwin E. Rich and Charles H. Wilson, 378–486. Cambridge: Cambridge University Press, 1967.

Briggs, Asa. *Victorian People: A Reassessment of Persons and Themes, 1851–67.* Chicago: University of Chicago Press, 1955.

Brion-Guerry, Liliane. *Le thème du "Triomphe de la mort" dans la peinture italienne.* Paris: Maisonneuve, 1950.

Bruck, Robert. *Die elsässische Glasmalerei.* Strasbourg: Heinrich, 1902.

Brundage, James A. *Law, Sex, and Christian Society in Medieval Europe.* Chicago: University of Chicago Press, 1987.

Bucher, François. *The Pamplona Bibles*. New Haven: Yale University Press, 1970.

Buchheit, Gert. *Hitler der Feldherr*. Rastatt: Grote, 1958.

Buchner, Ernst. *Das deutsche Bildnis der Spätgotik und der frühen Dürerzeit*. Berlin: Deutscher Verein für Kunstwissenschaft, 1953.

Bulst, Neithard. "Der schwarze Tod. Demographische, wirtschafts- und kulturgeschichtliche Aspekte der Pestkatastrophe von 1347–1352. Bilanz der neueren Forschung." *Saeculum* 30 (1979): 45–67.

Bulwer-Lytton, Edward. *England and the English* (1883). Chicago: University of Chicago Press, 1970.

Burdach, Konrad, ed. *Vom Mittelalter zur Reformation*, vol. 3:1, *Der Ackermann von Böhmen*, ed. Alois Bernt and Konrad Burdach. Berlin: Weidmann, 1917.

Burnett, John, ed. *Destiny Obscure. Autobiographies of Childhood, Education and Family from the 1820s to the 1920s*. London: Lane, 1982.

Butler, Jon. *Awash in a Sea of Faith: Christianizing the American People*. Cambridge, Mass.: Harvard University Press, 1990.

Butler, Samuel. *The Way of All Flesh*. Harmondsworth: Penguin, 1966.

Byers, Edward. "Fertility Transition in a New England Commercial Center: Nantucket, Massachusetts, 1680–1840." *Journal of Interdisciplinary History* 13 (1982): 17–40.

Byron, George Gordon. *Correspondence*, vol. 2, ed. John Murray. London: John Murray, 1922.

Cahn, Walter. "The 'Tympanum' of Saint-Pierre at Étampes: A New Reconstruction." *Gesta* 25/1 (1986): 119–26.

Calkins, Robert G. "Liturgical Sequence and Decorative Crescendo in the Drogo Sacramentary." *Gesta* 25 (1986): 17–23.

Camazine, Scott, and James Sneyd. "A Model of Collective Nectar Source Selection by Honey Bees: Self-organization Through Simple Rules." *Journal of Theoretical Biology* 149 (1991): 547–71.

Campbell, Donald T., and Robert C. Jacobs. "The Perpetuation of an arbitrary tradition through several generations of a laboratory microculture." *Journal of Abnormal and Social Psychology* 62 (1961): 649–58.

Carco, Francis. *La danse des morts comme l'a décrite François Villon*. Geneva: Milieu du Monde, 1944.

Carlyle, Thomas. *Carlyle's Complete Works*, vol. 12. Boston: Estes and Laureat, 1885.

Carr-Saunders, A. M. *The Population Problem. A Study in Human Evolution*. Oxford: Clarendon Press, 1922.

Cerati, Marie. *Le Club des Citoyennes Républicaines Révolutionnaires*. Paris: Éditions Sociales, 1966.

Chamoux, Antoinette, and Cécile Dauphin. "La contraception avant la Révolution française: L'exemple de Châtillon-sur-Seine." *Annales: Économies, Sociétés, Civilisations* 24 (1969): 662–84.

Chaney, Edward F., ed. *La danse macabré des charniers des Saints Innocents à Paris*. Manchester: Manchester University Press, 1945.

Chateaubriand, François-René de. *Oeuvres romanesques et voyages*, vol. 1. Paris: Gallimard, 1969.

Chaunu, Pierre. "Postface." In Jacques Dupâquier et al., *Histoire de la population française*, vol. 2, *De la Renaissance à 1789*, 553–63. Paris: Presses Universitaires de France, 1988.

Chesnais, Jean-Claude. *La transition démographique. Étapes, formes, implications économiques. Études de séries temporelles (1720–1984) relatives à 67 pays*. Paris: Presses Universitaires de France, 1986.

———. "La transition démographique. Étapes, formes, implications économiques. Études de séries temporelles (1720–1984) relatives à 67 pays. Présentation d'un Cahier de l'Ined." *Population* 41 (1986): 1059–70.

Chihaia, Pavel. *Immortalité et décomposition dans l'art du Moyen Âge.* Madrid: Fondation Culturelle Roumaine, 1988.

Christie, A. G. I. *English Medieval Embroidery.* Oxford: Clarendon Press, 1938.

Clark, James M. *The Dance of Death in the Middle Ages and the Renaissance.* Glasgow: Jackson, 1950.

Closets, François de. *Le bonheur en plus.* Paris: Denoël, 1974.

Coale, Ansley J. "The Decline of Fertility in Europe since the Eighteenth Century as a Chapter in Demographic History." In *The Decline of Fertility in Europe,* ed. Ansley J. Coale and Susan Cotts Watkins, 1–30. Princeton, N.J.: Princeton University Press, 1986.

Coale, Ansley J., and Susan Watkins, eds., *The Decline of Fertility in Europe.* Princeton, N.J.: Princeton University Press, 1986.

Coale, Ansley J., and Melvin Zelnik. *New Estimates of Fertility and Population in the United States. A Study of Annual White Births from 1855 to 1960 and of Completeness of Enumeration in the Censuses from 1880 to 1960.* Princeton, N.J.: Princeton University Press, 1963.

Cohen, Kathleen. *Metamorphosis of a Death Symbol. The Transi Tomb in the Late Middle Ages and the Renaissance.* Berkeley: University of California Press, 1973.

Cohn, Samuel K., Jr. "The Black Death: End of a Paradigm." *American Historical Review* 107 (2002): 703–38.

———. *The Black Death Transformed: Disease and Culture in Early Renaissance Europe.* London: Arnold, 2002.

———. *The Cult of Remembrance and the Black Death. Six Renaissance Cities in Central Italy.* Baltimore: Johns Hopkins University Press, 1992.

———. *Death and Property in Siena, 1205–1800. Strategies for the Afterlife.* Baltimore: Johns Hopkins University Press, 1988.

———. "Group Proces." In *Clio's Psyche* 7 (2000): 146–48.

———. *Women in the Streets. Essays on Sex and Power in Renaissance Italy.* Baltimore: Johns Hopkins University Press, 1996.

Cole, Thomas R. "Family, Settlement, and Migration in Southeastern Massachusetts, 1650–1805: The Case for Regional Analysis." *New England Historical and Genealogical Register* 132 (1978): 171–85.

Collins, Marcia. *The Dance of Death in Book Illustration.* Columbia, Mo.: Ellis Library, 1978.

Correas, Gonzalo. *Vocabulario de refranes y frasas proverbiales,* 1627, ed. Louis Combet. Bordeaux: Institut d'Études Ibériques et Ibéro-Américaines de l'Université de Bordeaux, 1967.

Croix, Alain. *La Bretagne aux 16e et 17e siècles.* Paris: Maloine, 1981.

Crown, Carol Uhlig. "The Winchester Psalter and 'L'enfance du Christ' Window at St. Denis." *The Burlington Magazine* 117 (1975): 79–83.

Crozet, René. *L'art romain en Saintonge.* Paris: Picard, 1971.

Dahl, Erik. "Nuaillé-sur-Boutonne." In Société Française d'Archéologie, *Congrès archéologique de France,* 114th session, La Rochelle, 1956, pp. 297–303.

Darnton, Robert. *The Forbidden Best-Sellers of Pre-Revolutionary France.* New York: Norton, 1995.

David, Paul A., and Thomas A. Mroz. "Evidence of Fertility Regulation Among Rural French Villagers, 1749–1789. A Sequential Econometric Model of Birth-Spacing Behavior." *European Journal of Population* 5 (1989): 1–26, 173–206.

Davidson, Cathy N. *Revolution and the Word. The Rise of the Novel in America.* New York: Oxford University Press, 1986.

Deaux, George. *The Black Death 1347.* London: Hanish, 1969.

Degler, Carl N. *At Odds. Women and the Family in America from the Revolution to the Present.* New York: Oxford University Press, 1980.

Demos, John. "Notes on Life in Plymouth Colony." *William and Mary Quarterly,* third series, 22 (1965): 264–86.

———. "Oedipus and America: Historical Perspectives on the Reception of Psychoanalysis in the United States." *Annual of Psychoanalysis* 6 (1978): 23–39.

———. "Shame and Guilt in Early New England." In *Emotion and Social Change. Toward A New Psychohistory,* ed. Carol Z. Stearns and Peter Stearns, 69–85. New York: Holmes & Meier, 1988.

Demus, Otto. *Romanesque Mural Painting.* New York: Thames and Hudson, 1970.

Deschamps, Eustache. *Oeuvres complètes,* ed. Queux de Saint-Hilaire, vol. 2. Paris: Didot, 1880.

Desforges, Jacques. "La loi Naquet." In *Renouveau des idées sur la famille,* ed. Robert Prigent, pp. 103–10. Paris: Presses Universitaires de France, 1954.

Dillenberger, Jane. *Style and Content in Christian Art.* London: SCM, 1965.

Dimier, Louis. *Les danses macabres et l'idée de la mort dans l'art chrétien.* Paris: Bloud, 1908.

Dinzelbacher, Peter. "La divinità mortifera." In *La peste nera: dati di una realtà ed elementi di una interpretazione. Atti del XXX Convegno storico internazionale. Todi, 10–13 ottobre 1993,* 137–54 and figs. 1–12. Spoleto: Centro Italiano di Studi sull'Alto Medioevo, 1994.

———. "Die tötende Gottheit: Pestbild und Todesikonographie als Ausdruck der Mentalität des Spätmittelalters und der Renaissance." In *Zeit, Tod und Ewigkeit in der Renaissanceliteratur,* ed. James Hogg, vol. 2, 5–138. Salzburg: Institut für Anglistik und Amerikanistik der Universität Salzburg, 1986.

Dobrzeniecki, Tadeusz. "Medieval Sources of the Pietà." *Bulletin du Musée National de Varsovie* 8 (1967): 5–24.

Domarus, Max, ed. *Hitler. Reden und Proklamationen 1932–1945,* 4 vols. Munich: Süddeutscher Verlag, 1965.

Drinker, Cecil K. *Not So Long Ago.* New York: Oxford University Press, 1937.

[Drysdale, George.] *The Elements of Social Science; or, Physical, Sexual, and Natural Religion.* London: Truelove, 1854. No longer anonymous from 1886. London: Standring, from 1905.

Dubruck, Edelgard. *The Theme of Death in French Poetry of the Middle Ages and the Renaissance.* The Hague: Mouton, 1964.

Duby, Georges. *Fondements d'un nouvel humanisme 1280–1440.* Geneva: Skira, 1966.

Dugatin, Lee Alan. *Cooperation Among Animals. An Evolutionarty Perspective.* New York: Oxford University Press, 1997.

Duncan, Carol. "Happy Mothers and Other New Ideas in French Art." *Art Bulletin* 15 (1973): 570–83.

Dupâquier, Jacques. "La constitution de la famille en France au XVIIe et au XVIIIe siècles." In *Family Building and Family Planning in Pre-Industrial Societies,* ed. John Roger, 25–31. Uppsala: University of Uppsala, 1980.

———. "Révolution et population." In *Histoire de la population française,* vol. 3, *De 1789 à 1914,* ed. Jacques Dupâquier, 63–115. Paris: Presses Universitaires de France, 1988.

———, et al. *Histoire de la population française,* vol. 3, *De 1789 à 1914.* Paris: Presses Universitaires de France, 1988; paperback Quadrige, 1995.

———. "Sur les débuts de la contraception en France ou les deux malthusianismes." *Annales: Économies, Sociétés, Civilisations* 24 (1969): 1391–1406.

Dupâquier, Jacques, and Marcel Lachiver. "Du contresens à l'illusion technique." *Annales: Économies, Sociétés, Civilisations* 36 (1981): 489–92.

Durkhein, Émile. *Le suicide. Étude de sociologie.* Paris: Alcan, 1975.

Easterlin, Richard E. "Population Change and Farm Settlement in the Northern United States." *Journal of Economic History* 36 (1976): 45–83.

Ebner-Eschenbach, Marie von. *Aus Spätherbsttagen*. Berlin: Paetel, 1901.

Eichbaum, Gerda. "Jugendprobleme im Spiegel der deutschen Dichtung (1880–1930)." *Zeitschrift für deutsche Bildung* 7 (1931): 612–21.

Eliot, Thomas Stearns. *The Waste Land. A Facsimile and Transcript of the Original Drafts Including the Annotations of Ezra Pound*, ed. Valerie Eliot. San Diego: Harcourt Brace, 1971.

Emerson, Ralph Waldo. *The Complete Essays and Other Writings*. New York: Modern Library, n.d.

Erasmus, Desiderius. *The Education of a Christian Prince*, tr. Lester K. Born. New York: Octagon, 1973.

Ferber, Stanley H. "Jean Pucelle and Giovanni Pisano." *The Art Bulletin* 66 (1984): 65–72.

Festy, Patrick. *La fécondité des pays occidentaux de 1870 à 1970*. Paris: Presses Universitaires de France, 1979.

Fichte, Johann Gottlieb. *Sämmtliche Werke*, vol. 2. Berlin: Veit, 1845.

Fine, Agnès. "Enfant et normes familiales." In Jacques Dupâquier et al., *Histoire de la population française*, vol. 3, 436–58. Paris: Presses Universitaires de France, 1988.

Flandrin, Jean-Louis. *Familles: parenté, maison, sexualité dans l'ancienne société*. Paris: Hachette, 1976.

Flinn, Michael W. *The European Demographic System*. Baltimore: Johns Hopkins University Press, 1981.

Forsyth, William H. *The Pietà in French Later Gothic Sculpture: Regional Variations*. New York: Metropolitan Museum of Art, 1995.

Fourastié, Jean. *Le grand espoir du XXe siècle*, 1949, updated. Paris: Gallimard, 1989.

Franks, Nigel R. "Army Ants: A Collective Intelligence." *American Scientist* 77 (1989): 139–45.

Fromm, Erich. *To Have Or To Be?* New York: Harper & Row, 1976.

Funkenstein, Amos. *Perceptions of Jewish History*. Berkeley: University of California Press, 1993.

Furst, Lilian R. "Novalis' *Hymnen an die Nacht* and Nerval's *Aurélia*." *Comparative Literature* 21 (1969): 31–46.

Galbraith, John Kenneth. *The Affluent Society*, 1958, fourth edition. Boston: Houghton Mifflin, 1984.

———. "*The Affluent Society* Revisited." In *The Affluent Society*, fourth edition, xi–xxxvii. Boston: Houghton Mifflin, 1984.

Ganiage, Jean. *Trois villages d'Île de France. Étude démographique*. Paris: Presses Universitaires de France, 1963.

Gaukey, David. *Demography. The Study of Human Population*. New York: Saint Martin's, 1985.

Gautier, Étienne, and Louis Henry. *La population de Crulai paroisse normande. Étude historique*. Paris: Presses Universitaires de France, 1958.

Giachetti, J.-C., and M. Tyvaert. "Argenteuil (1740–1790)." *Annales de démographie historique 1969*: 40–61.

Gide, André. *Les nourritures terrestres*. Paris: Gallimard, 1947.

Glixelli, Stefan. *Les cinq poèmes des trois morts et des trois vifs*. Paris: Champion, 1914.

Godineau, Dominique. "Masculine and Feminine Political Practice during the French Revolution, 1793. Year III." In *Women and Politics in the Age of Democratic Revolution*, ed. Harriet B. Applewhite and Darline G. Levy, 61–80. Ann Arbor: University of Michigan Press, 1990.

Goodwin, Sarah Webster. *Kitsch and Culture. The Dance of Death in Nineteenth-Century Literature and Graphic Arts*. New York: Garland, 1988.

Gordon, Michael. *The American Family in Social-Historical Perspective*. New York: St. Martin's, 1973.

Goubert, Pierre. *L'ancien régime,* vol. 2. Paris: Armand Colin, 1973.

———. "Historical Demography and the Reinterpretation of Early Modern French History. A Research Review." *Journal of Interdisciplinary History,* 1 (1970): 37–48.

———. "Legitimate Fertility and Infant Mortality in France During the Eighteenth Century: A Comparison." In *Population and Social Change,* ed. D. V. Glass and Roger Revelle, 321–30. London: Edward Arnold, 1972.

Gouesse, Jean-Marie. "En Basse-Normandie au XVIIe et XVIIIe siècles: Le refus de l'enfant au tribunal de la pénitence." *Annales de démographie historique 1973:* 231–61.

———. "Parenté, famille et mariage en Normandie au XVIIe et XVIIIe siècles. Présentation d'une source et d'une enquête." *Annales: Économies, Sociétés, Civilisations,* 27 (1972): 1139–54.

Grabar, André. "L'asymétrie des relations de Byzance et de l'Occident dans le domaine des arts au moyen âge." In *Byzanz und der Westen. Studien zur Kunst des europäischen Mittelalters,* ed. Irmgard Hutter, 9–24. Vienna: Österreichische Akademie der Wissenschaften, 1984.

Gracián, Baltasar. *Obras completas,* ed. Arturo del Hoyo. Madrid: Aguilar, 1967.

———. *Obras completas,* vol. 1. Madrid: Atlas, 1969.

Graeve, Mary Ann. "The Stone of Unction in Caravaggio's Painting for the Chiesa Nuova." *The Art Bulletin* 40 (1958): 223–38.

Granville-Barker, Harley. *The Voysey Inheritance.* London: Heinemann, 1967.

Graus, Franti_ek. *Pest - Geissler - Judenmorde. Das 14. Jahrhundert als Krisenzeit.* Göttingen: Vandenhoeck & Ruprecht, 1987.

Gravenkamp, Curt. *Marienklage: Das deutsche Vesperbild im vierzehnten und im frühen fünfzehnten Jahrhundert.* Aschaffenburg: Pattloch, 1948.

Graves, Robert. *Goodbye To All That.* Garden City, N.Y.: Doubleday, [1929] 1957.

Greenblatt, Stephen. *Renaissance Self-Fashioning. From More to Shakespeare.* Chicago: University of Chicago Press, 1980.

Greven, Philip J., Jr. *Four Generations: Population, Land, and Family in Colonial Andover, Massachusetts.* Ithaca: Cornell University Press, 1970.

Haak, Bob. *Rembrandt. His Life, His Work, His Time.* New York: Abrams, n.d.

Hahlweg, Werner. *Der Friede von Brest-Litowsk. Ein unveröffentlichter Band aus dem Werk des Untersuchungsausschusses der Deutschen Verfassungsgebenden Nationalversammlung und des Deutschen Reichstages.* Düsseldorf: Droste, 1971.

Halder, Franz. *Kriegstagebuch,* vol. 2, ed. Hans-Adolf Jacobsen. Stuttgart: Kohlhammer, 1963.

Hall, Edward T. *The Hidden Dimension.* New York: Doubleday, 1966.

Hamann, Richard. *Die Holztür der Pfarrkirche zu St. Maria im Kapitol.* Marburg: Verlag des Kunstgeschichtlichen Seminars, 1926.

Hamann, Richard, and Kurt Wilhelm-Kästner. "Die Plastik." Section 2 of *Die Elisabethkirche zu Marburg und ihre künstlerische Nachfolge,* 317–64. Marburg: Kunstgeschichtliches Seminar der Universität, 1929.

Hammerstein, Reinhold. *Tanz und Musik des Todes. Die mittelalterlichen Totentänze und ihr Nachleben.* Bern: Francke, 1880.

Hareven, Tamara K. "Family History at the Crossroads." *Journal of Family History* 12 (1987): ix–xxii.

Hasse, Max. "Studien zur Skulptur des ausgehenden XIV. Jahrhunderts," *Städel-Jahrbuch,* Neue Folge 6, 99–128. Munich: Prestel, 1977.

Hauptmann, Gerhart. *Sämtliche Werke,* 10 vols. Frankfurt: Propyläen, 1962–1966.

Hause, Steven C., with Anne R. Kenney. *Women's Suffrage and Social Politics in the Third French Republic.* Princeton, N.J.: Princeton University Press, 1984.

Hawel, Peter. *Die Pietà: Eine Blüte der Kunst.* Würzburg: Echter, 1985.

Hay, Denys. *Europe. The Emergence of an Idea.* Edinburgh: Edinburgh University Press, 1957.

Hayum, Andrée. *The Isenheim Altarpiece. God's Medicine and the Painter's Vision*. Princeton, N.J.: Princeton University Press, 1989.

Hecht, Jacqueline. "Le Siècle des Lumières et la conservation des petits enfants." *Population* 47 (1992): 1589–1620.

Heimann, Adelheid. "The Capital Frieze and Pilasters of the Portail Royal." *Journal of the Warburg and Courtauld Institutes*, 31 (1968): 73–102.

Helm, Rudolf. *Skelett- und Todesdarstellungen bis zum Auftreten der Totentänze*. Strasbourg: Heitz, 1928.

Henke, Josef. *England in Hitlers politischem Kalkül 1935–1939*. Boppard am Rhein: Harald Boldt, 1973.

Henrikson, Gören. "Das Nürnberger Dokument 386-PS (das 'Hossbach-Protokoll'). Eine Untersuchung seines Wertes als Quelle." In *Probleme deutscher Zeitgeschichte*, Lund Studies in International History 2 (Stockholm: Läromedelsförl, 1971): 151–94.

Henry, Louis. "Fécondité des mariages dans le quart sud-est de la France de 1670 à 1829." *Population* 33 (1978): 855–82.

———. "Fécondité des mariages dans le quart sud-ouest de la France de 1720 à 1829." *Annales: Économies, Sociétés, Civilisations* 27 (1972): 612–40, 977–1023.

———. "Some Data on Natural Fertility." *Eugenics Quarterly* 8 (1961): 81–91.

Henry, Louis, and Jacques Houdaille. "Fécondité des mariages dans le quart nord-ouest de la France de 1670 à 1829." *Population* 28 (1973): 873–924.

Herlihy, David. *The Black Death and the Transformation of the West,* ed. Samuel K. Cohn. Cambridge, Mass.: Harvard University Press, 1997.

———. *Medieval and Renaissance Pistoia. The Social History of an Italian Town, 1200–1430*. New Haven: Yale University Press, 1967.

Herlihy, David, and Christine Klapisch-Zuber. *Les Toscans et leurs familles*. Paris: Fondation Nationale des Sciences Politiques, 1978.

Hess, Moses. *Ausgewählte Schriften,* ed. Horst Lademacher. Cologne: Melzer, 1962.

Higgs, Robert, and H. Louis Stettler, III. "Colonial New England Demography: A Sampling Approach." *William and Mary Quarterly,* third series 27 (1970): 282–94.

Hillgruber, Andreas. *Deutschlands Rolle in der Vorgeschichte der beiden Weltkriege*. Göttingen: Vandenhoeck & Ruprecht, 1967.

———. *Hitlers Strategie: Politik und Kriegführung, 1940–1941*. Frankfurt: Bernard & Graefe, 1965.

Hitler, Adolf. *Mein Kampf*. Munich: Eher, 1935.

Hofstätter, Hans H. "Bethlehemitischer Kindermord." In *Das Münster* 43 (1990): 341–46.

Honour, Hugh. *Neo-Classicism*. Harmondsworth: Penguin, 1968.

———. *Romanticism*. New York: Harper & Row, 1979.

Horn, Wolfgang. "Ein unbekannter Aufsatz Hitlers aus dem Frühjahr 1924." *Vierteljahrshefte für Zeitgeschichte* 16 (1968): 280–94.

Horrox, Rosmary, ed. *The Black Death*. Manchester: Manchester University Press, 1994.

Houdaille, Jacques. "La fécondité des mariages de 1670 à 1829 dans le quart nord-est de la France." *Annales de démographie historique 1876*: 341–91.

Huet, G. "La danse Macabré." In *Le moyen âge*, second series, 20 (1917–1918): 148–67.

Hufton, Olwen H. *The Poor of Eighteenth-Century France, 1750–1789*. Oxford: Clarendon Press, 1974.

———. "Women and the Family Economy in Eighteenth-Century France." *French Historical Studies* 11 (1975): 1–22.

———. "Women in Revolution." *Past & Present* 53 (1971): 90–108.

Huizinga, Johan. *The Waning of the Middle Ages,* tr. F. Hopman. London: Arnold, 1924.

Hunt, Lynn. "Révolution française et vie privée." In *Histoire de la vie privée*, vol. 4, *De la Révolution à la Grande Guerre*, ed. Michelle Perrot, 21–51. Paris: Seuil, 1987.

Ibsen, Henrik. *Hedda Gabler and Three Other Plays,* ed. and trans. Michael Meyer. Garden City, NY: Doubleday, 1962.

———. *Samlede verker,* 6 vols. Oslo: Gyldendal Norsk, 1978.

———. *The Wild Duck,* ed. and trans. Dounia B. Christiani. New York: Norton, 1968.

Jäckel, Eberhard. *Hitlers Weltanschauung. Entwurf einer Herrschaft.* Tübingen: Hermann Leins, 1969.

Jäckel, Eberhard, and Axel Kuhn, ed. *Hitler. Sämtliche Aufzeichnungen 1905–1924.* Stuttgart: Deutsche Verlags-Anstalt, 1980.

Jacobsen, Hans-Adolf. *Nationalsozialistische Aussenpolitik 1933–1938.* Frankfurt: Alfred Metzner, 1968.

Jacobsen, Hans-Adolf, and Werner Jochmann, ed. *Ausgewählte Dokumente zur Geschichte des Nationalsozialismus 1933–1945.* Bielefeld: Neue Gesellschaft, 1966.

James, Henry. *What Maisie Knew.* Harmondsworth: Penguin, 1966.

James, William. *The Principles of Psychology,* 1890, vol. 1. New York: Henry Holt, 1904.

Janson, H. W. *History of Art,* second edition. Englewood Cliffs, N.J.: Prentice Hall, 1977.

Jochmann, Werner, ed. *Im Kampf um die Macht. Hitlers Rede vor dem Hamburger Nationalklub von 1919.* Frankfurt: Europäische Verlagsanstalt, 1960.

Kaiser, Gert. *Der tanzende Tod.* Frankfurt: Insel, 1982.

Kantrow, Louise. "Philadelphia Gentry: Fertility and Family Limitation among an American Aristocracy." *Population Studies* 34 (1980): 21–30.

Kaplan, Edward K., ed. and trans. *Mother Death. The Journal of Jules Michelet 1815–1850.* Amherst: University of Massachusetts Press, 1984.

Kartsonis, Anna D. *Anastasis. The Making of an Image.* Princeton, N.J.: Princeton University Press, 1986.

Kastner, Georges. *Les danses des morts. Dissertations et recherches historiques, littéraires et musicales sur les divers monuments de ce genre qui existent ou ont existé tant en France qu'à l'étranger, accompagnées de la danse macabre, grande ronde vocale et instrumentale, paroles d'Édouard Thierry, musique de Georges Kastner.* Paris: Brandus, Pagnerre, 1852.

Kates, Gary. "'The Powers of Husband and Wife Must Be Equal and Separate': The Cercle Social and the Rights of Women, 1790–91." In *Women and Politics in the Age of Democratic Revolution,* ed. Harriet B. Applewhite and Darline G. Levy, 163–80. Ann Arbor: University of Michigan Press, 1990.

Kerber, Linda K. "'I Have Don... much to Carrey on the War': Women and the Shaping of Republican Ideology after the American Revolution." In *Women and Politics in the Age of Democratic Revolution,* ed. Harriet B. Applewhite and Darline G. Levy, 227–57. Ann Arbor: University of Michigan Press, 1990.

Kern, Stephen. *The Culture of Love. Victorians to Moderns.* Cambridge, Mass.: Harvard University Press, 1992.

———. "Explosive Intimacy: Psychodynamics of the Victorian Family." *History of Childhood Quarterly* 1 (1974): 439–61.

Keyfitz, Nathan. *Applied Mathematical Demography.* New York: Wiley, 1977.

Keyfitz, Nathan, and Wilhelm Flieger. *Population: Facts and Methods of Demography.* San Francisco: Freeman, 1971.

Kilbourne, Larry. "The Fertility Transition in New England: The Case of Hampton, New Hampshire, 1655–1840." In *Generations and Change. Genealogical Perspectives in Social History,* ed. Robert M. Taylor, Jr., and Ralph J. Crandall, 203–14. Macon, Ga.: Mercer University Press, 1986.

Klapisch-Zuber, Christine. "La famille médiévale." In Jacques Dupâquier et al., *Histoire de la population française,* vol. 1, 479–89. Paris: Presses Universitaires de France, 1988.

Klepp, Susan E. "Revolutionary Bodies: Women and the Fertility Transition in the Mid-Atlantic Region, 1760–1820." *Journal of American History* 85 (1998): 910–45.

Knodel, John E. *The Decline of Fertility in Germany, 1871–1939*. Princeton, N.J.: Princeton University Press, 1974.

———. "Espacement des naissances et planification familiale: une critique de la méthode Dupâquier-Lachiver." *Annales: Économies, Sociétés, Civilisations* 36 (1981): 473–88, 493–94.

Knodel, John E., and Étienne Van de Walle. "Lessons from the Past." In *The Decline of Fertility in Europe*, ed. Ansley J. Coale and Susan Cotts Watkins, 390–419. Princeton, N.J.: Princeton University Press, 1986.

Koch, Friedrich. *Heinrich von Kleist: Bewusstsein und Wirklichkeit*. Stuttgart: Metzler, 1958.

Koehler, Wilhelm. *Die karolingischen Miniaturen*. Berlin: Deutscher Verein für Kunstwissenschaft, 1960.

Koerber, Adolf-Viktor von, ed. *Adolf Hitler. Sein Leben und seine Reden*. Munich: Boepple, [1923].

Körte, Werner. "Deutsche Vesperbilder in Italien." *Kunstgeschichtliches Jahrbuch der Bibliotheca Hertziana* 1 (1937): 1–138.

Kötzsche-Breitenbruch, Liselotte. "Zur Ikonographie des bethlehemitischen Kindermordes in der frühchristlichen Kunst." *Jahrbuch für Antike und Christentum* 11/12 (1968/1969): 104–15.

Krönig, Wolfgang. *Rheinische Vesperbilder*. Mönchengladbach: Kühlen, 1967.

———. "Rheinische Vesperbilder aus Leder und ihr Umkreis." *Wallraf-Richartz-Jahrbuch* 24 (1962): 97–191.

Krausnick, Helmut. "Judenverfolgung." In Martin Broszat, Hans-Adolf Jacobsen, and Helmut Krausnick. *Konzentrationslager, Kommissarbefehl, Judenverfolgung*, 281–448. Olten: Walter-Verlag, 1965.

Kuhn, Axel. *Hitlers aussenpolitisches Programm. Entstehung und Entwicklung 1919–1939*. Stuttgart: Klett, 1970.

Künstle, Karl. *Ikonographie der christlichen Kunst*, vol. 1. Freiburg im Breisgau: Herder, 1928.

Küppers, Leonhard. "Marienklage." In *Die Gottesmutter. Marienbild in Rheinland und in Westfalen*, vol. 1, ed. Leonhard Küppers, 277–90. Recklinghausen: Bongers, 1974.

Kursell, Otto von. *Adolf Hitlers Reden*. Munich: Boepple, 1925.

Lachiver, Marcel. *La population de Meulan du XVIIe au XIXe siècle (vers 1600–1870). Étude de démographie historique*. Paris: SEVPEN, 1969.

Lafontaine-Desogne, Jacqueline. *Histoire de l'art byzantin et chrétien d'Orient*, second edition. Louvain-la-Neuve: Institut Orientaliste, 1995.

———. "Iconography of the Cycle of the Infancy of Christ," In *The Kariye Djami*, ed. Paul A. Underwood, vol. 4, 195–241. Princeton, N.J.: Princeton University Press, 1975.

Landry, Adolphe. *La révolution démographique*. Paris: Sirey, 1934.

Langer, William L. "Checks on Population Growth: 1750–1850." *Scientific American* 226 (1972): 93–99.

Lapeyre, André. *Les façades occidentales de Saint-Denis et de aux portails de Laon*. Paris: Lapeyre, 1960.

Laqueur, Walter. *Russia and Germany*. Boston: Little, Brown, 1965.

Leasure, J. William. "La baisse de la fécondité aux États-Unis de 1800 à 1860." *Population* 37 (1982): 607–19.

———. "A Hypothesis About the Decline of Fertility. Evidence from the United States." *European Journal of Population* 5 (1989): 105–17.

Le Bras, Hervé. "Coït interrompu, contrainte morale et héritage préférentiel." *Communications* 44 (1986): 47–70.

Le Play, Frédéric. *L'organisation de la famille*. Paris: Téqui, 1871.

Lesthaeghe, Ron. "On the Social Control of Human Reproduction." *Population and Development Review* 6 (1980): 527–48.

Levy, Darline G., and Harriet B. Applewhite. "Women, Radicalization, and the Fall of the French Monarchy." In *Women and Politics in the Age of Democratic Revolution*, ed. Harriet B. Applewhite and Darline G. Levy, 81–107. Ann Arbor: University of Michigan Press, 1990.

Lill, Georg. "Die früheste deutsche Verspergruppe." *Der Cicerone* 16 (1924): 660–62.

Lisini, Alessandro, and Fabio Iacometti, eds. *Cronache sinesi*. Rerum italicarum scriptores, vol. 15, part 6. Bologna: Zanichelli, 1931–1937.

Livi Bacci, Massimo. "Social-Group Forerunners of Fertility Control in Europe." In *The Decline of Fertility in Europe*, ed. Ansley J. Coale and Susan Cotts Watkins, 182–200. Princeton, N.J.: Princeton University Press, 1986.

Lowenthal, Leo. *Literature, Popular Culture, and Society*. Palo Alto, Calif.: Pacific Books, 1961.

Lunghi, Elvio. "La decorazione pittorica della chiesa." In Marino Bigaroni, Hans-Rudolf Meier, and Elvio Lunghi. *La basilica di Santa Chiara in Assisi*, 204–30. Perugia: Quattroemme, 1994.

Lutz, Wolfgang. "Factors Associated with the Finnish Fertility Decline since 1776." *Population Studies* 41 (1987): 463–82.

Madaule, Jacques. "La famille dans la littérature française." In *Renouveau des idées sur la famille*, ed. Robert Prigent, 120–29. Paris: Presses Universitaires de France, 1954.

Maguire, Henry. *Art and Eloquence in Byzantium*. Princeton, N.J.: Princeton University Press, 1981.

———. "The Classical Tradition in the Byzantine Ekphrasis." In *Byzantium and the Classical Tradition. University of Birmingham Thirteenth Spring Symposium of Byzantine Studies, 1979*, ed. Margaret Mullett and Roger Scott, 94–102. Birmingham: Center for Byzantine Studies, University of Birmingham, 1981.

———. "The Depiction of Sorrow in Middle Byzantine Art." *Dumbarton Oaks Papers* 31 (1977): 123–74.

Maigron, Louis. *Le romantisme et les moeurs: Essai d'étude historique et sociale d'après des documents inédits*. Paris: Champion, 1910.

Mâle, Émile. *L'art religieux de la fin du Moyen Âge en France*. Paris: Armand Colin, 1944.

Markowitz, Joel. *The Psychodynamic Evolution of Groups*. New York: Vantage, 1969.

Maser, Werner. *Hitlers Briefe und Notizen. Sein Weltbild in handschriftlichen Dokumenten*. Düsseldorf: Econ, 1973.

Matossian, Mary Kilbourne. *Poisons of the Past. Molds, Epidemics, and History*. New Haven: Yale University Press, 1989.

McInnis, Marvin. "The Fertility Transition in Europe and America." In *Family Building and Family Planning in Pre-Industrial Societies*, ed. John Rogers, 1–15. Uppsala: University of Uppsala, 1980.

McLaren, Angus. "Abortion in France: Women and the Regulation of Family Size 1800–1914." *French Historical Studies* 10 (1978): 461–85.

Meiss, Millard. *French Painting in the Time of Jean de Berry. The Boucicaut Master*. London: Phaidon, 1968.

———. *Painting in Florence and Siena after the Black Death*. Princeton N.J.: Princeton University Press, 1951.

———. "Sleep in Venice: Ancient Myths and Renaissance Proclivities." *Proceedings of the American Philosophical Society* 110 (1966): 348–82.

Mellini, Gian Lorenzo. *Giovanni Pisano*. Venice: Electa, [1970].

Millet, Gabriel. *Monuments byzantins de Mistra. Matériaux pour l'étude de l'architecture et de la peinture en Grèce aux XIVe et Xve siècles*. Paris: Leroux, 1910.

———. *Recherches sur l'iconographie de l'évangile aux XIV, XV et XVI siècles, d'après les monuments de Mistra, de la Macédoine et du Mont-Athos*, second edition. Paris: Boccard, 1960.

Mitterauer, Michael, and Reinhard Sieder. *Vom Patriarchat zur Partnerschaft. Zum Strukturwandel der Familie.* Munich: Oscar Beck, 1977.

Möbius, Paul J. *Über Entartung.* Wiesbaden: Bergmann, 1900.

Mollaret, Henri H., and Jacqueline Brossollet. *La peste, source méconnue d'inspiration artistique.* Antwerp: Koninklijk Museum voor schone Kunsten, 1965.

Mollat, Michel, and Philippe Wolff. *Ongles bleus. Jacques et Ciompi. Les révolutions populaires en Europe aux XIVe et Xve siècles.* Paris: Calmann-Lévy, 1970.

Monick, Eugene. *Evil, Sexuality, and Disease in Grünewald's Body of Christ.* Dallas: Spring, 1993.

Montaigne, Michel de. *Essais,* ed. Albert Thibaudet. Paris: Gallimard, 1950.

Morel, Bénédict-Auguste. *Traité de dégénérescences physiques, intellectuelles et morales de l'espèce humaine.* Paris: Baillière, 1857.

Morganstern, Anne McGee. "The La Grange Tomb and Choir." *Speculum* 48 (1973): 52–69.

Morrow, Richard B. "Family Limitation in Pre-Industrial England: A Reappraisal." *Economic History Review* 31 (1978): 419–28.

Mroz, Thomas A., and David R. Weir. "Structural Change in Life Cycle Fertility During the Fertility Transition: France Before and After the Revolution of 1789." *Population Studies* 44 (1990): 61–87.

Musée des Beaux-Arts, Lyon. *Bronzes antiques de Sardaigne,* exhibition catalogue. Lyon: Musée des Beaux-Arts, 1954.

Musée d'Orsay, Paris. *Le dernier portrait,* exhibition catalogue. Paris: Réunion des Musées Nationaux, 2002.

Naquet, Alfred. *Le divorce.* Paris: Dentu, 1876.

———. *Religion, propriété, famille.* Paris: Poupart-Davyl, 1869.

———. *Vers l'union libre.* Paris: Félix Juven, 1908.

Nightingale, Florence. *Cassandra,* 1852. Old Westbury, NY: The Feminist Press, 1979.

Nochlin, Linda. *Realism.* Harmondsworth: Penguin, 1971.

Nohl, Johannes. *The Black Death, A Chronicle of the Plague,* trans. C. H. Clarke. New York: Harper, 1924.

Nolan, Kathleen. "Narrative in the Capital Frieze of Notre-Dame at Estampes." *The Art Bulletin* 71 (1989): 166–84.

Noonan, John T., Jr. *Contraception. A History of Its Treatment by the Catholic Theologians and Canonists.* Cambridge, Mass.: Harvard University Press, 1965.

———. "Intellectual and Demographic History." In *Population and Social Change,* ed. D. V. Glass and Roger Revelle, 115–35. London: Edward Arnold, 1972.

Norton, Mary Beth. *Liberty's Daughters. The Revolutionary Experience of American Women, 1750–1800.* Boston: Little, Brown, 1980.

Offen, Karen. "Depopulation, Nationalism, and Feminism." *American Historical Review* 89 (1984): 648–76.

Olds, Clifton C. "Love and Death in the Art of the Later Middle Ages." In *Images of Love and Death in Late Medieval and Renaissance Art,* exhibition catalogue, ed. William R. Levin, 3–6. Ann Arbor: Museum of Art, University of Michigan, 1975.

O'Neill, Robert J. *The German Army and the Nazi Party 1933/39.* New York: Heinemann, 1966.

Ortega y Gasset, José. *La rebelión de las masas,* 1930. Buenos Aires: Espasa-Calpa, 1939.

Osterud, Nancy, and John Fulton. "Family Limitation and Age at Marriage: Fertility Decline in Sturbridge, Massachusetts 1730–1850." *Population Studies* 30 (1976): 481–94.

Packard, Vance. *The Hidden Persuaders.* New York: McKay, 1957.

———. *The Waste Makers.* New York: McKay, 1957.

Palazzo Pubblico, Siena. *Il gotico a Siena: miniature pitture oreficerie oggetti d'arte. Siena: Palazzo Pubblico, 24 luglio - 30 ottobre 1982.* Florence: Centro Di, [1982].

Panofsky, Erwin. *Early Netherlandish Painting. Its Origins and Character,* 2 vols. Cambridge, Mass.: Harvard University Press, 1958.

———. "Reintegration of a Book of Hours Executed in the Workshop of the 'Maître de Rohan.'" In *Medieval Studies in Memory of A. Kingsley Porter,* ed. Wilhelm R. W. Koehler, vol. 2, 479–99. Cambridge, Mass.: Harvard University Press, 1939.

———. *Tomb Sculpture. Four Lectures on Its Changing Aspects from Ancient Egypt to Bernini.* New York: Abrams, 1964.

———. "Zur künstlerischen Abkunft des Strassburger 'Ecclesiameisters.'" *Oberrheinische Kunst* 4 (1929/1930): 124–29.

Pascal, Blaise. *Oeuvres complètes,* ed. Jacques Chevalier. Paris: Gallimard, 1957.

Passarge, Walter. "Das deutsche Vesperbild im Mittelalter." In *Deutsche Beiträge zur Kunstwissenschaft,* ed. Paul Frank, vol. 1. Cologne: Marcan, 1924.

Perec, Georges. *Les choses.* Paris: France Loisirs, 1965.

Perrot, Jean-Claude. *Une histoire intellectuelle de l'économie politique XVIIe–XVIIIe.* Paris: École des Hautes Études en Sciences Sociales, 1992.

Perrot, Michelle. "Avant et ailleurs." In *Histoire de la vie privée,* vol. 4, *De la Révolution à la Grande Guerre,* ed. Michelle Perrot, 17–19. Paris: Seuil, 1987.

Pfister, Christian. "L'archevêque de Metz Drogon (823–856)." In *Mélanges Paul Fabre. Études d'histoire du moyen âge,* 101–45. Paris: Picard, 1902.

Phelps, Reginald. "Hitler als Parteiredner im Jahr 1920." *Vierteljahrshefte für Zeitgeschichte* 11 (1963: 274–330.

Pinder, Wilhelm. "Die dichterische Wurzel der Pietà." *Repertorium für Kunstwissenschaft* 42 (1920): 145–63.

———. *Die Pietà.* Leipzig: Seemann, 1922.

Pirandello, Luigi. *Maschere nude,* vol. 1. Milan: Mondadori, 1974.

Pirenne, Henri. *Histoire de Belgique des origines à nos jours,* vol. 1. Brussels: Renaissance du Livre, 1948.

Polzer, Joseph. "Aspects of the Fourteenth-Century Iconography of Death and the Plague." In *The Black Death and the Impact of the Fourteenth-Century Plague,* ed. Daniel Williman, 107–19. Binghamton, N.Y.: Center for Medieval & Early Renaissance Studies, 1982.

Porter, Roy. "'The Secrets of Generation Display'd': Aristotle's Masterpiece in Eighteenth-Century England." *Eighteenth-Century Life* 9 (1985): 1–21.

Preiss, Heinz, ed. *Adolf Hitler in Franken. Reden aus der Kampfzeit.* Nuremberg: [Der Stürmer], 1939.

Previtali, Giovanni. *Giotto e la sua bottega.* Milan: Fabbri, 1993.

Proctor, Candice E. *Women, Equality, and the French Revolution.* Westport, Conn.: Greenwood, 1990.

Ragusa, Isa, and Ruth Wilkins Sullivan. Letters to *The Art Bulletin* 69 (1987): 646–49.

Rawson, Beryl. "The Roman Family." In *The Family in Ancient Rome,* ed. Beryl Rawson, 1–57. London: Croon Helm, 1986.

Reiners-Ernst, Elisabeth. *Das freudevolle Vesperbild und die Anfänge der Pietà-Vorstellung.* Munich: Filser, 1939.

Reinhard, Marcel. "La Révolution Française et le problème de la population." *Population* 1 (1946): 419–27.

Reuter, Gabriele. *Aus guter Familie.* Berlin: Fischer, 1909.

Robertson, Ritchie. "Modernism and the Self." In *Philosophy and German Literature 1700–1990,* 150–96. Cambridge: Cambridge University Press, 2002.

Rodolico, Niccoló. *La democrazia fiorentina nel suo tramonto (1378–1382).* Bologna: Zanichelli, 1905.

Rogers, John. "The Study of Family Planning in Pre-Industrial Societies." In *Family Building and Family Planning in Pre-Industrial Societies,* ed. John Rogers, 41–51. Uppsala: University of Uppsala, 1980.

Rogers, Neville, ed. *The Complete Poetical Works of Percy Bysshe Shelley*. Oxford: Oxford University Press, 1972.

Rose, R. B. "Feminism, Women and the French Revolution." *Australian Journal of Politics and History* 40 (1994): 173–86.

Rosenberg, Jakob, Seymour Slive, and E. H. ter Kuile. *Dutch Art and Architecture 1600 to 1800*. Harmondsworth: Penguin, 1966, 1972.

Rosenfeld, Hellmut. *Der mittelalterliche Totentanz. Entstehung, Entwicklung, Bedeutung*. Cologne: Böhlau, 1954, 1968.

———. "Der Totentanz als europäisches Phänomen." *Archiv für Kulturgeschichte* 48 (1966): 54–83.

Rotzler, Willy. *Die Begegnung der drei Lebenden und der drei Toten*. Winterthur: Keller, 1961.

Salleron, Claude. "La littérature au XIXe siècle et la famille." In *Renouveau des idées sur la famille*, ed. Robert Prigent, 60–80. Paris: Presses Universitaires de France, 1954.

Santow, Gigi. "*Coitus interruptus* and the Control of Natural Fertility." *Population Studies* 49 (1995): 17–43.

Sauer, Wolfgang. "Die Mobilmachung der Gewalt." In Karl Dietrich Bracher, Wolfgang Sauer, and Gerhart Schulz, *Die nationalsozialistische Machtergreifung. Studien zur Errichtung des totalitären Herrschaftssystems in Deutschland 1933/34*. Cologne: Westdeutscher Verlag, 1962, 683–966. Cologne: Westdeutscher Verlag, 1962.

Sauerländer, Willibald. *Gothic Sculpture in France 1140–1270*. London: Thames and Hudson, 1972.

Saugnieux, Joël. *Les danses macabres de France et d'Espagne et leurs prolongements littéraires*. Lyon: Vitte, 1972.

Sauvy, Alfred. "Essai d'une vue d'ensemble." In *La prévention des naissances dans la famille. Ses origines dans les temps modernes*, ed. Hélène Bergues, 377–91. Paris: Presses Universitaires de France, 1960.

———. "Présentation." In *La prévention des naissances dans la famille. Ses origines dans les temps modernes*, ed. Hélène Bergues, 13–16. Paris: Presses Universitaires de France, 1960.

———. *La prévention des naissances*. Paris: Presses Universitaires de France, 1962.

Schäfke, Werner. *St. Maria im Kapitol*. Cologne: Wienand, n.d.

Schauenbourg, Baron de. "Mémoire du Baron de Schauenbourg." In Société Française d'Archéologie, *Congrès archéologique de France 1859*. Paris: Derache, 1859.

Schenk, Hans G. *The Mind of the European Romantics*. London: Constable, 1966.

Schiller, Gertrud. *Ikonographie der christlichen Kunst*, vol. 2, *Die Passion Jesu Christi*. Gütersloh: Gerd Mohn, 1968.

Schneider, Arthur von. "Ein frühes Versperbild vom Oberrhein." *Der Cicerone* 19 (1927): 10–14.

Schnitzler, Arthur. *Gesammelte Werke*, 7 vols. Berlin: Fischer, 1912.

Schumacher, Joseph. *Die Krankheitsdarstellungen der Volksepidemien in der deutschen Kunst vom fruhen Mittlealter bis einschliesslich XVI. Jahrhundert*. Bochum-Langendreer: Pöppinghaus, 1937.

Sebald, W. G. *Austerlitz*, trans. Anthea Bell. New York: Modern Library, 2001.

Seccombe, Wally. "Starting To Stop: Working-Class Fertility Decline in Britain." *Past and Present* 126 (February 1990): 151–88.

Servetus, Michael. *Christianismi restitutio*, 1553. Frankfurt: Minerva, 1966.

Shaw, George Bernard. *Collected Plays With Their Prefaces*, vol. 4. London: Max Reinhardt, 1972.

Shelley, Mary. *Frankenstein*. New York: Signet, 1983.

Siciliano, Italo. *François Villon et les thèmes poétiques du moyen âge*. Paris: Nizet, 1934.

Siegfried, André. *Tableau des partis en France*. Paris: Gallimard, 1930.

Simmel, Georg. *Philosophie des Geldes*, fifth edition. Berlin: Duncker & Humboldt, 1930.

Simon, Sonia C. "Studies on the Drogo Sacramentary: Eschatology and the Priest-King." Ph.D. dissertation, Boston University, 1975.

Smiles, Samuel. *Self-Help*. London: John Murray, 1859.

Smith, Daniel Scott. "The Dating of the American Sexual Revolution: Evidence and Interpretation." In *The American Family in Social-Historical Perspective*, ed. Gordon Michael, 321–35.

———. "The Demographic History of Colonial New England." *Journal of Economic History* 32 (1972): 165–83.

———. "'Early' Fertility Decline in America: A Problem in Family History." *Journal of Family History* 12 (1987): 73–84.

———. "Family Limitation, Sexual Control, and Domestic Feminism in Victorian America." In *A Heritage of Her Own. Toward a New Social History of American Women*, ed. Nancy F. Cott and Elizabeth Pleck, 222–45. New York: Simon and Schuster, 1979. (Reprinted from *Feminist Studies* 1 [1973]: 40–57.)

———. "A Homeostatic Demographic Regime: Patterns in West European Family Reconstruction Studies." In *Population Patterns in the Past*, ed. Ronald Demos Lee, 19–51. New York: Academic Press, 1977.

———. "The Peculiarities of the Yankees: the vanguard of the fertility transition in the United States." Unpublished paper for IUSSP seminar on Values and Fertility Changes, Sion (Switzerland), 1994.

———. "Population, Family and Society in Hingham, Massachusetts, 1635–1880," Ph.D. dissertation, University of California-Berkeley, 1973.

Sober, Elliott, and David Sloane Wilson. *Unto Others: The Evolution and Psychology of Unselfish Behavior*. Cambridge, Mass.: Harvard University Press, 1998.

Soldano, Bianca Tosatti. *Miniature e vetrate senesi del secolo XIII*. Genoa: Università di Genova, 1978.

Sommer, Theo. *Deutschland und Japan zwischen den Mächten 1935–1940*. Tübingen: Mohr, 1962.

Spagnoli, Paul G. "The Unique Decline of Mortality in Revolutionary France." *Journal of Family History* 22 (1997): 425–61.

Spengler, Joseph J. *France Faces Depopulation*. Durham, N.C.: Duke University Press, 1938.

———. *French Predecessors of Malthus: A Study in Eighteenth-Century Wage and Population Theory*. Durham, N.C.: Duke University Press, 1942.

Spicq, Ceslaus. *Agapè dans le Nouveau Testament: Analyse des textes*. 3 vols. Paris: Lecoffre, 1958–1969.

Stegemeier, Henri. *The Dance of Death in Folk-Song, with an Introduction on the History of the Dance of Death*. Chicago: private edition, 1939.

Stengers, Jean. "Les pratiques anticonceptionnelles dans le mariage au XIXe et au Xxe siècle: problèmes humains et attitudes religieuses." *Revue belge de philologie et d'histoire* 49 (1971): 403–81.

Stoetzel, Jean. *Les valeurs du temps présent. Une enquête*. Paris: Presses Universitaires de France, 1983.

Strindberg, August. *Dödsdansen*. Stockholm: Norstedt, 1988.

———. *Kammarspel*. Stockholm: Albert Bonnier, 1917.

Suckale, Robert. "Arma Christi." *Städel-Jahrbuch*, Neue Folge 6, 177–208. Munich: Prestel, 1977.

Sullivan, Ruth Wilkins. "Some Old Testament Themes on the Front Predella of Duccio's Maestà." *The Art Bulletin* 68 (1986): 597–609.

Swarzenski, Georg. "Italienische Quellen der deutschen Pietà." In *Festschrift Heinrich Wölfflin. Beiträge zur Kunst und Geistesgeschichte zum 21. Juni 1924, überreicht von Freunden und Schülern*, 127–34. Munich: Hugo Schmidt, 1924.

Swarzenski, Hanns. "Quellen zum deutschen Andachtsbild." *Zeitschrift für Kunstgeschichte* 4 (1935): 141–44.

Synge, John Millington. *Plays, Poems, and Prose.* London: Dent, 1941.

Tapié, Alain, ed. *Les vanités dans la peinture au XVIIe siècle. Méditations sur la richesse, le dénuement et la rédemption,* exhibition catalogue. Caen: Musée des Beaux-Arts, 1990.

TeBrake, William H. *A Plague of Insurrection. Popular Politics and Peasant Revolt in Flanders, 1323–1328.* Philadelphia: University of Pennsylvania Press, 1993.

Temkin-Greener, H., and A. C. Swedlund. "Fertility Transition in the Connecticut Valley: 1740–1850." *Population Studies* 32 (1978): 27–41.

Tenenti, Alberto. *Il senso della morte e l'amore della vita nel Rinascimento.* Turin: Einaudi, 1957.

———. *La vie et la mort à travers l'art du XVe siècle.* Paris: Armand Colin, 1952.

Théré, Christine. "Limitation des naissances et émancipation des femmes au XVIIIe siècle." In Association internationale des démographes de langue française, 1994, *Les modes de régulation de la reproduction humaine. Incidences sur la fécondité et la santé,* colloque international de Delphes, 6–10 October 1992, 425–38. Paris: Presses Universitaires de France, 1994.

Thorslev, Peter L., Jr. "Incest as Romantic Symbol." *Comparative Literature Studies* 2 (1965): 41–58.

Todini, Filippo. *La pittura umbra dal duecento al primo cinquecento,* vol. 1. Milan: Langanesi, 1989.

Tolstoy, Leo. *Kreutzerova Sonata.* Berlin: Bera, 1890.

Tomaselli, Sylvana. "Moral Philosophy and Population Questions in Eighteenth Century Europe." In *Population and Resources in Western Intellectual Traditions,* ed. Michael S. Teitelbaum and Jay Winter, 7–29. Cambridge: Cambridge University Press, 1989.

Traer, James F. *Marriage and the Family in Eighteenth-Century France, 1750–1789.* Ithaca: Cornell University Press, 1980.

Trapier, Elizabeth du Gué. *Valdés Leal. Spanish Baroque Painter.* New York: Hispanic Society of America, 1960.

Treue, Wilhelm. "Hitlers Denkschrift zum Vierjahresplan 1936." *Vierteljahrshefte für Zeitgeschichte* 3 (1955): 184–210.

Trigger, Bruce. *Early Civilizations: Ancient Egypt in Context.* Cairo: American University in Cairo Press, 1993.

Tselos, Dmitri. "The Pietà: Its Byzantine Iconographic Origins and Its Western Titular Diversity." *Annales d'Esthétique* 25–26 (1986–1987): 55–87.

Tuchman, Barbara. *A Distant Mirror. The Calamitous 14th Century.* New York: Knopf, 1978.

Turgenev, Ivan. *Sobranie sochinenii,* 10 vols. Moscow: State Publishing House for Literary Classics, 1961.

Turner, J. Scott. *The Extended Organism: The Physiology of Animal-Built Structures.* Cambridge, Mass.: Harvard University Press, 2000.

Tyrell, Albrecht, ed. *Führer befiehl... Selbstzeugnisse aus der 'Kampfzeit' der NSDAP.* Düsseldorf: Droste, 1969.

Vallès, Jules. *L'enfant.* Paris: Garnier-Flammarion, 1968.

Valmary, Pierre. *Familles paysannes au XVIIIe siècle en Bas-Quercy. Étude démographique.* Paris: Presses Universitaires de France, 1965.

Van de Walle, Étienne. "Allaitement, stérilité et contraception: les opinions jusqu'au XIXe siècle." *Population* 27 (1972): 685–701.

———. "Alone in Europe. The French Fertility Decline until 1850." In *Historical Studies of Changing Fertility,* ed. Charles Tilly, 257–88. Princeton, N.J.: Princeton University Press, 1978.

———. "Fertility Transition, Conscious Choice, and Numeracy." *Demography* 29 (1992): 487–502.

———. "Motivations and Technology in the Decline of French Fertility." In *Family and Sexuality in French History,* ed. Robert Wheaton and Tamara K. Hareven, 135–78. Philadelphia: University of Philadelphia Press, 1980.

Van de Walle, Étienne, and Helmut V. Muhsam. "Fatal Secrets and the French Fertility Transition." *Population and Development Review* 21 (1995): 261–79.

Vermeule, Emily. *Aspects of Death in Early Greek Art and Poetry.* Berkeley: University of California Press, 1979.

Viereck, George Sylvester. "Hitler the German Explosive." *American Monthly* 15 (1923): 235–38.

Vinovskis, Maris A. "A Multivariate Regression Analysis of Fertility Differentials Among Massachusetts Townships and Regions in 1860." In *Historical Studies of Changing Fertility* ed. Charles Tilly, 225–56. Princeton, N.J.: Princeton University Press, 1978.

———. "Socioeconomic Determinants of Interstate Fertility Differentials in the United States in 1850 and 1860." *Journal of Interdisciplinary History* 6 (1976): 375–96.

Vogelsang, Thilo. "Hitlers Brief an Reichenau vom 4. Dezember 1932." *Vierteljahrshefte für Zeitgeschichte* 7 (1959): 429–37.

———. "Neue Dokumente zur Geschichte der Reichswehr 1930–1933." *Vierteljahrshefte für Zeitgeschichte* 2 (1954): 397–436.

Vovelle, Michel. *Idéologies et mentalités.* Paris: François Maspero, 1982.

Wais, Kurt K. T. *Das Vater-Sohn Motiv in der Dichtung bis 1880.* Berlin: Gruyter, 1931.

———. *Das Vater-Sohn Motiv in der Dichtung 1880–1930.* Berlin: Gruyter, 1931.

Watkins, Susan Cotts. "Conclusions." In *The Decline of Fertility in Europe,* ed. Ansley J. Coale and Susan Cotts Watkins. Princeton, N.J.: Princeton University Press, 1986, 420–49.

Weinberg, Gerhart L., ed. *Hitlers zweites Buch. Ein Dokument aus dem Jahr 1928.* Stuttgart: Deutsche Verlags-Anstalt, 1961.

Weir, David R. "Estimation de la proportion de personnes limitant leur fécondité. France rurale 1740–1810." In *Modèles de la démographie historique,* ed. Alain Blum, Noël Bonneuil, and Didier Blanchet, 225–56. Paris: Presses Universitaires de France, 1992.

———. "Family Reconstitution and Population Reconstruction. Two Approaches to the Fertility Transition in France, 1740–1911." In *Old and New Methods in Historical Demography,* ed. David S. Reher and Roger Schofield, 145–58. Oxford: Clarendon Press, 1993.

———. "New Estimates of Nuptiality and Marital Fertility in France, 1740–1911." *Population Studies* 48 (1994): 307–31.

Wells, H. G. *Tono-Bungay.* New York: Random House, 1935.

Wells, Robert V. "Family History and Demographic Transition." *Journal of Social History* 9 (1975/1976), 1–19.

———. "Family Size and Fertility Control in Eighteenth-Century America: A Study of Quaker Families." *Population Studies* 25 (1971): 73–82.

———. *Revolutions in Americans' Lives. A Demographic Perspective on the History of Americans, Their Families, and Their Society.* Westport, Conn.: Greenwood, 1982.

Wenzel, Siegfried. "Pestilence and Middle English Literature." In *The Black Death: The Impact of the Fourteenth-Century Plague,* ed. Daniel Williman, 131–59. Binghamton, N.Y.: Center for Medieval and Early Renaissance Studies, 1982.

Wescher, Paul. *Jean Fouquet and His Time.* New York: Reynal & Hitchcock, 1947.

Wesemberg, Rudolf. *Frühe mittelalterliche Bildwerke: Die Schulen rheinischer Skulptur und ihre Ausstrahlung.* Düsseldorf: Schwann, 1972.

White, John. *Duccio: Tuscan Art and the Medieval Workshop.* New York: Thames and Hudson, 1979.

Wilde, Oscar. *Oscar Wilde,* ed. Isabel Murray. New York: Oxford University Press, 1989.

Williams, Ethel Carleton. "The Dance of Death in Painting and Sculpture in the Middle Ages." *Journal of the British Archaeological Association,* third series, 1 (1937): 229–57.

Wilson, David Sloane. "The Group Selection Controversy: History and Current Status." *Annual Review of Ecological Systems* 14 (1983): 159–87.

Wilson, David Sloane, and Elliott Sober. "Reintroducing Group Selection to the Human Behavioral Sciences." *Behavioral and Brain Sciences* 17 (1994): 585–604.

Wirth, Jean. *La jeune fille et la mort. Recherches sur les thèmes macabres dans l'art germanique de la Renaissance.* Geneva: Droz, 1979.

Withey, Lynne E. "Household Structure in Urban and Rural Areas: The Case of Rhode Island, 1774–1800." *Journal of Family History* 3 (1978): 37–49.

Wolf, Stephanie Grauman. *Urban Village. Population, Community, and Family Structure in Germantown, Pennsylvania 1683–1800.* Princeton, N.J.: Princeton University Press, 1976.

Wrigley, Edward Anthony. "Family Limitation in Pre-Industrial England." *Economic History Review* 19 (1966): 82–109.

———. "Fertility Strategy for the Individual and the Group." In *Historical Studies of Changing Fertility,* ed. Charles Tilly, 135–54. Princeton, N.J.: Princeton University Press, 1978.

———. "Marital Fertility in Seventeenth-Century Colyton: A Note." *Economic History Review* 31 (1978): 429–36.

———. *People, Cities and Wealth. The Transformation of Traditional Society.* Oxford: Blackwell, 1987.

Wynne-Edwards, V. C. *Animal Dispersion in Relation to Social Behavior.* Edinburgh: Oliver and Boyd, 1962.

Yasuba, Yasukichi. *Birth Rates of the White Population in the United States, 1800–1860. An Economic Study.* Baltimore: Johns Hopkins University Press, 1962.

Young, Alfred F. "The Women of Boston: 'Persons of Consequence' in the Making of the American Revolution, 1765–76." In *Women and Politics in the Age of Democratic Revolution,* ed. Harriet B. Applewhite and Darline G. Levy, 181–226. Ann Arbor: University of Michigan Press, 1990.

Young, Karl. *The Drama of the Medieval Church.* Oxford: Clarendon Press, 1933.

———. *Ordo Rachelis.* Madison: University of Wisconsin Press, 1919.

Zanetti, Dante E. *La demografia del patriziato milanese nei secoli XVII, XVIII, XIX.* Pavia: Università, 1972.

Zechlin, Egmont. "Ludendorff im Jahr 1915. Unveröffentlichte Briefe." *Historische Zeitschrift* 211 (1970), 316–53.

Ziegler, Philip. *The Black Death.* New York: John Day, 1969.

Zinc, Anne. *Azereix. La vie d'une communauté rurale à la fin du XVIIIe siècle.* Paris: SEVPEN, 1969.

Zola, Émile. *La terre.* Paris: Fasquelle, [1981?].

Index